Women's Lives/Women's Times

SUNY Series, Feminist Theory in Education
Madeleine Grumet, Editor

Women's Lives/Women's Times

NEW ESSAYS ON AUTO/BIOGRAPHY

ॐ

EDITED BY
Trev Lynn Broughton
and
Linda Anderson

State University of New York Press

Published by
State University of New York Press, Albany

For information, address State University of New York Press,
State University Plaza, Albany, N.Y. 12246

Production by M. R. Mulholland
Marketing by Theresa A. Swierzowski

Library of Congress Cataloging-in-Publication Data

Women's lives/women's times : new essays on auto/biography / edited by
    Trev Lynn Broughton and Linda Anderson.
        p.   cm. — (SUNY series, feminist theory in education)
    Includes bibliographical references and index.
    ISBN 0-7914-3397-8 (hardcover : acid free paper). — ISBN
0-7914-3398-6 (pbk. : acid free paper)
    1. Autobiography—Women authors. I. Broughton, Trev Lynn, 1959–
. II. Anderson, Linda, 1950–   . III. Series.
CT25.W66 1997
920.72—dc20   96-27662
                                                                    CIP

10 9 8 7 6 5 4 3 2 1

*This volume is dedicated to
our students in Women's Studies,
past and present.*

CONTENTS

ACKNOWLEDGMENTS

The authors gratefully acknowledge permission to use the following materials:

Quotations from *Sir Leslie Stephen's Mausoleum Book*, ed. Alan Bell, 1977, by permission of Oxford University Press.

Excerpt from "The Double Image," *To Bedlam and Part Way Back* by Anne Sexton. Copyright © *The Gift Giver*, © 1980 by Joyce Hansen. Reprinted by permission of Clarion Books/Houghton Mifflin Company. All rights reserved.

Excerpt from "To Bryher" by H. D. Copyright © H. D.: *Collected Poems 1912–1944*. Reprinted by permission of Carcanet Press.

Lines from "Origins and History of Consciousness," "To a Poet," Part XII of "Twenty-One Love Poems," "Sibling Mysteries," and "Transcendental Etude." Reprinted from *The Dream of a Common Language, Poems 1974–1977*, by Adrienne Rich, by permission of the author and W. W. Norton and Company, Inc. Copyright © 1978 by W. W. Norton and Company, Inc.

Letters between Winifred Holtby and Vera Brittain quoted by permission of Mr. Paul Berry, literary executor of the Holtby estate.

Ray Strachey's letters quoted by permission of the Lilly Library, Indiana University.

Passages from *Family Sayings* retranslated by Judith Woolf, by kind permission of Carcanet Press, proprietors of the English translation rights in the work of Natalia Ginzburg.

"The Beast" reprinted by permission of Bloodaxe Books Ltd. from *Life by Drowning: Selected Poems* by Jeni Couzyn (Bloodaxe Books, 1985).

PREFACE

In the nineteenth century the writing of autobiography under the title of *Life and Times* signalled the belief that an entire social landscape could happily come within the purview of an individual life. Not surprisingly this gesture of appropriation was the prerogative of national heroes—of statesmen and laureates—and looked surprisingly like presumption in anyone else. Another once familiar sub-genre—*Life and Opinions*—made explicit the wide interpretive frame which went with this view of autobiography: like Thomas Carlyle's Diogenes Teufelsdröckh, the autobiographer could appoint himself a Professor of Things in General.[1] Such universality was, of course, a masculine prerogative. As Carlyle's admirer, Geraldine Jewsbury joked to Jane Carlyle in 1849, a volume of "life and errors" was the most women were likely to aspire to.[2]

Our choice of title reflects the task of feminist revision that critics in the field of autobiography have undertaken since the early eighties: the error to be redressed, of course, was the iniquity of women's non-representation within the existing canon of autobiographical texts and criticism. With the publication in 1980 of Estelle C. Jelinek's *Women's Autobiography: Essays in Criticism*,[3] there was a decisive change in critical attitudes. Serious attention was accorded writing by women which had previously been regarded as non-existent, negligible, or crude. New connections were made between works such as diaries and letters, usually dismissed as peripheral, and the more formal writing of autobiography. Most importantly, it was demonstrated that in autobiography, more vividly and pressingly than elsewhere, gender and genre are reciprocally at stake.

The title we have chosen, however, also has another purpose. Through it we intend to signal what we see as the major theme of this volume of essays: the complex interrelation between the personal, the theoretical, and the political offered by women's autobiographical writing which thus seems to defy or exceed both generic and disciplinary boundaries. The relation between the "life" and "times" in women's autobiography is still to be worked out; that is, there can be no easy assertion that we simply know how the paradigmatic inscription of a life joins the historical and cultural specificity of its lived time or moment.

The challenge offered by women's autobiography is precisely in this complex weave between the metaphorical—the figures and products of writing—and their literal ground or reference. Like other recent feminist critics of autobiography, then, we perceive a danger in theory's tendency to generalize about the subject, to disenfranchise the "bios," the lived element of autobiography, and thus drown out the multiple voices of women's autobiography through the iteration of its own theme. The opportunity and risk presented by autobiography, we suggest, lies outside theory as we currently understand it, in the interrogation of theory, in the lack of fit between theory and practice, in the purchase that the specific can thus begin to obtain on the general. It is through autobiography and the experiments it allows, we argue, that feminists can begin to explore the conditions and limits of knowledge itself.

The conference from which the following papers originate attracted a preponderance of literary critics and literary historians, and in this respect it mirrors many of the feminist interventions in autobiographical studies that have issued from the United States. For this very reason it becomes important to stress that, although "autobiographical studies" freely exploit the excavations of literary historians, and take for granted literary critical concepts such as genre, narrative, and voice, in Britain at least, most of the curricular developments arising from the study of autobiography have taken place within departments of sociology and teacher education, or within the combatively interdisciplinary frameworks of the "new" universities, rather than in departments of literature.

The reasons why autobiographical studies should have been most enthusiastically promoted in contexts where the disciplinary boundaries have been less rigidly fixed are both historical and theoretical. First, it is important to acknowledge how the burgeoning of autobiography as a body of work and as a field of study has coincided historically with the modernist critique of "objectivity" in the social sciences and the corresponding demand for so-called "self-reflexivity" in sociological and anthropological research. Social scientists have been called on to examine the pressure of their own histories on their research methods—on the questions they ask and the answers they hear, and to weigh ethical and political issues of accountability and ownership. What happens, for example, when others' "lives" are appropriated as research data, and what is the impact of the research process on the life-histories of both researcher and respondent? Academics working in this field, therefore, have come face to face with questions of autobiography, often entering into a productive dialogue across disciplines with feminist literary accounts of the genre, and finding in the location and problematization of the "subject," an answer—or part of one—to the claims of enlightenment epistemology.

In recent times autobiography has also supported important developments in radical teaching. For many years, teachers working within adult literacy, access, and continuing education frameworks have promoted the reading and writing of life-history as both a mode of critique and a means of empowerment. Indeed, although it is widely accepted that the whole "turn to the autobiographical" received its initial impetus from the organizational patterns and discursive practices of "grassroots" politics in the 1960s and 70s, and in particular from feminism's revaluation of the personal as political, the extent to which this political momentum has been sustained in the classroom has seldom been acknowledged. Significantly, Maggie Humm has pointed to over three hundred institutions in which structured autobiographical work, with its processes of selection, ordering, and reflection is advocated as a way of transforming "life experience" into academic qualification, of accrediting and validating prior informal learning, or of introducing non-standard entrants to the interpretive, management, and planning routines of higher education. "In theory," Humm points out, "autobiography should allow men and women, gay men, lesbians and heterosexuals, black and white students, to be subjects and sources within their own world": though as her research reveals, such work may require modes of assessment as nuanced and self-reflexive as the autobiographies themselves.[4]

This pedagogical use of autobiography—its implementation in the classroom, as a subject which not only crosses disciplines but crosses the boundary between reader and writer and between theory and practice—has been highly significant. Students' autobiographies, family histories, self-portraits, and photo-albums have been extensively employed as a means of bringing to consciousness, and hence of exposing to evaluation and perhaps to change, everyday assumptions and "common sense" decisions. Jane Ribbens has argued that, as a process of thinking about the self's relationship to society, autobiography can enable students to inhabit and thus transform key sociological concepts such as "structure" and "agency," or "gender inequality."[5] Typically, such courses as Ribbens' encourage students to take control of the tools of analysis and develop new ones of their own. In Women's Studies, in particular, such exercises have proved invaluable in opening up debate about key (and highly fraught) questions such as the relationship between textual and political forms of representation; the usefulness to feminist politics of concepts of identity, identification, and difference; the category of "experience" and its role in feminist thinking; the significance, or otherwise, of the subjective in academic enquiry; and notions of individualism, authenticity, and consciousness. It is here, at the juncture between apprehension and theorizing, that the teaching of autobiography has proved most challenging and most disturbing. By insisting on, rather than obscuring, the embodied social dimension of the thinking self, autobiography as pedagogy can challenge the "objectivity," and thus the authority, of traditional disciplinary paradigms. Hence it almost inevitably disrupts what counts as "knowledge"—and just as controversially what counts as "credit"—in the academy.

We have conceived this book with the teaching of women's autobiography very much in mind. The book is divided into four sections, each highlighting the headings—"Historians of the Self," "Selves and Others," "Subjectivities," and "Lives in Practice"—important general topics, each containing a short introduction and a reading list. Our aim is to provide a book which functions both as a guide and a resource for teachers and students undertaking work in the rich and diverse area of women's autobiography.

Diversity is a key term and it is an issue that is both illustrated by, and returned to, in the essays themselves. At this moment in time it seems important to broaden the critical discussion of life-writing beyond the "usual suspects." Provocative and inspiring though they have been, the works of a few, invariably "literary," women—Woolf, Stein, de Beauvoir, Wolf, Angelou—have been in danger of foreclosing debate. We want to bring to a wider audience a range of texts familiar, if at all, only to specialists, and to encourage readers to look beyond the limits of this or any other anthology to the wealth of materials still scarcely recognized, much less acknowledged, as women's testimony.

Our additional aim is to illustrate some of the important trends in feminist autobiographical studies, signposting the most significant questions currently posed by students of the genre, and equipping newcomers with a variety of ways to address them. What issues are raised by the pressures on self-representation in the post-colonial moment? In what terms, in whose language, and to what effect can the "Other" woman speak? As Elspeth Probyn puts it: "Is it possible for the autobiographical voice not to be self-centered, and does attention to one's self have to produce a hierarchy of selves?"[6] What opportunities present themselves when we recognize the intercalation of biography and autobiography? Can the new emphasis on autobiography as a practice in the material world, and as a mode of cultural politics, enable us better to understand non-literary forms of life-writing? What is gained from intertextual study—from juxtaposing pairs or groups of "selves" from the same historical moment, or from setting men's autobiographies in the context of women's? What role has self-inscription played in women's political life? And what challenges do women's autobiographical writings pose to historiography: to the master narratives of class-formation, white supremacy, and nation-building, and to the concepts of chronology and periodicity which underpin them?

Lastly we hope this book will help to embolden students and teachers in many fields, but especially perhaps in Women's Studies, to explore the interdisciplinary valences and political potentialities of life-writing in their own teaching and research.

Notes

1. Thomas Carlye, *Sartor Resartus*, Kerry McSweeney and Peter Sabor, eds. (Oxford: Oxford University Press, 1987), p. 14.

2. Mrs. Alexander Ireland, ed. *Selections from the Letters of Geraldine E. Jewsbury to Jane Welsh Carlyle* (London: Longmans Green and Co., 1892), p. 337.

3. Bloomington: Indiana University Press, 1980.

4. "Autobiography and 'Bell-pins.'" In Vivienne Griffiths et al., *Writing Feminist Biography 2: Using Life Histories* (Manchester: Studies in Sexual Politics, University of Manchester, 1987), p. 17.

5. Jane Ribbens, "Fact or Fictions? Aspects of the Use of Autobiographical Writing in Undergraduate Sociology," *Sociology* 27 (February, 1993), pp. 67–80.

6. Elspeth Probyn, *Sexing the Self: Gendered Positions in Cultural Studies* (London and New York: Routledge, 1993), p. 94.

Suggested Reading

"Literary" and Literary-Historical Approaches

Anderson, Linda. *Women and Autobiography in the Twentieth Century* (Hemel Hempstead: Harvester Wheatsheaf, 1996).

Bell, Susan Groag and Yalom, Marilyn, eds. *Revealing Lives: Autobiography, Biography and Gender* (Albany: SUNY Press, 1990).

Benstock S., ed. *The Private Self: Theory and Practice of Women's Autobiographical Writing* (London: Routledge, 1988).

Brodzki, Bella and Schenck, Celeste, eds. *Life/Lines: Theorising Women's Autobiography* (Ithaca: Cornell University Press, 1988).

Gilmore, Leigh. *Autobiographics: A Feminist Theory of Women's Self-Representation* (Ithaca and London: Cornell, 1994).

Heilbrun, Carolyn G. *Writing a Woman's Life* (London: Women's Press, 1989).

Jelinek, Estelle C. *Women's Autobiography: Essays in Criticism* (Bloomington: Indiana University Press, 1980).

Lang, Candace. "Autobiography in the Aftermath of Romanticism." *Diacritics*, vol. 12 (Winter 1982), pp. 2–16.

Marcus, Laura. *Auto/biographical Discourses: Theory, Criticism, Practice* (Manchester: Manchester University Press, 1994).

Neuman, Shirley, ed. *Autobiography and Questions of Gender* (London: Frank Cass, 1991).

Nussbaum, Felicity A. *The Autobiographical Subject: Gender and Ideology in Eighteenth-Century England* (Baltimore: Johns Hopkins University Press, 1989).

Simons, Judy. *Diaries and Journals of Literary Women* (Basingstoke-Macmillan, 1990).

Smith, Sidonie. A Poetics of Women's Autobiography: *Marginality and the Fictions of Self-Representation* (Bloomington and Indianapolis: Indiana University Press, 1987).

Smith, Valerie. *Self-Discovery and Authority in African American Narratives* (Cambridge: Harvard University Press, 1987).

Stanton, Domna C., ed. *The Female Autograph.* (Chicago and London: University of Chicago Press, 1987).

Wong, Hertha Dawn. Sending My Heart Back Across the Years: *Tradition and Innovation in Native American Autobiography* (New York: Oxford University Press, 1992).

Interdisciplinary Approaches

Ashley, Kathleen, Gilmore, Leigh and Peters, Gerald, eds. *Autobiography and Postmodernism* (Amherst: University of Massachusetts Press, 1994).

Auto/Biography: Journal of the B.S. A Study Group on Auto/Biography.

Gagnier, Regenia. *Subjectivities: A History of self-representation in Britain, 1832–1920* (New York and Oxford: Oxford University Press, 1991).

Geiger, Susan. "Women's Life Histories: Method and Content." *Signs*, vol. 11, no. 2 (Winter 1986), pp. 334–51.

Gender and History: Special Issue on Autobiography, vol. 2, no. 2 (Spring 1990).

Hamilton, Paula. "Inventing the Self: Oral History as Autobiography." *Hecate*, vol. 16, nos. 1/2 (1990), pp. 128–33.

Magarey, Susan, ed. *Writing Lives: Feminist Biography and Autobiography.* *Australian Feminist Studies*, 1992.

Okely, Judith. "Anthropology and Autobiography: Participatory Experience and Embodied Knowledge." *Anthropology and Autobiography* (New York and London: Routledge, 1992), pp. 1–28.

Personal Narratives Group, ed. *Interpreting Women's Lives: Feminist Theory and Personal Narratives* (Bloomington and Indianapolis: Indiana University Press, 1989).

Popular Memory Group. "Popular Memory: Theory, Politics, Method." *Making Histories: Studies in History-Writing and Politics.* R. Johnson et al., eds. (London: Hutchinson, 1982), pp. 205–52 .

Probyn, Elspeth. *Sexing the Self: Gendered Positions in Cultural Studies* (London: Routledge, 1993).

Stanley, Liz. "On Auto/biography in Sociology." In *Sociology: Special Issue on Auto/biography in Sociology*, vol. 27, no. 1 (February 1993), pp. 41–52.

Steedman, Carolyn. *Past Tenses: Essays on Writing, Autobiography and History* (London: Rivers Oram Press, 1992).

Autobiography as Teaching/Learning

Humm, Maggie. "Subjects in English: Autobiography, Women and Education." *Teaching Women: Feminism and English Studies.* Ann Thompson and Helen Wilcox, eds. (Manchester: Manchester University Press, 1989), pp. 39–49.

———— . "Autobiography and 'Bell Pins.'" In Vivienne Griffiths et al. *Writing Feminist Biography 2: Using Life Histories. Studies in Sexual Politics* (Manchester University, 1987).

King, Kim. "Using Retrospective Autobiographies as a Teaching Tool." *Teaching Sociology*, vol. 15 (October 1987), pp. 410–13.

Metcalfe, Marion, Towers, Timothy and Abbs, Peter (Pateman, Trevor, ed.). *Autobiography and Education* (Education Area, University of Sussex, 1986).

Ribbens, Jane and Students from Oxford Polytechnic. *The Personal and the Sociological: The Use of Student Autobiography in Teaching Undergraduate Sociology* (Oxford Polytechnic, 1991).

Ribbens, Jane. "Facts or Fictions? Aspects of the Use of Autobiographical Writings in Undergraduate Sociology." In *Sociology: Special Issue on Auto/biography in Sociology*, vol. 27, no. 1 (February 1993), pp. 81–92.

Swindells, Julia ed. *The Uses of Autobiography* (London: Taylor and Francis, 1995).

PART I

Historians of the Self

INTRODUCTION

In her introduction to *The Penguin Book of Women's Lives*, Phyllis Rose writes of her "wild excitement" when her elderly mother announced she had written her memoirs. Mrs Davidoff's memoirs turn out to be a list of words on the back of a contract bridge score card: "milk 2 / ice / trolley—El / radio / meter / beer / A&P / laundry / Staten Island / movies." The words, it transpires, are aides-mémoire for a spoken account of the technological changes her mother has witnessed in eighty years of daily life in New York City. Fascinating as all this is, Rose admits to a pang of disappointment: "I wanted the psychological inside scoop on my family. . . . There were things about my mother I really wanted to know."[1]

The anecdote encapsulates two moments in the feminist scholar's relationship to autobiographical texts. The first is the researcher's intake of breath when she stumbles across a bundle of letters in an attic, or uncut pages in a musty volume of memoirs. The second, of course, is that perplexed feeling when, opening the envelopes or cutting the pages, she discovers that the answers offered inside do not quite match the questions she is asking, or when she finds that her accustomed ways of reading slide off the surface of the writing.

Both sensations—the elation and the deflation—are partly to do with what has been called the historian's "massive transferential relationship to the past": the fact that what we look for hardest is by definition what we miss (as we might miss our own childhood, for instance, or some fantasized unity with our mother).[2] But the feminist historian faces further difficulties. For one thing, in many cultures ideologies of femininity require of women a range of qualities incompatible with public self-representation: reticence, modesty, propriety, humility, discretion. The Collective's study of Englishwomen's life-writing in the seventeenth century shows that, whether women actively endorse or teasingly subvert such ideologies, the records they leave, if any, will pose particular challenges to the reader hoping for the "inside scoop." Furthermore, as these early writings also show, appeals to experience and stategies of disclosure may be couched in conventional discourse—in the language of the Bible for instance.

Nor is the problem reducible to ideologies of femininity. As all contributors to this section demonstrate, the self-inscriptions of women are seldom of the kind preserved in, much less as, the "historical record"—the more so if, like Jolly's subject Maimie Pinzer, they are marginalized by virtue of disability, ethnicity, sexual identity, or occupation. And because of this, the subjectivities such texts record, whether in a mnemonic for an oral narrative, a family album, a bundle of letters, a garden, or a quilt, are often not what we currently recognize as "selves."

In other words, a snug fit has evolved between the liberal humanist "poetics" of autobiography and individualist (read masculinist, bourgeois, Eurocentric) modes of subjectivity. Regenia Gagnier has usefully outlined the mode of selfhood we have come to expect from autobiography:

> a meditative and self-reflective sensibility; faith in writing as a tool of self-exploration; an attempt to make sense of life as a narrative progressing in time, with a narrative typically structured upon parent/child relationships and familial development; and a belief in personal creativity, autonomy and freedom for the future.[3]

The modes of literacy, leisure, family-life, aspiration, and change assumed by this literary model of subjectivity have been inaccessible to all but a few subjects in the recent past; inevitably, it fails adequately to account for many of the works addressed in this book. However the model cannot straightforwardly be dismissed as irrelevant to our reading practices, since its dominance not only means that many varieties of women's life-writing are not recognized as autobiography, but that some are not legible as "texts" at all.[4]

Historian Carolyn Steedman has dramatized this problematic in the troubling encounter between Victorian social explorer Henry Mayhew and an eight-year-old girl selling watercresses on the streets of London. Prompted to describe her life, the girl produces a narrative in which work is her identity rather than an attribute of it, and in which her experience of childhood is determined by her role in a precarious family economy. Mayhew, according to Steedman, is disconcerted. He (we) can't tell if what she calls her "toys" are really the family's meagre furniture, or whether the little girl "minds" a baby for love, or money, or both. The "things" in her narrative—"pieces of fur, the bunches of cress, the scrubbed floor"—do not share the same meanings as found in the paraphernalia of middle-class family life of more "literary" narratives. They do not "resonate": they do not seem to function as metaphors for anything outside themselves, and so we cannot make a satisfying story of them.

The little girl's testimony so confounds Mayhew's notions of childhood, dependence, and work that in important ways he cannot see her.[5] His problem—the historian's problem, let us say—is thus not necessarily lack of "evidence," but lack of an appropriate frame within which to see it as such. It is precisely the appearance of flatness in the marginal stories—in the testimony of the watercress girl, for example—that produces the effect of depth in culturally-central canonical stories . As Steedman puts it, "there is no kind of narrative that can hold the two together (though perhaps history can)."[6] The challenge—the challenge women's autobiography poses to history—is not to displace one set of stories with another, but as Rendall's essay suggests, patiently to reconstruct the frameworks within which marginalized "self-historians" have made sense of their lives.

In Britain this work was begun by Julia Swindells, who argued that Victorian working women, excluded from dominant modes of both individualist and class-conscious self-representation, construct subjectivities by calling on genres and conventions in which women are at least visible, if often in idealized form. She points to the way such women call upon novelistic or melodramatic styles in order to underwrite their judgements and experiences—especially when violating convention by articulating their dilemmas as women.[7] Many readers have followed Swindells' lead in looking to these gendered eruptions of "the literary" for what Jolly, in this volume, calls "evidence of past consciousness."

But while literary discourse may have special significance in a context such as mid-Victorian Britain, in which print culture in general and fiction in particular have a prominent place in the national imaginary, other moments and contexts will privilege different discourses: the scriptural, the psychological, or the pedagogical, for example.[8] Hence, Rendall in this volume follows Regenia Gagnier in exploring the multiple, intersecting generic frameworks evident in working women's lifewritings, and in paying close attention to the practical uses of literacy rather than simply to autobiography as self-actualization for its own sake. (The texts examined here find women writing the self in order to lead others to salvation, to make money, to secure patronage, to counteract slander. . . .) Gagnier's rhetorical approach brings into clear focus the struggle lifewriting represents—in all the works discussed in this section—to create, secure, and maintain communities of support. Life-writing may, as Alberti's reading of Ray Strachey's letters illustrates, be a means of ensuring moral support in the face of emotional upheaval or political struggle; one only has to turn from Ray Strachey to Maimie Pinzer to see that it may be, simultaneously, a plea for material help in the face of poverty, desertion, or dispossession.

The rhetorical urgency of such documents has encouraged our contributors to resist purely deconstructive approaches to the "textual self" and to reclaim some notion of writing as agency. From their various perspectives as literary, social, and political historians, they converge with Liz Stanley (a sociologist) and Regenia Gagnier (a cultural historian) in emphasizing the diverse uses of autobiography in women's lives. In various ways they justify Liz Stanley's defense of the "common reader" of autobiography: one who "recognizes the power and importance of referentiality in autobiography writing and is capable of reading in an active way, recognizing both the fragility of "the self" and its constitution in and through the everyday behaviours, events, persons, of the life."[9] Cumulatively, our contributors to this section suggest that it is only through an understanding of subjectivity in, and as, active engagement with the material world, rather than just as textual "effect" or just as "product" of historical determination, that we can restore to women life-writers their dignity as "self-historians."

Notes

1. Introduction, *The Penguin Book of Women's Lives* (London: Viking, 1994), p. 36.

2. Carolyn Steedman, *Past Tenses: Essays on Writing, Autobiography and History* (London: Rivers Oram Press, 1992), p. 201.

3. Regenia Gagnier, *Subjectivities: A History of Self-representation in Britain 1832–1920* (New York and Oxford: Oxford University Press, 1991), p. 39.

4. Ranjana Khanna's discussion of Mahasweta Devi's story "Draupadi" in this volume throws further light on this problem.

5. Carolyn Steedman, *Landscape for a Good Woman: A Story of Two Lives* (London: Virago Press,1986), pp. 128–39.

6. Steedman, *Landscape*, p. 139.

7. Julia Swindells, *Victorian Writing and Working Women* (Cambridge: Polity, 1989).

8. I am indebted to the doctoral research of Ruth Symes, Centre for Women's Studies, University of York, for pointing out the special function of pedagogical discourse in late eighteenth-century Englishwomen's autobiography.

Further Reading

Gagnier, Regenia. *Subjectivities: A History of Self-Representation in Britain, 1832–1920* (New York and Oxford: Oxford University Press, 1991).

Gender and History (Special Issue on Autobiography and Biography), Vol. 2, No. 1 (Spring 1990).

Nussbaum, Felicity A. *The Autobiographical Subject: Gender and Ideology in Eighteenth-Century England* (Baltimore: Johns Hopkins University Press, 1989).

Personal Narratives Group, *Interpreting Women's Lives: Feminist Theory and Personal Narratives* (Bloomington and Indianapolis: Indiana University Press, 1989).

Riley, Denise. *Am I that Name? Feminism and the Category of Women in History* (London: Macmillan, 1988).

Scott, Joan W. "Experience" in Judith Butler and Joan W. Scott, eds., *Feminists Theorize the Political* (London and New York: Routledge, 1992), pp. 22–40.

Sheridan, Dorothy. "Writing to the Archive: Mass-Observation as Autobiography," *Sociology*, vol. 27, no. 1 (February 1993), pp. 27–40.

Smith, Lee. *Oral History* (London: Picador, 1989).

Sommer, Doris. "'Not just a personal story': Women's testimonies and the plural self." In Bella Brodzki and Celeste Schenck eds., *Life/Lines: Theorising Women's Autobiography* (Ithaca: Cornell University Press, 1988), pp. 107–30.

Spence, Jo and Holland, Patricia, eds. *Family Snaps: The Meaning of Domestic Photography* (London: Virago Press, 1991).

Stanley, Liz. *The Auto/biographical I: The Theory and Practice of Feminist Auto/biography* (Manchester: Manchester University Press, 1992), part II.

Steedman, Carolyn. *Landscape for a Good Woman: A Story of Two Lives* (London: Virago, 1986).

——— . *Past Tenses: Essays on Writing, Autobiography and History* (London: Rivers Oram Press, 1992).

Swindells, Julia. *Victorian Writing and Working Women* (Cambridge: Polity, 1985).

——— . "Liberating the Subject? Autobiography and 'Women's History.'" In The Personal Narratives Group, eds., *Interpreting Women's Lives: Feminist Theory and Personal Narratives* (Bloomington and Indianapolis: Indiana University Press, 1989), pp. 24–38.

Walker, Alice. *In Search of Our Mothers' Gardens* (New York: Harcourt Brace Jovanovich, 1983).

1

"Life Has Done Almost as Well as Art": Deconstructing The Maimie Papers

Margaretta Jolly

Autobiographical writing has been a central resource in feminist projects to reconceptualize both "history" and "literature" in terms that recognize women's contributions and the dynamics of gender relations. However, over the last decade or so, these projects of recovery have been challenged by the postmodern strategy of deconstruction whereby the status of historical or empirical "knowledge" is radically problematized.[1] Far from abandoning the personal and experiential records that autobiography offers us, however, some feminists have become fascinated with them as discursive constructions of self, pitting deconstruction against reconstruction, literary critical reading of genre against historical reading of experience.[2] But doubts begin to nag. How well, some feminists are asking, does postmodernist theory meet the needs of the oppressed?[3] Its invitation to deconstruct the subject can undermine the very terms of identity needed for self-representation. This chapter evaluates deconstructive methods by looking at how they might apply—or fail to apply—to a concrete example: the life and writing of Maimie Pinzer. Only by foregrounding individual histories can we really sense what is at stake in the larger philosophical exchange between postmodernism and feminism.

This analysis of *The Maimie Papers* is undertaken for two reasons. As the copious, intimate, and extremely powerful letters of a disabled, Jewish, working woman and ex-prostitute, they represent the kind of hidden history infinitely precious to many feminists and other radical readers. In addition, *The Maimie Papers* require us to re-evaluate letters, and more specifically, letter-collections, as a form that has been unduly neglected in the study of autobiographical writings, particularly since, as this chapter argues, the epistolary life-story poses an interesting challenge to deconstruction.[4] My underlying suspicion is that theories that purport to do away with individualism are often disrespectful of their subjects' own terms of self-representation. But let Maimie Pinzer set the terms of the debate herself:

> Goodness knows, I am old enough—but I do like to think I have some youth left and with [Miss Brown] it is impossible. For she condemns everything that has anything to do with life and the joy of living. She starts to talk—and it gives me a pain in the ear. Such platitudes and rot! As though any people can be classed off and nicely packeted away, according to a system. I know *every one* individual is different from any other person that has ever existed, for they have a different combination of things in their get-up. . . . She says, being a successful stenographer, I have proven I couldn't ever be anything else successfully. I like to tease her; so I say I expect some day to write short stories successfully— though to date I have never tried to write one single word. It gets her goat (to use the vernacular) when I say that—and I enjoy seeing her getting enraged at my impudence.[5]

What are *The Maimie Papers*?

The letters of Maimie Pinzer were "discovered" by the feminist historian Ruth Rosen in the Schlesinger Library at Radcliffe College. They had been written to Fanny Quincy Howe, who had kept them for more than half a century, until her daughter donated them to the library in 1971. Rosen, with Sue Davidson, edited and published the letters in 1977.[6]

Maimie Pinzer,[7] born in 1885, was the daughter of lower-middle-class Russian-Jewish immigrants who had settled in Philadelphia. When she was thirteen, her father was brutally murdered, and she was forced to leave school to help at home. She began work in a department store and socialized with young men there. After staying out several nights with one of the boys she had met there, Maimie was arrested at the instigation of her mother, who then refused to come and get her daughter out of the police cell where she had been taken that night. Maimie ended up in the Magdalen Home, "a sort of mild reform school for girls that had gone astray," and after her release in 1899 worked intermittently as a prostitute until 1910.[8] By then she had lost an eye, probably due to syphilis, had suffered thirty-nine surgical operations, and was under treatment for morphine addiction. At this point, Mr. Welsh, a dubious Christian social worker, put her in touch with a wealthy Gentile Bostonian, Fanny Quincy Howe, as a possible patron with "moral" influence. Surprisingly, twelve years of intense and sustaining correspondence followed, although the two women met only twice. But Fanny Howe's letters disappeared with Maimie Pinzer, in 1922. Philip Toynbee speculates that "from all that we learn of Maimie from this selection of her own letters . . . if there had been any hint of condescending patronage or sanctimonious reproach in Fanny Howe's letters Maimie would never have bothered to write back."[9]

During those twelve years Maimie Pinzer left her stolid husband to become the mistress of Ira, an infatuated Jewish businessman whom she eventually married in 1917. She tried to make good seeking secretarial work in New York and Toronto, established her own women's stenography company until the war pushed her out of business, and finally ended up discovering what she said was her "lifework": helping young prostitutes off the street. But this is to suggest a resolution, a happy ending, when the challenge of this story, both historically and aesthetically, is its denial of any such closure. The last, brief letter in the collection is dated four years after the rest, from a hotel in Chicago in 1922. This anti-ending—bristling with enigmas—is perhaps the most potent reminder that this is history, not fiction.[10]

Invoking history against fiction, however, is a dangerous move when dealing with autobiography. Autobiography's intrigue is precisely its confusion of those disciplinary boundaries: a confusion that is particularly intense in a text with as much "literary" appeal as *The Maimie Papers*. Doris Lessing, comparing Maimie's letters to Richardson's epistolary classic *Clarissa*, says that "life has done almost as well as art."[11] However it is precisely what lies trapped between life and art, history and fiction, that we most need to find terms for— that is, Maimie's sense of self, her consciousness. Negotiating a space between the disciplines for that "almost art" is no simple matter. And if we then wish to "deconstruct" that sense of self, we will inevitably find ourselves deconstructing the disciplinary frameworks that define themselves through it. By moving between historical and literary critical perspectives on *The Maimie Papers* I hope to show the fascination of this tension between "deconstructing the self" and "reconstructing the past" and ultimately, that it can be part of the same interdisciplinary project.

The Maimie Papers in Historical Context

We are lucky to have a ready-made historical context for *The Maimie Papers*, since Ruth Rosen, the editor of the letters, used them substantially in *The Lost Sisterhood*, her book on prostitution in the so-called Progressive Era. Maimie's extant letters coincide with the height of the era and, as Rosen interprets them, they exemplify some characteristic tensions within prostitution and working women's lives at the time. The mania for reform that gives the period its name has been interpreted as a coming-to-consciousness of the effects of the rapid industrialization and explosive population growth, boosted by mass immigration, during the last quarter of the nineteenth century.[12] The middle classes swept into the burgeoning immigrant, working-class, and industrial communities to "clean up vice," pressed for protective legislation and set up social welfare organizations. Of all the social causes, the campaign against prostitution was the most fervent and widespread. For about twenty years, the reformers fought both laissez-faire government and the powerful interests in the trade who argued for "regulation" rather than "abolition," eventually gaining government support for abolition by 1916. The social significance of the era's reforms is still contentious. Did they provide much needed welfare? Or were they a complex apparatus of social control over the lives of the poor, deviant, or needy?[13] As regards prostitution, Rosen argues persuasively that prostitutes themselves gained nothing overall from the campaigns for reform.

Maimie Pinzer's experiences as both the recipient and the dispenser of this kind of proto-social work seem to exemplify the ambiguity and often utter futility of such reform efforts. The reasons why Maimie Pinzer entered prostitution tally very closely with what Rosen's critical review of the literature suggests made women choose to become prostitutes. Although most women entered prostitution for basically economic reasons, reformers' surveys suggest that a high percentage came from families distinguished not by their poverty, but by the experience at some point of a severe disruption of the family economy. Rosen argues further that considering that both prostitutes and non-prostitutes faced the same bleak occupational prospects—their economic and social mobility blocked by class, gender, and sometimes disability and ethnic identity—family instability may have been an important factor in women's decisionmaking. This certainly makes much sense of Maimie Pinzer's experiences subsequent to her father's brutal murder when she was thirteen. It also throws light on Maimie Pinzer's sense of never fitting into any circle, and her anguish when she writes of her estrangement from her family. The fact that, as the letters attest, she fights against miserable impoverishment rather than return to prostitution makes their refusal to forgive or accept her harder still:

> They all hate me, I must be somehow at fault or why doesn't one of them like me? . . . I've got 3 brothers, a mother and many uncles and aunts and I can't turn to one of them and my brother said he'd consider I'd done the family a kindness if I would get off the Earth.[14]

But as manifest as the tone of remorse is in *The Maimie Papers*, more so is Maimie's defiance and sharp-sighted criticism of "respectable" society's hypocrisy: a strain that Rosen identifies as a hallmark of the "subculture" of prostitution. Walkowitz pushes this further in her analysis of prostitution in Victorian England. Rather than stressing the negative effects of a "broken family home," she speculates that it may have been precisely the lack of strict family socialization that allowed girls to question their opportunities more boldly: sexual and social defiance finding an outlet in prostitution.[15] In addition to this, Rosen tells us that central to prostitutes' own perceptions of their lives was that the trade was a better option—"easier work"—than the common alternatives, factory work or domestic service. In Maimie Pinzer's early letters, the temptation to "go back" was particularly strong, as Maimie found herself trapped in a loveless marriage with the hopeless Albert, a bricklayer whom she had married for economic security only to find that the chronic unemployment situation meant she was more likely to bring in money than he. Maimie explains to Fanny:

> I always felt that if a person sincerely wanted to work they could readily find work, even though it was not exactly the sort of work they prefer, and I still believe that, so the plain truth must be that I do not sincerely want to work . . . Of course, there is scrubbing of floors and dish washing to be considered—and since I wouldn't do that, it is plain to be seen I do not sincerely want to work . . . You know, Mrs. Howe, that I never had any luxuries, and been reared a domestic, that would not seem so absolutely not-possible, but I lived in a luxurious home until I was sixteen, and then for years after that had the easy life that immoral living brings, and I just cannot be moral enough to see where drudgery is better than a life of lazy vice.[16]

In the light of Rosen's and Walkowitz's historical accounts, it would seem that the tensions we feel so sorely in Maimie Pinzer's letters originate in historical conditions rather than in her individual character. If Maimie Pinzer's letters continually testify to her "outcast" status and the suffering that it caused her, then we can locate this in the historical moment in which prostitutes were made "an outcast group."[17] However, the symbiotic relationship between Rosen's history and her edition of Maimie Pinzer's letters invites us to contextualize Rosen herself, particularly in the way she "uses" the letters. Her formulation of prostitution as "not much different from the alternative" options facing working women stresses prostitutes' power within a limited set of choices. Using autobiographical sources, and especially direct quotations, allows her to render "agency" as a textual effect. The drawback is that it tends to elide the difficulties of resurrecting "voices" from texts that deconstruction has forced us to acknowledge. Let us take up her insistence on women's personal struggle, and move into the more dangerously tenuous evidences of past consciousness.

Redemption in the Promised Land: Models of Self

I consider the subjective dimension of the letters by looking at some textual characteristics of Maimie Pinzer's "autobiographical voice," specifically as she discusses her sense of identity. I try to focus this by comparing the letters to the autobiography of the contemporary Jewish woman writer Mary Antin. The publication of Mary Antin's autobiography *The Promised Land* (1912) provoked Maimie to reflect on her own "story" as a Jewish woman of "humble origin"[18] and particularly, on her ambitions to write. These reflections are given an interesting twist when Maimie Pinzer meets Mary Antin briefly in 1912.[19]

The Promised Land told of the Antin's family's immigration to the U.S. in 1894 when she was thirteen, after escaping from anti-Semitic persecution in the Russian Pale. The book chronicles their struggles on arrival in Boston and Antin's eventually joyful acculturation during her adolescence. The book's publication crowned her success in escaping the "ghetto." Antin's autobiography is fascinating for the proto-modernist language of her description of "self-generation" as she insists that "I am absolutely other than the person whose story I have to tell." While many have seen her autobiography as a sentimental glorification of the American Dream,[20] this exposure of the process of self-construction both represents and problematizes a political self-making as an American Jew. Her description of her self-generation—she even offers a kind of rebirth for her parents—acknowledges the traditional Judaic investment in the continuity of the people while adroitly inverting it, in a fascinating synthesis of the American and Jewish dreams.[21] Antin writes of her earliest memories of life in Polotzk:

Of the interior of the house I remember only one room, and not much of the room as the window, which had a blue sash curtain, and beyond the curtain a view of a narrow, walled garden, where deep-red dahlias grew. The garden belonged to the house adjoining my grandfather's, where lived the Gentile girl who was kind to me.

Concerning my dahlias I have been told that they were not dahlias at all, but poppies. As a conscientious historian I am bound to record every rumour, but I retain the right to cling to my own impression. Indeed, I must insist on my dahlias, if I am to preserve the garden at all. I have so long believed in them, that if I try to see *poppies* in those red masses over the wall, the whole garden crumbles away, and leaves me a gray blank. I have nothing against poppies. It is only that my illusion is more real to me than reality. And so often do we build our world on an error, and cry out that the universe is falling to pieces, if anyone but lift a finger to replace the error with truth.[22]

Antin's memory of the childhood garden is about the importance of her own perception in the most general sense. The dahlias of illusion are preferable to the poppies of truth. Yet it is notable that this evocation of a classic autobiographical trope—the garden of childhood—is twisted so that she is outside the "narrow walled garden": it belongs to the Gentile girl next door. This fact, combined with her characteristic move into philosophical rhetoric, produces a disconcerting yet seductive tension between our sense of a child's and an adult's perspective. Her charming little-girl's self assertion ("I retain the right to cling to my own impression") is arch and there is a whisper of cynicism in her adult conclusion that "so often do we build our world on an error." I suggest that this passage implicitly represents the general tension in her autobiography between a desire for—or perhaps her forced acceptance of—historical continuity as a Jew and an assertion of radical self-making to the point of discarding the objective world, or her own past, for her "own impressions."

The Maimie Papers is likewise a tale of self-generation after a forced break from the past. As the story of a second-generation immigrant, however, it is very much a disillusioned sequel in which self-construction is more like reconstruction, and this is reflected, at the level of form, in the difference between Antin's public and rhetorical representation, and the privatized realism of Maimie Pinzer's letters.

Maimie's description of meeting Antin provides a good point at which to compare their self-representations, especially since it elicited a childhood memory that startlingly echoes the style of Antin's text. It appears to be Fanny Howe who was responsible for Maimie's introduction to the famous writer and it is quite clear that Maimie viewed Antin as a possible "contact." Maimie is apprehensive however:

> I don't resent her wishing to know more of me or Ira or his family; still I feel much as I did when you wrote to me the first time . . . The fact she is one of my own race and from humble origin should make me feel she really is the sort I ought to like—but I am afraid she is not like "Mrs. Howe."[23]

These feelings are borne out in their eventual fraught rendezvous at Antin's house, and Maimie's account of it to Fanny is as poignant as it is witty. Antin was unresponsive to all Maimie's topics of conversation, especially those that touched on Antin's own origins:

> I ventured further (thinking this topic—our Race—was her pet one, judging from a letter or two that she wrote me, and also from her stories), that I recalled when I was a little girl, how I had been given permission to pick some roses (one Sunday afternoon) in a well-filled garden belonging to a fine Christian gentleman who was friendly with me . . . I picked about ten roses—as much as I could then hold (I was seven or eight years old). And after about four or five such Sundays, he went with me into the garden, and asked me why I did not take a white rose or a pink one? And I said that I didn't want to pick them until they were ripe. For I no doubt thought they started white, became pink, and then red. I heard this story told by him to many visitors at his home after that; and in every case I heard comment which, even as a child, I remember, had great bearing on the fact that I was a Hebrew, and the brighter colours naturally appealed to me. Oh yes: it seems—though Mr. Webb explained, and I understood—I never wanted a rose other than a red one. And once—when the red were about gone—I refused any, rather than take the paler ones. I thought this might interest her. But she only commented that one's tastes were most likely the result of one's environment—and as I glanced about the room. I thought she had better have left it to the Race.[24]

Her suggestion that her refusal to pick any but the red roses signifies her "Hebraic" taste for bright colours, along with the evident "privilege" of being in this man's garden, exoticizes her in a manner typical of Antin's self-presentation. At the same time, in striking contrast to Antin's childhood garden, the anecdote is strangely evocative of fairy tale: there is the hint of a fantasy of plenitude in the characterization of the garden as "well-filled," and of herself as carrying "as much as she could . . . hold," and this is compounded by the symbolic testing of her identity as she chooses from the three colors of the roses. Maimie has never mentioned this mysterious Mr. Webb before (in the published letters) although it is interesting that his name echoes that of another "fine Christian gentleman," the social worker Mr. Welsh who took her up as a Jewish girl ripe for redemption. Furthermore, Maimie Pinzer's description of her relationship with Mr. Webb carries the latent sexualization of her references to Mr. Welsh. Roses are the age-old Christian symbol for love and femininity—the gradations of Mr. Webb's roses from white to pink to red are surely suggestive of the sexualization of innocent girlhood. The scene bears an obvious similarity to the Beauty and the Beast story, and we can develop this theme to see a kind of exchange between Maimie and the gentleman of her "self," but also particularly her sexuality, for a rose.[25] The implication that she is there on sufferance as a poor girl is underwritten by her Jewishness, and the sexualized language figures not only her gender but her racial and class "otherness" in the Christian bourgeois world.

To return to the encounter between Maimie and Antin, Antin refuses Maimie's description of her childhood garden as a token of their common identity. She certainly refuses to take up the hint that there may have been exploitation and oppression in Maimie's childhood "privilege," as there was in her own "exclusion" from the garden of her childhood. Maimie Pinzer's final acerbic parting shot that "glancing about the room, I thought she had better left it to the Race," is a cynical comment on Mary Antin's political reputation and on her own exoticized version of the redeemed self. In her detachment, and in Maimie's confidence to Fanny, she subverts the model of selfhood—a Jew redeemed by the American Dream—on which Mary Antin has made her name. But she also makes explicit the latent trouble of gender that Antin's autobiography attempts to ignore. The model of selfhood Maimie looks to remains Mrs. Howe, although on the way home, she feels that it is Fanny, as much as Mary Antin, who has inexplicably failed her:

> The funny part of it was that somehow, the day we went, I kept you in mind and sort of expected her to be of your sort; and I felt downcast on my return, as though you had failed me.[26]

Redemption for both Mary and Maimie Pinzer, but far more quietly and completely for Maimie, is on terms that prevent their common

identification as Jewish women and point up the vulnerability Maimie
Pinzer ultimately faces in her own possibilities for redemption through
the writing of her life for Fanny Howe.

The kind of discursive analysis I have attempted here aims to give
access to the more subjective dimension of the autobiographical text.
But this presupposes a relation of text to history—as knotted up in the
notion of selfhood—that can be picked apart. Maimie Pinzer, for whom
a great deal hung on the possibility of a gap—or a space—between a self
and its writings, was acutely aware of the limits of reading. Responding
to Fanny Howe's suggestion that she should meet Mary Antin, she had
written:

> I will make this suggestion: You know her only from her writings,
> and while one's writings are generally supposed to reflect one-
> self, one's character, etc., that would not always prove correct, as
> some are very clever with the pen and would trick one. So until
> such time as either you or I meet her—if either of us ever do—sup-
> pose you do not tell her *all* about me—leaving out the ugly part,
> until you feel sure she would not condemn me.[27]

Let us now step into the gap between text and consciousness by asking
who is the Maimie Pinzer we can know "only from her writings?"

You Know Her Only From Her Writings

I want to pursue our quest for Maimie Pinzer's consciousness in
the light of the work of Julia Swindells, who has attempted to bring
together poststructuralist, materialist, and feminist theory directly in
relation to women's autobiographical writing. Swindells' premise,
elaborated in her fascinating book, *Victorian Writing and Working
Women* (1985), is that one cannot freely "invent" a self but must always
negotiate it within given discourses and especially the dominant discourse. In her formulation, women autobiographers will be forced to
negotiate "conflicting subjectivities." Thus subjectivity is separate
from the author (and plural) but is nevertheless a phenomenon that in
the public domain of writing may be more or less available, and more
or less appropriate to the writer's material interests, depending on
one's position in the production of culture. When we read autobiography, therefore, we must look again to those ubiquitous textual
"cracks"—though neither for precisely historical nor psychological
information but rather as evidence of an intersection of different discourses, or "intertextuality." This evidence tells us not about the writer

directly, but about the terms upon which s/he wrote. For British nine-teenth-century working women autobiographers, these terms were severe:

> For working women, particularly in the first half of the nineteenth century, the models of social advance . . . barely exist in any form, in the social formation. Neither can working women call upon a clearly defined class consciousness which unites the social group, working women. What working women autobiographers have to do therefore, given that absence . . . is to construct subjectivities by calling on particular representations, particular genres, in which women are at least visible, though frequently in a reified, ide-alised form.[28]

Unlike working men's autobiographies of the same period, therefore, which are "frequently organized around particular notions of advance in waged labor" or, stereotypically, the "rags to riches" plot, many nine-teenth-century working women turn to fiction, melodrama, or romance, to represent their lives "as if 'the literary' itself is the key (possibly the only) means of construction of self."[29] This recourse to the literary is not only a search for available female models. Swindells' examination of the points in a text where such intertextuality can be found suggests that "it almost invariably means that experience has moved into the most fraught areas of sexuality, of 'women's issues' as that category allocated to women as not public, kept from articulation."[30] Just as women find it difficult to construct identities around a narrative of career, therefore, they also find the terms lacking for a public articulation of what is defined as "the personal."

The interest of Swindells' argument is that it is aimed not at evi-dently rewritten or fabricated "testimonies" of working women, but precisely at those texts we would wish to cherish as letting us hear, even if faintly, that voice of a sister in the past. This is where she draws attention to the popular view that the more literary an autobiography, the greater its individuality and authenticity. On close examination this is a paradoxical claim based on an assumption that literary discourse is less determined, more individually expressive than other discourses. What it conceals more fundamentally is the ideological nature of indi-vidualism itself. From this point of view, the frequency with which *The Maimie Papers* is compared to an epistolary novel, and a most individual one at that, makes it even more vital to place such an apparently authen-tic and remarkable document historically, as subject to the same restric-tions as working women whose voices either did not survive, or did so as the overt projections of reformers' moral concerns.[31]

In applying Swindells' theory to *The Maimie Papers*, the first point to note is that the letters were produced overtly as part of a reconstruction of Maimie Pinzer's identity, at least initially. In other words, the correspondence was initiated on terms which forced her to negotiate Christian, bourgeois and, in the case of Mr. Welsh, patriarchal judgements. Let us examine Maimie's second letter to Fanny Howe from this perspective:

> I am not working at anything, and I am ashamed to admit it, for I always felt that if a person sincerely wanted to work they could readily find work, even though it was not exactly the sort of work they prefer, and I still believe that, so the plain truth must be that I do not sincerely want work. In my mind, I explain my inability to get work this way. I am not fitted for any work that is a trade, as stenography etc.; and as for the sort of work that a general education and some "horse sense" fits you for, I cannot work at that for that is almost always clerking in the public stores, and where they see me they will not employ me because of the appearance I present with this patch on my eye. I am invariably told that they will be glad to take me on when I—or rather my eye—"get well." Of course there is scrubbing of floors and dish washing to be considered—and since I wouldn't do that, it is plain to be seen I do not sincerely want to go to work. I could not need money any worse than I do, and yet I would not do work of that sort, so I must admit that I am not serious when I say I would do any sort of work.[32]

Maimie Pinzer is here talking of a painful, obviously pressing situation—being out of work—and yet what comes over is her own distance from that reality. "In my mind, I explain my inability to get work this way." The language also distances her from her disability, for which she suffers such serious discrimination ("the appearance I present") although she then collapses together this distinction between "appearance" and "mind" in the confusion of "I" and her "eye." The conversation between Maimie and Fanny/the reader is played out as the internal dialogue in Maimie's head. She thus appears to wrestle with her conscience rather than to demand or even merely express the need for money. More specifically, we could pick up the way that the meaning of the idea of "sincerity" fluctuates. The first time it is used it serves unambiguously to condemn Maimie's profession to be desperate for work, when she evidently has not found any. The aphoristic moralism of "if a person sincerely wanted to work" is echoed in her repeated conclusion that she must not sincerely want to work. But a detachment has occurred: she applies the moral to herself but shows that it does not fit—the "plain truth must be"; "it is plain to be seen." Her insincerity in saying that she would work at anything is transformed into her sincerity about being "above" scrubbing of floors and dish washing. Which is to say that she appeals to Fanny's gentility through a subtle assertion of her own, crucially advanced through a moral rhetoric of truth and sincerity rather than of the issue at hand, work.

By the time Maimie meets Mary Antin in 1912, her relations with Fanny have changed, and it is important to bear in mind that the letters are written to a woman to whom Maimie professes great love. Nevertheless, those overdetermined appeals to sincerity, while not necessarily untruthful, are arguably part of a discourse that mystifies the social differences between the two women, as well as Maimie's work, particularly when that work is prostitution. An overt case of this idealization is when Maimie does "drop back" into prostitution. Although the letters evidence her struggles, monetary and emotional, over the decision to leave her husband for Ira, her wealthier lover, the plot and the language make a dramatic move from realism to romance. Ira arrives with roses and a diamond brooch, transports her to a hotel suite in New York "almost like a doll's house, it is so pretty and small."[33]

We could liken the "plot" of *The Maimie Papers* to eighteenth-century epistolary novels, in which a female heroine suffers all sorts of social, but crucially sexual, indignities as a test of her virtue. After her rude expulsion (by the proverbial "bad mother") from the comfortable life she'd had before the murder of her father, Maimie Pinzer is virtue besieged, having to negotiate the improprieties forced upon her because of her class, disability, and ethnicity, as well as her gender. However, if these produce possible examples of the intertextuality that Swindells identifies, Maimie's accounts to Fanny are never programmatic, even in the early letters. Letter thirteen, for example, begins:

> My trolley is twisted again; that is I am "off again," and that means I can't think but that everything is going to the bow-wows. I think it's a scurvy trick on my part to write to you in this mood, but I can't or won't help it . . .[34]

She follows with a tale of her attempts to find the rent after learning that Albert, her husband, has been laid-off again. She ends up phoning one of her old contacts, but only dines with him. In the end, because she is hungry and unable to refuse the man's attentions, she comes home sick, drunk, and remorseful:

If I was "blue" all week, last night's sweet escapade has given me a monopoly on all the Blues in the world. Somehow I feel I ought not to tell you all this, for I think it will pain you, but then, I don't want to keep that one ugly out. For I have said all along to myself that I was writing you—my other self—just as I would write were I keeping a faithful diary.

I would like to read your mind when you read this letter. I don't think you would be angry, but still you might be disgusted. It surely doesn't seem as though your and Mr. Welsh's encouraging letters helped me much. Well, there is no use sitting here condemning myself. I am to you what I am to myself; so it is rank waste of time expressing my opinion of myself, when you know my worth—or, rather, worthlessness—just as well as I do. I wonder whether you knew I was off again, when you did not hear from me.

I will go to bed now, as it is twenty-five minutes of five and I am sleepy; but I wish I could end this appropriately—cleverly I mean—as you do in the letter in The Opal.

Perhaps after all I had better say goodnight.[35]

The slang (often self-consciously placed in inverted commas) and the exaggerated claim to own the monopoly of the world's sadness give us a wry and worldly-wise Maimie, not altogether serious about her confession. But equally, the childlike appeals to Fanny's all-knowing powers, and the painful redundancy of her honesty, counteract this detachment: "You know my worth—or, rather, worthlessness—just as well as I do." Her wish—and inability—to find an end to the letter as "appropriate" as that as Fanny's letter in her novel *The Opal* suggests the fragility of her narrative as much as it does the weight of discursive influence.

The problem of finding an appropriate ending is a good point at which to bring out the ambiguity of Swindells' method of reading autobiography. Her suggestion that narrative advance in autobiography is dependent on discursive opportunity can lead to an extremely determinist view of culture. The logic of such a political deconstruction would read the brief, almost anonymous final letter of *The Maimie Papers*, dated tantalizingly four years later than the previous one, as the confirmation that, in terms of her writing to Fanny, no continuing story remains possible for this heroine. But instead we could see that last letter as the point at which Maimie is liberated from the reading of her life, or at the least, the point at which history takes over and distinguishes itself from discourse. Consider the mysterious, almost inscrutable tone of her concluding paragraphs:

> You haven't any idea of what I am thinking these days. I want to write you fully and ask your advice . . . but just now I can't go into it, except to give you a hint and ask you to think about it.
>
> I want to go to school—i.e., I want to take up the study of something. I am fearful lest my equipment is inadequate. I haven't any idea of what I should aim for, and above it all, I am so afraid that I overestimate the worthwhileness of it. I haven't discussed this with Ira, mainly because in his estimation I know now more than anyone alive! However, I know what I have yet to know.
>
> My love to you all,
>
> Maimie.[36]

But it is this distinction of history from discourse that deconstruction, and its attack on the self, radically undermines. If Maimie cannot be anything other than a "textual effect" for present readers, the text in its opacity can have only one dimension, the ideological. To privilege the text to this extent, in other words, is to say that history and ideology are one and the same. In the case of autobiographical writing, it is to say that an individual in a position of powerlessness cannot truly be said to be able to "write history," becoming instead the poignant mouthpiece for their oppressors.[37] In my final section I will consider these implications of deconstruction by contrasting it with a different kind of textual analysis that may offer more positive terms for the relation of text, self, and history.

Possibility, History and *The Maimie Papers*

It seems obvious to me that the most vital and pressing part of the experience of reading *The Maimie Papers* is the sense of Maimie Pinzer changing, and more generally, of temporality in the narrative itself. However, the monolithic and deterministic story that emerged from my "scientific" reading of *The Maimie Papers* in the last section does not appear to encourage a sense of the historicity of the present. Could it be that there is a contradiction between the premises of a materialist discursive reading of history and its results? A muddle between determination and determinism? The attention to structure, linguistic and political, that is the prerequisite of these approaches, can lead to a very static analysis. In response I want to argue that the sense of the self-in-history, rather than being a capitulation to a humanist and idealist notion of a coherent self, is a textual effect in its own right, indeed the primary textual effect of *The Maimie Papers*. Finding terms for this will therefore recognize the centrality of the text without sacrificing the radical effect of reading the letters, which is the apprehension of individual agency.

Throughout the letters we experience the turgidity, the tautness of a prose that follows, or so it would convince us, every tributary and twist of a geographically, economically, and emotionally unstable life. Its qualities are those of flux, process, contingency, surprise, paradox, irony. Yet these are inextricably bound to the concreteness of the plot which refuses schematization. Although we can identify discourses of martyrdom, literary genre, and maturation, partly as a result of the editing, the text that cries out for attention involves the movement between Fanny's and Maimie's "positions" as both ironic and unstable, and this is only one aspect of the irony and instability of the general relationship between the narrating and the experiencing "I." This is a chameleon relation that is intensified by the proximity in time between these two selves. Maimie Pinzer constantly rehearses the immediate past and projects anxiously or determinedly into the future. Furthermore this task of self-construction is endless: of course, what she plans or predicts does not happen, or it happens differently. She can write at one moment and not the next.

Dorrit Cohn's study of consciousness in narrative fiction, *Transparent Minds*, provides us with some terms for this kind of self-representation.[38] Cohn argues that first-person narration by definition projects an experiencing self which parallels the narrator's relationship to the protagonist in third-person narration. But in first person narration, evidently, the narrating self is linked existentially as well as functionally to the experiencing one. In *The Maimie Papers*, letters in which we feel privy to intense self-revelation or at least, continual self-presentation, these two selves appear very closely linked. This narrative effect becomes obvious when we compare the letters to Mary Antin's autobiography, in which the two categories of selves are set so far apart that they appear totally severed, as, moreover, the "present" Antin argues is her conscious strategy. Antin's younger "past" self is thus presented as if it were a character in a third-person narrative, indeed objectified to such an extent that the authorial self seems to be totally preserved from the reader, while the earlier one becomes a sounding board for the general philosophical reflections that sustain the autobiography. In *The*

Maimie Papers, the narrating self has no such structural privilege, and this is obviously one of the essential means by which we are convinced of both the letters' literalness and their psychological credibility. Retrospection, exposition, cathartic expression—there is constant variation in the intensity and temporality of this relationship between Maimie Pinzer writing and Maimie Pinzer living. This is partly to insist on the obvious fact that these are letters and we will experience them with all the contingency of the genre. The epistolary form, albeit within the overall economy of her exchange with Fanny, continually threatens any structure of advance that would situate the "I" through the abstraction of a literary genre. Furthermore, can we not help but feel that every part of the narrative is relevant in ways that exceed the terms of "identifiable" discourses—Maimie Pinzer's expenses; her love of her dog; the wonderful name of her dog, Miss Poke; the confrontation with her mother over whether using Listerine mouthwash was a "lewd practice?"

Yet there are difficulties with situating this brief discussion of the epistolary form of *The Maimie Papers* within my previous arguments about ideology and history. By countering the abstracting effects of the ideological reading I considered earlier, am I inappropriately comparing the structural characteristics of the text as a narrative, and the structural relations of its production? It is arguable indeed that the writing and the reading relations that produced the letters were schematic in a way that the plot is not. Yet, since both involve the application of literary critical technique to an historical text. I am bound to observe that the first offers a much more inclusive and representative description of the experience of reading the text than the second, which is so selective in its technique that we sometimes wonder whether it is necessary to have read the whole text in the first place. By denying the narrative its spontaneity and by culling discursive "instances" to serve as parables of cultural determination, we lose the most radical effect of reading the letters, which is the sense of the self-in-history. This evidently is not just a question of validating the lay-reader's response to the text. It is crucial to how we use the text *as* history, particularly in the still-burning question of retrieving past consciousness.

It is my conviction that what we could call the aesthetics of the letters ironically provides the strongest argument against the poststructuralist attack on history. This is because the passage of time is so strongly implicated in the letters and because, as narrative form, the letter-collection represents particularly clearly the tension between structure and anti-structure. If the epistolary form can become a test case for maintaining a structural analysis that resists closure or stasis, it also inevitably returns us to what we know as history. These are the philosophical implications of my insistence that the narrating self remain in tension with the projected "self-written," that the "I" always extend beyond or behind the moment of its utterance. I am saying, in other words, that it is in recognizing individual consciousness in *The Maimie Papers* as a primary textual effect, that we find the grounds to argue that it be read as more than that: as a textual effect that can and should tell us about real struggles that are other than, or, extra-textual. How we then understand the nature of that reality is another debate, but one logical direction would be to follow on from anthropological perspectives to look at the role of form and story in everyday life.[39] At any rate this is to take the text's index of struggle more on its own terms. It is also to pay tribute to what we sense is precisely an existential investment in Maimie Pinzer's writing. *The Maimie Papers*, by representing to us a woman struggling with life and writing within the boundaries that history allowed her, reminds us that the point about history is that it could have been different. Perhaps it is appropriately ironic to finish by quoting Maimie on her difficulty in answering philanthropists' letters: "I have such a horror of writing to persons that I feel are not specially interested in me as a person, but in me as a *question* (if you know what that means)."[40]

Notes

1. For an excellent introduction to the theory of deconstruction, see Jonathan Culler, *On Deconstruction: Theory and Criticism after Structuralism* (London: Routledge, 1989).

2. See for example Shari Benstock, ed., *The Private Self: Theory and Practice of Women's Autobiographical Writing* (London: Routledge, 1988).

3. Linda Anderson, for example, has observed that the post-modernist theory of the "fragmented subject" obscures women's route to the decentered self and may be as much based on falsely universal claims as was the humanist Romantic self. At this historical moment, she suggests, feminists need to keep some notion of a unified selfhood as it is our primary interest to analyze the relation of subjectivity to the outside world. Linda Anderson, Women's Studies seminar discussion: York, 1989.

4. For exceptions, see Charles A. Porter, ed., "Men/Women of Letters," *Yale French Studies* (No. 71, Yale University Press, 1986); Elizabeth Goldsmith, ed., *Writing the Female Voice: Essays on Epistolary Literature* (Boston: Northeastern University Press, 1988); and Linda S. Bergmann, "The Contemporary Letter as

Literature," *Women's Studies Quarterly* (Fall/Winter 1989, Vol. 17), 128–39. The latter is one of only two articles to discuss *The Maimie Papers* in literary critical terms.

5. Ruth Rosen and Sue Davidson, eds., *The Maimie Papers* (1977. London: Virago, 1979), pp. 186–87.

6. Rosen, *The Maimie Papers*, pp. xi–xii.

7. Maimie Pinzer is a pseudonym given by Rosen and Davidson.

8. She also worked in various secretarial jobs, as an actor, and as a nude model for art classes.

9. Philip Toynbee, "Sisters in Affliction," rev. of *The Maimie Papers*, ed. Ruth Rosen, *Observer*, 16 Sept. 1987: p. 36.

10. This is the end of the story in published form: Ruth Rosen in a letter to the author, Dec. 1993, told me that she has found only sparse and tenuous evidence of Maimie's subsequent life and no mention of further communication with Fanny.

11. Doris Lessing, "Doris Lessing on The Maimie Papers," rev. of *The Maimie Papers*, ed. Ruth Rosen, *The Literary Review* 5 Oct. 1979: pp. 4–7.

12. See for example Richard Hofstadter, *The Age of Reform* (London: Jonathon Cape, 1962).

13. Ellen Carol Du Bois, "Working Women, Class Relations and Suffrage Militance: Harriet Stanton Blatch and the New York Woman Suffrage Movement, 1894–1909." *The Journal of American History*, Vol. 74 (1), June 1987: pp. 34–59.

14. Ruth Rosen, *The Lost Sisterhood: Prostitution in America, 1900–1918* (Baltimore and London: Johns Hopkins University Press, 1982), p. 161.

15. Judith Walkowitz, *Prostitution and Victorian Society: Women, Class and the State* (New York: Cambridge University Press, 1980).

16. Rosen, *The Maimie Papers*, p. 3.

17. The phrase comes from Judith Walkowitz's study of prostitution in Victorian Britain, referred to above, although I think it is applicable also to prostitution in the Progressive Era.

18. Rosen, *The Maimie Papers*, p. 114.

19. Mary Antin, *The Promised Land* (London: William Heineman, 1912).

20. Suzanne Koppelman chides Ludwig Ledwisohn amongst others for this criticism in Suzanne Koppelman, "Mary Antin," *Dictionary of Literary Biography Yearbook*, ed. Jean W. Ross. Gale Research Company, 1985, pp. 225–32.

21. Suzanne Koppelman has traced other ways in which Antin reinscribed orthodox Judaic beliefs as American secular enlightenment in ibid., pp. 225–32.

22. Mary Antin, *The Promised Land*, p. 81.

23. Rosen, *The Maimie Papers*, pp. 113–14.

24. Rosen, *The Maimie Papers*, p. 162.

25. I am indebted to Trev Broughton for this suggestion.

26. Rosen, *The Maimie Papers*, p. 167.

27. Rosen, *The Maimie Papers*, p. 114.

28. Julia Swindells, *Victorian Writing and Working Women: The Other Side of Silence* (Cambridge: Polity Press, 1985), p. 11.

29. Swindells, *Victorian Writing*, p. 140.

30. Swindells, *Victorian Writing*, p. 140.

31. The historian Anne Butler, for example, refers to "the frustrations" of dealing with "fraudulent memoirs piously written by non-prostitutes" and "tracts of reformed prostitutes" in Anne Butler, *Daughters of Joy, Sisters of Misery: Prostitutes in the American West, 1865–1890* (Urbana and Chicago: University of Illinois Press, 1985), endnotes.

32. Rosen, *The Maimie Papers*, p. 3.

33. The implication of Maimie's reconstruction via writing her life for Fanny is ironically played out again between Maimie and Ira, where Maimie manages to inspire Ira to make a large sale for much needed money by leaving him a six-page letter of encouragement at the breakfast table, as well as reading him Fanny's novel. "Isn't that almost like a fairy tale?" she asks Fanny Rosen. *The Maimie Papers*, p. 92.

34. Ibid., p. 29.

35. Rosen, *The Maimie Papers*, p. 32.

36. Rosen, *The Maimie Papers*, p. 416.

37. See Swindells' suggestion that some discourses would be more "appropriate" than others for working women (for example, ones which would not reify or obscure their labor as their sex).

38. Dorrit Cohn, *Transparent Minds: The Representation of Consciousness in Fiction* (Princeton: Princeton University Press, 1978).

39. For example, see The Personal Narratives Group, ed., *Interpreting Women's Lives: Feminist Theory and Personal Narratives* (Bloomington and Indianapolis: Indiana University Press, 1989).

40. Rosen, *The Maimie Papers*, p. 285.

2

"A Short Account of My Unprofitable Life": Autobiographies of Working Class Women in Britain c. 1775–1845

Jane Rendall

In 1834 Eliza Macauley, farmer's daughter, actress, and lecturer, wrote that as a "self-historian" "I am desirous . . . of being known and understood." To her "Auto-Biography"[1] was "the most interesting species of biographical literature . . . because the most authentic."[2] Yet for other working women, like Elizabeth Evans, the lace-worker who told of her "unprofitable life," such a public commitment to self-history was more difficult. Sarah Martin, dressmaker, also regretted the "strange impropriety" and "egotistical appearance" of the history of her life.[3] Hannah Carnes, needlewoman, displacing herself as subject, wrote of her life rather as "a short account of the Lord's dealings with my soul."[4] Mary Ann Ashford, servant and sweetseller, offered the "various events of her own life" not as a romance but as "the real truth" for the amusement of "matter-of-fact persons."[5]

Since the publication of David Vincent's pioneering *Bread, Knowledge and Freedom* in 1981, social historians have recognized the challenge of recovering such histories.[6] Vincent wrote of the contribution they could make to the understanding of radical culture in Britain in the first half of the nineteenth century. Such a culture was rooted in the occupational experience of the male working class, though it drew upon the traditions of spiritual autobiography and oral reminiscence. While these narratives were largely given coherence and shape by the occupational identity of their authors, they were also informed and structured by a sense of progress, both collective and individual, towards the "knowledge and freedom" to which radical artisans aspired. Vincent suggested that there was an ambiguous relationship between such autobiographies and the emergence of the canonical male autobiographical writings of the eighteenth and early nineteenth centuries, of Rousseau, Gibbon, and Wordsworth. Such working-class male narratives represented the collective aspirations of their class, yet, molded within an individualist and bourgeois culture, they also charted a history of the self rewritten with optimism and, for many, pride. Vincent noted with regret that his survey of 142 autobiographies included only six by women.

Feminist historians have written of the extent to which the radical political culture of the early nineteenth century had the male subject, with his identity shaped by his possession of skilled labor and the headship of a household, at its heart.[7] Yet the experiences of economic and industrial change, of urbanization and the shifting family economy, were different for working-class men and working-class women, even though working-class women, single or married, were accustomed to labor from an early age. If single, they might be mobile, might pursue and change occupation, yet the most common location of their labor remained a household. Apprenticeship and skilled trades for women were a diminishing possibility throughout this period. Women's occupations were less likely to be lifelong, more likely to change as they moved from single life to marriage and motherhood, and in response to shifting forms of production and definitions of women's work. Working-class women were measurably less literate than either working-class men or middle-class women.[8]

Sally Alexander argues that:

> feminist history has to emancipate itself from class as the organising principle of history, the privileged signifier of social relations and their political representations.

Drawing upon psychoanalytic theory, she suggests the possibilities of an historical approach to the study of subjectivity, one which through its writing of desire and fantasy might also simultaneously incorporate "the social naming and placing among kin, community, school, class, which are always historically specific."[9]

Regenia Gagnier's recent work, *Subjectivities* (1991), suggests a pluralistic approach to the study of subjectivities, an approach defined not by its relationship to a classical canon rooted in an individualistic and Enlightenment tradition, but by the varieties of material and cultural experience, everyday practices and literary form, found in working-class autobiographies.[10] She has written of such autobiographers as shaping the identities of their narratives through discursive engagement with different sets of collective, mutual, and familial loyalties—frequently defined in oppositional terms. In this essay, writing as a historian, I argue that the continuing recovery of working-class women's autobiographical texts will make possible further exploration of the complex identities constructed within such narratives. For there is a far wider range of autobiographical writing within the period 1750–1850 on which to draw than has been acknowledged. In a preliminary survey of a range of standard bibliographical sources and historical works, I have identified fifteen pieces of autobiographical writing by working-class women, from circa 1775 to circa 1845.[11] None of these were used by Vincent in *Bread, Knowledge and Freedom*. They represent a very disparate grouping, posing immediate problems of definition.

One definition, used by Julia Swindells, would include all those women who had to work for their living.[12] But here there are problems of self-identification, in relation to class. There would be a much wider pool of writing to be discussed here, if the works of women such as Hannah Robertson, Alice Davis, and the female sailor, Mary Anne Talbot, who chart their social decline from a higher status to debtors' prisons and destitution, were included.[13] The marvellous recollections of the governess Ellen Weeton, and the equally spirited memoirs of Hannah Kilham, radical Methodist, Quaker, and missionary to Sierra Leone, who kept a school on widowhood, have been excluded, since they identified themselves with the middle ranks of society.[14] And although it is an important document, I have excluded, because of its very distinctiveness, the only slave-narrative published in Britain by a woman in this period, the *History of Mary Prince*.[15]

The problems underlying a gendered understanding of class difference become apparent in considering these disparate works. The unevenness of economic change within this period makes it, for most social and economic historians, a transitional period in the formation of a working class from the plebian culture of a pre-industrial society. Such unevenness makes it difficult to chart the boundaries between, for instance, the families of small farmers and respectable artisans, and the larger numbers of the very poor, all of whom are represented here. The autobiographies considered range geographically, from the Essex domestic servant to the Ulster spinner, from the Nottinghamshire weaver to the Devon nursemaid. Yet only one of the female autobiographers discussed here defined herself in terms of an occupational identity: Jane Jowitt, "the Poor Poetess." Although she was a barrister's daughter, Jane Jowitt is included among these fifteen narratives because of the care with which she inscribed herself as a "poor woman" in her text, precisely setting out the labor and the relationships which defined that term. She became a soldier's wife, she "always got plenty of needlework from the officers' ladies," and "when General Smith sent his butler to get a female that was handy at getting a plain English dinner," she became a cook.[16]

Yet all these autobiographers were at different times employed in whatever task came to hand. The most common occupation was service, at different levels, followed by keeping a shop and hawking goods across the country, needlework and dressmaking, spinning, weaving, and teaching. Keeping a school did not necessarily imply status or formal education. Mary Porteus opened a school for small children shortly after she learned to write. Even lengthy experience did not necessarily constitute an occupational identity. Mary Ann Ashford wrote that her seventeen years in service constituted only a third of her life so that the best title for it would be "what it really is—the Life of a Licensed Victualler's Daughter."[17]

These narratives vary greatly in their length and presentation, from the six pages by Eliza Smith to the 164 by Margaret Davidson. An immediate problem is that of editorial mediation. Only those by Mary Ann Ashford, Ann Candler, Hannah Carnes, Jane Jowitt, and Eliza Macauley were published during the author's lifetime. It was common practice for the nineteenth-century editor to build a memoir around fragmentary autobiographical pieces, diaries, and letters, in his, and here it is uniformly his, creation of a life. Such works have been used only where autobiographical writing forms the most important source for a life, and in which very substantial selections have been incorporated into editorial narrative, such as those of Mary Porteus and. Johanna Brooks. Margaret Davidson, the Irish Methodist, was blind and dictated the complex record of her life, to her editor "taken down verbatim almost as she herself delivered it."[18] These texts were all written within this period and may therefore look back to some sixty years earlier, as do those of Margaret Davidson and Mary Saxby.

In looking at these texts, I want to consider, as Gagnier does, the diversity of "master-narratives" which frame them, the different loyalties and overlapping identities upon which their writers draw.[19] Only Eliza Macauley, a London Owenite, lecturer and writer, participated, marginally, in that radical culture analyzed by Vincent, Hall, and Alexander.[20] I will suggest seven possible alternative frames of reference, which constantly overlap within this group of texts, and differ slightly from Gagnier's: the spiritual autobiography, the repentance narrative, the world of oral story, the petition, the genre of romantic fiction, the language of middle-class womanhood, and the life-cycle of the family economy.

The commonest informing principle structuring these works is the spiritual autobiography.[21] Such autobiographies told the story of individual search for illumination, of a life of constant self-abnegation and self-exploration. The spiritual autobiography was not limited to a single denomination. Like Sarah Martin's it could be written with a posthumous publication in mind, as part of a collective missionary impulse offering a model of spiritual struggle, for the conversion of others. The servant, Miriam Sheriff, wrote of her life:

> Encouraged by the Word of God, and in consequence of the entreaties of a dear child, who by the hand of God was made useful to my poor soul, by teaching me the Word of God, and how to pray over it; which I consider was the first step in leading me to a saving knowledge of my Saviour and myself: I now take a review of my life, and how the Lord has led me, by a way I knew not, that he might bring me to a city of habitation.[22]

The Quaker example offered women the chance to speak in public and travel as ministers, powers which set them at odds with gender conventions. Wesleyan Methodism offered a model of the spiritual journey in the individual's progression from a sinful past to a first awareness of the potential saving grace of God, to repentance, to justification and a new birth, the continuing stage of going on to perfection, and the ultimate unachievable goal of entire sanctification. Women made that journey, as they extended their prayers to public testimony in class or public meeting, to exhorting, expounding, and even giving an exegesis of biblical texts in public preaching. Margaret Davidson's narrative was one of constant travel in such testimony. The Wesleyan Methodist Conference imposed a ban on women's public preaching in 1803 . Yet women from the dissident Methodist sects, like Hannah Carnes, Elizabeth Evans, Mary Porteus, and the Bible Christian Johanna Brooks, continued to travel and to preach.[23] In their writings, there are claims to an autonomy defined against the authority of parents and husbands, and claims too to a public voice which might concern later editors.[24]

A particular form of the spiritual autobiography was the repentance tract, usually encouraged, sometimes forged, by middle-class patrons. The outstanding example here is Mary Saxby's *Memoirs of a Female Vagrant* (1806) written with the encouragement of a local minister, who provided an editorial commentary, and published her work through the Society for Bettering the Condition of the Poor to display "the vices and miseries of a vagrant life."[25] Saxby, the daughter of a London silk-weaver, ran away from home, and joined a company of travelling gypsies, living with one of them before she married. The miseries of her life, as she encountered prison and the workhouse, the violence of her husband, and the bearing of ten children, are recounted before "the most pleasing part of my story," her conversion, through the reading of a seventeenth-century tract and the ministry of Methodist preachers.[26] The short narrative of Eliza Smith, written from prison before transportation, is largely formulaic, but Elizabeth Kenning, a runaway cotton-spinner who turned to prostitution and drink, offers a detailed and circumstantial account of her salvation by the ladies who took her to the Liverpool Penitentiary where she remained, crippled and bedridden for most of the period from 1813 to her death in 1829. There she came to play a "zealous and judicious part" in the guidance of penitents, as well as to write poems such as her verse "On a review of my past unprofitable life, and of the goodness of God in directing my wandering steps to the Liverpool Female Penitentiary."[27]

There are also here intimations of lives lived close to an oral culture, though this is not always easy to identify, partly because of the editorial presence. Mary Ann Ashford begins her own narrative with a recounting of her parents' lives which goes beyond the mere placing of origins. She tells the story of her father's first place as a servant, of the tragi-comic episode which turned him into a tanner, as a well-known and much rehearsed family anecdote.[28] The editor of Mary Porteus' work noted the "many every-day incidents that Mrs Porteus's observant faculties and tenacious memory enabled her to relate," but he reprinted few of them.[29] Mary Saxby on the road became a ballad-singer, and though her writing is in the form of a spiritual autobiography, it is also a lively story of her travels, an almost picaresque narrative. It was condemned by one reviewer in the *Evangelical Magazine* for its inclusion of so much unnecessary and improper detail of a past life.[30]

One autobiographical form which could be deployed, always with the possibility of subversion of the formulaic, was the petition. Ann Candler's brief autobiography was prefixed to a small volume of poems written mainly from the workhouse, as a petition for support. Jane Jowitt, in her old age, besides earning her living as a letter-writer to her local community, also wrote poetry for the local gentry. The poor poetess, like the uneducated poet, might hope for the sponsorship of patrons of the upper and middle classes. Of the autobiographies discussed here, it is striking how many of the authors also wrote and published poetry: the prison reformer Sarah Martin, the evangelical preachers Hannah Carnes and Caroline Hopwood, the converted vagrant Mary Saxby, and the repentant thief Elizabeth Kenning all did so, besides Ann Candler and Jane Jowitt. Such writing might offer a statement of personal exploration of experience, and be a means of financial support, but it could also appeal directly to the expectations of patrons.[31] The writing of a life in such a context could mean the recounting of its miseries and of the writer's struggles, in terms designed to appeal to the patron. Ann Candler's volume was published by a small local subscription.

Within these works, patronage was a continuing theme. In old age, a lack of financial resources could mean reflection not on past achievements or a life of material or educational progress, but on present destitution; the grant or refusal of outdoor relief and the expectation of the workhouse figure in a number of these autobiographies. Writing poetry, allied to a life which matched dominant expectations of worth, might constitute a claim for support. A parallel, however bleak, might be the life-stories found in the almshouse petitions of elderly women, a source as yet unexplored for this period. Eliza Macauley tells of her mother, in service with the Countess of Conyngham for seven years, witnessing the Countess' reception of such petitioners.[32] Even in an industrializing society, these deferential relations of dependence and subordination could structure women's lives, though they were not entirely unquestioned. In her study of the early eighteenth century poet Mary Collier, Donna Landry signalled Collier's "apparent resignation to an unchanging social order" as coexisting with a literary ambition and "textual resistance."[33] The coexistence of such resignation with forms of resistance can also be found within these texts, notably the narratives of Jane Jowitt and Mary Ann Ashford, as can the more explicit resistance of Eliza Macauley.

Both Eliza Macauley and Mary Ann Ashford defined their own narratives in contrast to those of romantic fiction. Ashford, in her preface, wrote of the origin of her own autobiography in seeing advertisements for a work called "Susan Hopley, or the Adventures of a Maidservant" (1841).[34] Disappointed to find this a work of fiction, Ashford insisted, in contrast, on the plain truth of her tale—though she could still draw upon the conventions of such fiction in her account of an attempt at seduction. Eliza Macauley presented the first issues of her memoirs in a fictionalized account of the life of her mother, "Elizabeth, or A Tale of Truth." She too wrote of the absence of the poor from the heroines of romance:

The heroines of romance are mostly, indeed we may say invariably, persons of high birth and noble parentage. It would be an
innovation upon all the rights of fiction, should a novel writer
presume to draw the attention of her readers to a heroine of
obscure origin. Nobility of mind, coupled inferiority of birth—
fame and renown crowning the labors of an obscure individual,—
are incongruities appertaining only to *real life*.[35]

Autobiography, then, might validate the aspirations of the heroines of
the poor.

Middle-class women too, in the course of the eighteenth century,
were to develop their own genres of autobiographical writing, as the
private world acquired a new set of meanings, and the boundaries of
gender were more sharply differentiated. The domestic management
of the household, and the woman's task of moral education within it,
could be contrasted with the varieties of public life open to different
classes of men. The developing language of "woman's mission" might
take those moral responsibilities into a wider world. Felicity Nussbaum
and Mary Jean Corbett have recently begun the study of the autobiographical writing of eighteenth- and nineteenth-century middle-class
women.[36] Within the group examined here, Sarah Martin's narrative of
a life committed to philanthropic endeavor can be read in the light of
the developing discourse of "woman's mission."

More significant in a number of these works is the continuing
struggle for survival within that family economy to which all members
were expected to contribute, though in which the wife and mother car-
ried a major burden. Courtship for the young servant or needlewoman
was marked by a period, perhaps a long one, of saving and looking forward to the pragmatic responsibilities of establishing a household.
Once married, her life was shaped by daily provision for the family,
and by the responsibilities of caring for dependent children and placing
them in suitable employment as they grew older. It was punctuated by
the trials, the disasters, and the successes of the family. Mary Ann
Ashford records her careful savings, and her achievements in placing
one son in a foundation school, and her daughter Victoria in a good
place in service. Mary Porteus also recorded how she kept to her
mother's maxim "Owe no man anything" while maintaining her family on her husband's casual and meagre earnings of six shillings a
week.[37]

Within these autobiographies, there is room to explore the overlapping of these frameworks in the structuring of individual lives, in far
more depth than can be done here. The role played by these overlap-

ping generic frameworks in the structuring of individual working
women's lives is richly suggestive for future research. For now two
themes—representations of sexual and marital relationships, and of
class deprivation and difference—will offer a brief glimpse of the complexity and diversity of these materials.

These narratives deal more explicitly with sexuality than those
male autobiographies studied by Vincent. Swindells has pointed to the
use of the melodramatic genre in anecdotes of seduction such as in
Mary Ann Ashford's narrative.[38] Yet the theme is present not only in
the secular but also in the spiritual narratives. Margaret Davidson
recounts her early sinfulness, in the "inordinate affection" she conceived for a young preacher, "her body and mind" both disordered for
about six months: she trembled and blushed at his presence, and "the
distress of my soul was inconceivable."[39] But she tells also of an
attempted rape by the father of a young woman friend, with whom
she had to share a bedroom:

> He opened not his mouth till I had undressed myself; then he
> began to enquire what kept me up so late, "Why (said I) I thought
> you were asleep" to which he answered, "I was dreaming that I
> was in a house where there was none with me but a young girl in
> bed, and making haste to her, I said I will lie down with you."
> Before I could recover from my surprise, he was wafted, quick as
> thought, to the bed where I lay, as if the infernal Dragon had lent
> him wings. Being fast imprisoned in his arms,, without a possi-
> bility, by my own strength, of getting free I instantly cried to the
> God that delivered Daniel out of the den of Lions, to rescue me
> from the hands of my enemy.[40]

The biblical reference would be familiar to her readers; she related at
length the battle to save herself and her final escape.

Mary Saxby recorded that as a vagrant she was fortunate to
escape becoming a prostitute, and that as a ballad singer, she was "in
that line of life which attracted the notice of men."[41] She recollected
her good fortune in escaping assault by a group of sailors, saved only
by the providential interposition of a local farmer. But she wrote of
cohabitation with her gypsy husband, and of being forced to become
his secondary wife or servant to his first wife. She refused to marry a
second man with whom she lived "lest he should use the child ill: and
as it was not then customary for travellers to marry, I saw no evil in
it."[42] She told her story clearly, defending the rationality of decisions
taken according to custom, yet a custom which is also offered retro-

spectively as evidence of her own sin. There is in this narrative a lingering defense of popular assumptions, not yet entirely displaced by evangelical morality.

Jane Jowitt tells of the engineer officer, the Irish gentleman who visited too frequently, against whom her mother, in a dream, warned her:

> [she] spoke to me respecting this gentleman, warning me in the most solemn manner to take care of myself, for this man intended my destruction, after giving me this advice, she said REMEMBER, and gave me a slap on the breast which awoke me; I was very much terrified and was in a violent perspiration, although I knew it was but a dream: on going to the table to wash myself, I found that the print of my mother's hand was quite visible on my chest, and of a high colour. . . .[43]

Jowitt's narrative is of a childhood of loss, of an absent and unfaithful father, of a mother dying when she was eight. In her adulthood, she travelled independently, supporting herself, maintaining her claims to respectability and decency in the face of poverty, keeping her better birth and parentage a secret. Her dream recalled that standard of sexual morality appropriate to a higher class in her own adult life and marriage, restated her own knowledge of her origins, her fears of the "Irish gentleman"—again recalling her own Dublin origins—never conveyed to her husband. Recalled, recreated, the telling of past resistance to seduction and rape, of the preservation of chastity by the vulnerable, could be a way of stressing the integrity of self.

Familial relationships are central to most of the autobiographies described here: this is of course a marked contrast to those male autobiographies described by Vincent. Most of the accounts of relationships between husbands and wives are shaped by a history of conflict. This may be described in terms which suggest battles over resources, and over failure to meet expectations of marriage, expectations of support in surviving and caring for children, of shared codes of behavior and religious experience. Ann Candler was deserted by her soldier husband, who was given to drinking, "utterly degraded in appearance, manners and morals," so that her account—addressed to her subscribers—is one of "an unhappy marriage, for nearly forty years."[44]

Mary Ann Ashford and Jane Jowitt both explicitly contrasted their relatively happy first marriages with less successful second marriages. Ashford's account is matter-of-fact, unsentimental. The proposal took place without any courtship, by a tradesman whom she hardly knew, when she was a servant about to lose her place. There are lingering regrets, regrets exemplified in the tale told of a possible alternative, of the Quaker gentleman who appeared on the scene too late, an opportunity missed. But the tradesman shoemaker made a good if elderly husband. He had more money than she expected, he worked for his family, he saved. "We acted fair and candid towards each other"; but we learn more of the family economy than of intimate relations.[45] Ashford's second husband was also elderly—and she was his fourth wife. He was less honest and continuously ailing, so that she increasingly took the responsibility for all family affairs.

Jane Jowitt recounts her first meeting with a young tradesman in Ireland, who enlisted and was sent to Dover: losing her own money, she followed him as a hawker and married him, a marriage never regretted:

> he behaved towards me in the kindest and most affectionate manner possible, was sober, strictly honest and industrious and respectable . . .[46]

The contrast with a second husband is striking: her account begins:

> An artful old man . . . had his eye constantly on my house; the front door being usually open in fine weather, he could see me writing or selling some of my poetry, and had an idea that it would be a good job to get me for a wife . . .[47]

Though she took out a reference on this prospective husband, it proved unreliable; she who had been moderately prosperous, was left by his drinking and abusiveness, and theft of her property, in a state of destitution. The contrasts are exactly made, the tales told define expectations of a husband still within the bounds of a family economy rather than of middle-class domesticity.

One notable source of conflict emerges within the spiritual narrative, that between the converted wife and unredeemed husband. Hannah Carnes wrote of her enemies as "those of my own house."[48] After her conversion, Mary Saxby's husband, frequently drunk, threatened to throw a boiling pot over her. She describes anecdotally with biblical reference, her lengthy attempts to win him over: the impact of their son's death, his backslidings, his money difficulties, his drinking companions. Yet finally in his last illness, conversion was achieved, as he rejected even "a little good beer . . . when he exceedingly wanted it," "the company and conversation of his old associates" and the services of a woman who was an "old pot-companion" to lay him out after death—he begged she would not touch his body. Such a resolution marks the high point of the narrative.[49]

In the spiritual narratives of Mary Porteus and Johanna Brooks a direct conflict with husbands over their preaching arose, a conflict which was to be resolved only by conversion. Johanna Brooks describes what happened after her return from preaching to a large congregation:

> My dear husband did not speak to me all that night, nor even when he rose in the morning. At eight o'clock I sent the two children to call him to breakfast. He entered the house and then went into the garden, and brought a rod, with which he struck me several times, every stripe leaving a mark.

The tale is both domestic and biblical: the "stripes" are borne by reflecting upon "the precious truth, that 'by *his* stripes we are healed'" (Isaiah lv; 1 Peter ii). Johanna Brooks justified her actions by Matthew x. 34, 35:

> I came not to send peace, but a sword. For I am come to set a man at variance against father, and the daughter against her mother, and the daughter in law against her mother in law.[50]

The sword is taken up. From her domestic isolation onwards, the narrative is one of conversion, not only of congregations, but of the grace finally accorded to her parents and husband—or put in an alternative way, of an empowerment achieved, of a source of strength within family relationships.

Conventions of gender may be both confirmed and challenged in such narratives. The claim to preach in public challenged not merely familial authority but that of public worlds. Johanna Brooks confronted not only the authority of parents and husband, but raised her voice in the local Anglican church, was thrown out by her husband and parish officers, and threatened with the church court; yet she records with satisfaction that she was called to see her vicar in his last illness, that he acknowledged her actions to be right, and, praying with him, she saw him achieve justification.[51] Joel ii.28 is a much quoted text: "I will pour out my spirit on all flesh; and your sons and your daughters shall prophesy." Hannah Carnes generalized:

> About this time the Lord was pouring out His spirit in a particular manner on his handmaidens . . . He hath chosen the weak things of this world, to confound the things that are mighty.[52]

The drive to conversion might find expression in forms which parallel the activities of middle-class women. Sarah Martin's conversion led her to "point others to the foundations of joy"; from teaching in a Sunday School, she felt first "a strong desire to visit the poor in the workhouse" and then those in Yarmouth Prison. The reading of Scriptures and the reform of conditions in the prison were to dominate her life for twenty-four years. Her account is marked first by her encounters with sick and aged women in the workhouse, and by accounts of individual woman prisoners: although from other evidence it is clear much of her time was also spent in teaching and setting to work male prisoners.[53] For Martin there was a conflict between her need to earn a living, and her desire to continue this work. She could support herself as a dressmaker, and her time could be freed by "a lady" paying for one day's work. But the time given to dressmaking dwindled and by 1838 she had given it up, to rely on the providential support of sympathizers, freed from anxiety for the future: "Now my life is my own, my time is for the prisoners, according to my conscience before God."[54]

Most of the autobiographies discussed here—like male working-class autobiographies—record a material deprivation, and a constant anxiety in the face of unpredictable economies, though there are also some differences from the male texts. The absence of food plays a significant part in Margaret Davidson's narrative. She wrote of her exhaustion at living for days together on a little bread and water, of her gratitude for receiving a small quantity of meal, of the temptation of a very little sugar and even of her desire for salt herrings. She also wrote of determination to spin for her keep, yet of still being unable to support herself, reliant on a small parish offering and help from Methodist friends. Such help was variable and unreliable. In her travelling she might be "indulged upon feathers" or "mortified upon straw," entertained in the parlor or "exposed to smoke and soot and the insults of servants in the kitchen."[55] The whole pattern of support and survival was evidence of providential intervention, such divine grace bestowed where an individual woman's striving for independence could not succeed. That same reliance upon providential grace, juxtaposed to a pride in independence yet recognizing the inability of a woman to earn a wage which could support herself and others may be read in the life of Mary Porteus, who tells of a series of providential interventions, of a Christmas dinner unexpectedly provided, a confinement paid for, a rent due relieved, and a son apprenticed.

Yet relief could be harder to come by without the support of a religious community. On the death of Jane Jowitt's husband, she was first refused outdoor relief, then permitted one shilling and sixpence a week. Opportunistically, on the death of Lady Fitzwilliam, she addressed her poetry first to Earl Fitzwilliam, and then to other local dignitaries, on significant events in their families. Her poetry illustrates a relationship of dependence and patronage, yet also one of enterprise. The tale told in her narrative is not one of self-pity; but of walking to York from Sheffield, selling her verses on the way, giving her bread to an old Irishman, and making thirty shillings on her trip. Yet after a stroke she too looked for a home to end her days, and to the possibility of an "asylum for aged widows" to be built by two local ladies.[56] The appeal to the patronage of one's own sex could be an important resource, one which might properly reward a life of struggle and self-reliance.

Similarly, much of the latter part of Mary Ann Ashford's life-history is taken up by her battles against those wielding the powers of patronage. Her interview to enter a lying-in hospital is preceded by an extraordinary dream of:

> a porcupine which lay at my feet, and its quills kept going off like squibs . . . at last . . . it suddenly burst open, and the face of a very cross, ugly old man came forth.[57]

The "porcupine" might perhaps recall that continuing campaigner against Old Corruption, William Cobbett, whose complete works, including his more conservative *Life and Adventures of Peter Porcupine* were republished, abridged, in 1835.[58] In any case, she met this face again at her interview by four or five elderly men, who, cross-examining her, rejected her application. Both her husbands were employed in an army school for soldiers' children, the Duke of York's Royal Military School, Chelsea, which she names Fairy Land. Her first-born child attracted the notice of the Duchess of Kent, after whom she was named Victoria Maria Louisa, some nine months before the birth of the Duchess's daughter, Princess Victoria. In Ashford's struggles to secure the widow's pension due to her from her first husband, she tells of making the rounds of "persons in authority," her constant supplications refused, the only kindness received from the Duchess's gifts. But in her last battle she was successful, for a petition to Queen Adelaide secured superannuation and backpay to her second husband. Here personal and female intervention finally gave success at the expense of bureaucratic authority.

Eliza Macauley in her *Autobiographical Memoirs* both understood, and for herself defiantly discounted, the appeal to patronage:

> I write my life, because I wish it should be written; I send it to the world, because I wish it should be read; and above all, I send it

forth, because I desire to make advantage by its sale! This, though a secondary motive, is nevertheless a very prominent one. The hey-day of my youth is past . . . I would not willingly eat the bread of dependance, or wait till the day of destitution comes, before I make one final effort to shield myself from the perils which have so often attended the declining years of talent and industry.[59]

And, having published her own memoirs with the aid of subscribers, she proposed to establish a "moveable repository," along the lines of a travelling library, to advertise and sell her work.

The range of these narratives cannot be discussed simply in the context of the radical culture of "bread, knowledge, and freedom," though they may help us in the rewriting of women's participation in such a culture.[60] The appeal to patronage, the spiritual autobiography and its conflicts, and the female writer's narrative of service and the family economy could, overlapping, help to structure the self recreated in such works. Spiritual journeys and the life-cycles of the family could offer competing and overlapping coherences. Conversion offered a secure persona, the most important step on the ladder to perfection; and in a secular context the literate and determined woman writer might shape a coherent identity from her familial and laboring roles, though she could never free herself from the random and destructive blows of desertion, economic disaster, and death. Within their narratives, individual women mapped out and imagined their journeying through these harsh territories for themselves.

Notes

I thank the editors of this volume, and Nicole Ward Jouve, for their helpful comments on this paper.

1. Evans, "Memoir," vol. I, 145.

2. [Macauley], *Autobiographical Memoirs*, 1835, 10.

3. Martin, *Brief Sketch*, 31.

4. Carnes, *Life*, Preface.

5. Ashford, *Life*, iv.

6. David Vincent, *Bread, Knowledge and Freedom: A Study of Nineteenth-Century Working-Class Autobiography* (London and New York: Methuen, 1981).

7. Catherine Hall, "The Tale of Samuel and Jemima: Gender and Working-Class Culture in Early-Nineteenth-Century England," in *White, Male and Middle-Class: Explorations in Feminism and History* (Oxford: Polity Press, 1992), 124–50.

8. For an introduction to these themes, see Jane Rendall, *Women in an Industrializing Society: England 1750–1880* (Oxford: Basil Blackwell, 1990). On the literacy of working-class women, see W. B. Stephens, *Education, Literacy and Society, 1830–1870: The Geography of Diversity in Provincial England* (Manchester: Manchester University Press, 1987); David Vincent, *Literacy and Popular Culture: England 1750–1914* (Cambridge: Cambridge University Press, 1989).

9. Sally Alexander, "Women, Class and Sexual Difference." *History Workshop* 17 (Spring 1984): 133–34.

10. Regenia Gagnier, *Subjectivities: A History of Self-Representation in Britain, 1832–1920* (New York and Oxford: Oxford University Press, 1991).

11. The works of reference used were: Earl Kent Brown, *Women of Mr. Wesley's Methodism*, Studies in Women and Religion, no. 11 (New York: Edwin Mellen Press, 1983); John Burnett, David Mayall, and David Vincent, eds., *The Autobiography of the Working Class: An Annotated Critical Bibliography*, vols. 1 and 3 (Brighton: Harvester Press, 1984 and 1989); Gwenn Davis and Beverly A. Joyce, eds., *Personal Writings by Women to 1900: A Bibliography of American and British Writers* (London: Mansell, 1989); S. Barbara Kanner, *Women in English Social History 1800–1914: A Guide to Research*, vol. 3, *Autobiographical Writings* (New York and London: Garland, 1987); W. B. Matthews, *British Autobiographies: An Annotated Bibliography of British Autobiographies Published or Written before 1951* (Berkeley: University of California Press, 1955); Janet Todd, *A Dictionary of British and American Writers 1660–1800* (London: Methuen, 1987); Julie Wheelwright, *Amazons and Military Maids: Women Who Dressed as Men in Pursuit of Life, Liberty and Happiness* (London: Pandora, 1989); Deborah M. Valenze, *Prophetic Sons and Daughters: Female Preaching and Popular Religion in Industrial England* (Princeton, N.J.: Princeton University Press, 1985); and "Cottage Religion and the Politics of Survival," in *Equal or Different: Women's Politics 1800–1914*, ed. Jane Rendall (Oxford: Basil Blackwell, 1987), 31–56. The list makes no claim to be inclusive and no extensive searches were made for locally-printed materials.

12. Julia Swindells, *Victorian Writing and Working Women: The Other Side of Silence* (Oxford: Polity Press, 1985), 125–35.

13. Alice Davis, *A Brief Sketch of the Life and Sufferings of Alice Davis, only daughter of an officer deceased and heir at law to an hereditary estate, the wrongs which she suffered and the oppressions, hardships and deprivations which she endured* (London: J. Barfield, 1831); Hannah Robertson, *The life of Mrs. Robertson . . . who though a grand-daughter of Charles II has been reduced . . . from splendid affluence to the greatest poverty* (Derby: J. Drewry, 1791); Mary Anne Talbot, "The Intrepid

Female, or surprising life and adventures of Mary Anne Talbot, otherwise John Taylor," *Kirby's Wonderful and Scientific Museum*, II (1804): 160–225.

14. [Hannah Kilham] *Memoir of the late Hannah Kilham; chiefly compiled from her journal . . .* , ed. Sarah Biller (London: Darton & Harvey, 1837); [Ellen Weeton] *Miss Weeton's Journal of a Governess*, 2 vols., ed. J. J. Bagley (Newton Abbot: David & Charles, 1969).

15. [Mary Prince], *The History of Mary Prince, a West Indian slave, related by herself* (London: 1831, reprint, ed. Moira Ferguson, London: Pandora, 1987).

16. Jowitt, *Memoirs*, 16, 21–33.

17. Ashford, *Life*, iv.

18. [Davidson], *Extraordinary Life*, 2.

19. Gagnier, *Subjectivities*, 151.

20. Barbara Taylor, *Eve and the New Jerusalem: Socialism and Feminism in the Nineteenth Century* (London: Virago, 1983), 71.

21. However, I have excluded the purely spiritual meditation, like that, for instance, of Isabel Hood, servant and flax-spinner of Elgin, since her "record of spiritual experience of a humble Christian woman" is never placed within the material framework of her life. Isabel Hood, *Memoirs and Manuscript of Isabel Hood*, ed. Rev. John Macdonald, 2nd ed. (Edinburgh: no publisher, 1841). For discussion of women's spiritual autobiographies, see Felicity Nussbaum, *The Autobiographical Subject: Gender and Ideology in Eighteenth-Century England* (Baltimore: Johns Hopkins University Press, 1989), ch. 7.

22. Sheriff, *Care of divine providence*, 5.

23. Women from these Methodist sects are heavily represented among these autobiographies, thanks to Deborah Valenze's close study of female preachers within them, in her *Prophetic Sons and Daughters*, and "Cottage Religion and the Politics of Survival."

24. See, for instance, [Porteus], *Power of Faith*, Preface.

25. Saxby, *Memoirs*, v.

26. Ibid., 35ff.

27. Kenning, *Some account*, 22–24.

28. Ashford, *Life*, 5–7.

29. [Porteus], *Power of Faith*, 44.

30. *Evangelical Magazine*, XIV (July 1806): 324–25.

31. See David Vincent, *Literacy and Popular Culture*, 215; Roger Lonsdale, ed., *Eighteenth-century Women Poets: An Oxford Anthology* (Oxford: Oxford University Press, 1989), xxvi–vii.

32. Macauley, *Autobiographical Memoirs* (1835), 21–22. The Countess of Conyngham later founded Lady Conyngham's Charity, whose records, including the petitions of poor women, are held in the Borthwick Institute of Historical Research, University of York, LCT/C2.

33. Donna Landry, *The Muses of Resistance: Laboring-Class Women's Poetry in Britain, 1739–1796* (Cambridge: Cambridge University Press, 1990), 69–77.

34. The title of the first edition of this novel, by Catherine Crowe, published in 1841, was, however, *Adventures of Susan Hopley, or, Circumstantial Evidence*, 3 vols. (London: Saunders and Otley, 1841). Saunders and Otley also published Mary Ann Ashford's *Life*. Catherine Crowe's novel was reprinted only in 1852 as *Susan Hopley, or the Adventures of a Maidservant* (London: G. Routledge & Co.). It recounts in three volumes Susan Hopley's increasingly gothic and fantastic adventures across the European continent.

35. [Macauley], *Autobiographical Memoirs* (1835), 21–22.

36. Mary Jean Corbett, *Representing Femininity: Middle-Class Subjectivity in VIctorian and Edwardian Women's Autobiographies* (New York and Oxford: Oxford University Press, 1992); Nussbaum, *The Autobiographical Subject*, ch. 9.

37. [Porteus], *Power of Faith*, 35.

38. Swindells, 151–52.

39. [Davidson], *Extraordinary Life*, 13–14.

40. Ibid., 27–29.

41. Saxby, *Memoirs*, 12.

42. ibid., 7, 12–13, 17–20.

43. Jowitt, *Memoirs*, 22–23.

44. Candler, *Poetical Attempts*, 14–15.

45. Ashford, *Life*, 58–62.

46. Jowitt, *Memoirs*, 20.

47. Ibid., 31.

48. Carnes, *Life*, 31.

49. Saxby, *Memoirs*, 46–51.

50. [Brooks], *Handmaid of the Lord*, 33–34.

51. Ibid., 18–20, 62–63.

52. Carnes, *Life*, 27.

53. Martin, *Brief Sketch*, 8–11.

54. Ibid., 11, 26.

55. [Davidson], *Extraordinary Life*, 106–7.

56. Jowitt, *Memoirs*, 36–37, 49–51.

57. Ashford, *Life*, 64–65.

58. William Cobbett, *Selections from Cobbett's Political Writings: Being a complete abridgement of the 100 volumes which comprise the writings of "Porcupine" and the "Weekley Political Register"* . . . , 6 vols., ed. John M. Cobbett and James P. Cobbett (London: Ann Cobbett, 1835).

59. [Macauley], *Autobiographical Memoirs* (1835), 13.

60. I should like to acknowledge my debt here to Helen Rogers' D. Phil thesis: "Gender, Power and Knowledge: Women and Radical Culture 1830–1860" (University of York, 1995).

Autobiographies Cited

Ashford, Mary Ann. *Life of a Licensed Victualler's Daughter. Written by herself* (London: Saunders and Otley, 1844).

[Brooks, Johanna]. *A Handmaid of the Lord: Some Records of the Life of Johanna Brooks* (London: Morgan & Chase, [1868]).

Candler, Ann. *Poetical Attempts . . . with a short narrative of her life* (Ipswich and London: J. Raw, 1803).

Carnes, Hannah. *The Life of Hannah Carnes. Compiled from her own papers. Which form a journal of her life, from her childhood to the present time,—her call to labour in the vineyard of Christ, and her travels through different parts of England, describing some interesting death-bed scenes* (Weymouth: B. Barnes, 1838).

[Davidson, Margaret]. *The Extraordinary Life and Christian Experience of Margaret Davidson (as dictated by herself)*, ed. Edward Smyth (Dublin: printed for the editor, 1782).

Evans, Elizabeth. "Memoir of Mrs. Elizabeth Evans," in *Biographical Sketches of the Lives and Public Ministry of Various Holy Women, whose eminent usefulness and successful labours in the Church of Christ have entitled them to be enrolled among the great benefactors of mankind*, 2 vols., ed. Z. Taft (London: 1825, 8), Vol. 1, 145–58.

Hopwood, D. Caroline. *An account of the life and religious experiences of D. Caroline Hopwood of Leeds, deceased* (Leeds: E. Baines, 1801).

Jowitt, Jane. *Memoirs of Jane Jowitt, the Poor Poetess aged 74 years, written by herself* (Sheffield: J. Pearce Jun., 1844).

Kenning, Elizabeth. *Some account of the life of Elizabeth Kenning, chiefly drawn up by herself* (Bradford: printed by H. Wardman, 1829).

Macauley, Elizabeth Wright. *Autobiographical Memoir of Miss Macauley* (London: published for the author, no date).

———. *Autobiographical Memoirs of Miss Macauley, written under the title of Elizabeth, or "A Plain and Simple Tale of Truth"* (London: Charles Fox, 1835).

Martin, Sarah. *A Brief Sketch of the Late Sarah Martin; of Great Yarmouth; with extracts from the Parliamentary Reports on Prison; her own prison journals &c &c* (Yarmouth: C. Barker, 1844, reprint; London: Religious Tract Society, 1847).

[Porteus, Mary]. *The Power of Faith and Prayer exemplified in the Life and Labours of Mary Porteus, late of Durham, who for fourteen years was a travelling preacher, and twenty-two years a local preacher in the Primitive Methodist connexion. "A Mother in Israel"* (London: R. Davies, Conference-offices, 1862).

Saxby, Mary. *Memoirs of a Female Vagrant. Written by herself. With illustrations*, ed. Samuel Greatheed (Dunstable: J. W. Morris, 1806, reprint; London: Religious Tract Society, 1820).

Sheriff, Miriam. *The care of divine providence and the comforts of true religion, as exhibited in a narrative and extracts from the journal of Miriam Sheriff (late servant to Mrs. Austen of Colchester) written by herself during a painful affliction of eight years*, 5th edition (London: no publisher, 1835).

Smith, Eliza. *Memoir of Eliza Smith, who was transported for shoplifting, written by herself*, with some introductory remarks by [Mary Jane Knott] (Dublin: no publisher, 1839).

3

"Pondering All These Things in Her Heart": Aspects of Secrecy in the Autobiographical Writings of Seventeenth-Century Englishwomen

Elspeth Graham, Hilary Hinds, Elaine Hobby, and Helen Wilcox[1]

Autobiography is always inevitably bound up with issues of secrecy. What is told and not told, through conscious and unconscious decisions about inclusions and exclusions, is the primary choice in the process of self-writing. The interplay of revelation and secrecy is the essential element in the autobiographical act, fundamental to both the control of meaning and the possibility of self-construction. But to examine the role of secrecy in the autobiographical writing of seventeenth-century Englishwomen is particularly exciting for two reasons. Firstly, autobiography as a genre was not conceptualized or recognized until the late eighteenth century, so the range of options for self-representation was especially broad within the fluidity of literary discourses in the earlier period. Secondly, the autobiographical process had a particular urgency and intensity for women, a quality which probably arises from the contradictory subject-positions offered to them in seventeenth-century discourse and society.[2]

In this chapter we explore a variety of ways in which the autobiographical writings of seventeenth-century Englishwomen are contained within, and yet thrive upon, secrecy. By examining four very different texts, we seek to highlight several aspects of the creative concealments operating within autobiography, a mode of writing which in the hands of early modern women is poised between the humility and the power of concealment. The constraints on women and their relationship to self-disclosure in the seventeenth century are hinted at in the biblical text on which our title is based: "But Mary kept all these things, and pondered them in her heart."[3] In the case of the Virgin Mary, "these things"—the momentous events of the first Christmas and the knowledge of her son's holiness—are not to be talked about but instead are humbly tucked away in the privacy of her own heart. However, such secrecy gives her a hidden reserve of enormous strength while allowing her at the same time to maintain an outward appearance of proper modesty.

The autobiographical texts considered here together challenge us to broaden our definition of secrecy. It can range from necessary or fearful privacy to the intimacy of a shared secret or the mystery of one withheld. We trace, in turn, the paradoxes of disclosure and dissolution in Alice Thornton's remembrances; the multiple selves of Anne Wentworth hidden within the biblical language of her self-justification; the tactical secrecy of Katherine Philips' closet lesbian poetry; and the excitedly conspiratorial imaginings of Elizabeth Delaval's meditations. Lying behind our discussion of the four texts are two main purposes: to introduce these early modern women's autobiographical writings to the wider readership they deserve, and to consider some fundamental questions about women's self-writing and the essential agency of secrecy. Prominent among the issues we consider are the shifting borderline of public and private in early modern women's lives, the dangers of slander and betrayal at a time when a good name was so vital a commodity for women, the creation of textual selves, and the relationship between reader and text in the mutual secrecy of autobiography.

Secrecy, Disclosure and Control in Alice Thornton's
A Book of Rembrances (c. 1668).

Secrecy and revelation, twin impulses shaping self-writing, play a crucial role in Alice Thornton's *A Book of Rembrances*.[4] Together they cause tensions in the working of the text, but at the same time facilitate the self-definition of the autobiographical subject. In this consideration of Thornton's work, we are concerned with the ways in which issues of secrecy and disclosure, and moments of self-articulation and self-dissolution, are interlocked.

A Book of Rembrances comes to us in a particularly unfixed form. It is probably the first of the several versions of her autobiography which Thornton produced. It differs significantly from the more widely-known version, *The Autobiography of Mrs. Alice Thornton of East Newton, Co. York*, published by the Surtees Society in 1873. This nineteenth-century edition is, in fact, a conflation of versions, in which events and passages have been re-ordered, producing an apparently coherent life-story, where description of personal experience is surrounded by comment on national and political issues and in which there is considerably more detail and explanation of key events than in the more raw and fragmentary *A Book of Rembrances*. The *Autobiography* is much more public than the *Book*; it contextualizes, and it is consciously explanatory. There is, for instance, a full account of Thornton's marriage, which is merely noted in the *Book*; there is revelation of her feelings about her husband at the time of their marriage; there is a discussion of detailed financial transactions. *A Book of Rembrances* is less a fleshed-out autobiography in the form most familiar to us in the twentieth century than a quite literal-minded record of every deliverance (from death, accident, illness, periods of emotional distress, religious melancholy, or general unpleasantness) that Thornton or members of her family suffered. We do not have a definite date for its composition, but it is likely that this attempt at self-writing was made soon after her husband's death in 1668 and drew on journal entries made throughout the period 1626–1668.

The *Book* can be seen to be shaped by several impulses. It draws on the model of *Psalms* and assimilates the discourse of *Psalms* throughout, using reference to forms derived from *Psalms* in an active manner, but also echoing phrases and spiritual paradigms of suffering and comfort more unconsciously.[5] Another equally clear but more secular motivation lying behind Thornton's continuation of her *Book*, the expansions in its later parts and the eventual circulation of it among members of Thornton's family in manuscript form, is evident in Thornton's desire and need to vindicate herself and her husband from accusations of financial mismanagement throughout their married life. A third motivation to write is her husband's death and the events surrounding it, intensifying the theme of loss, mourning, and suffering which informs the *Book* as a whole. But it is possible to read the episodes occurring at the end of her *Book*, not as the culmination of Thornton's losses, but, in terms of impetus, as the trigger to her preoccupation with self-writing (as opposed to making erratic note-form journal entries) and formally as a source of her predication of selfhood on suffering and deliverance. Although *A Book of Rembrances* is concerned throughout with loss, including description of a series of deaths (of cousins and uncles, her sister, her children and the exemplary good death of her mother), it is the intensity of loss articulated at its end that seems to transform the text

and the autobiographical project. Thornton's self emerges most strongly
out of the greatest and most intensely experienced threats to self
through loss and suffering. Paradoxically, it is an apparently identity-
depriving loss which drives her to self-articulation.

The final passages of *A Book of Rembrances* (pp. 157–63) bring
together key threats to Thornton's identity: her husband's sickness and
death, outrage at the "slanderous" imputations made against Thornton
and her husband by Mary Breaks (Thornton's "bosom's friend"), and
Thornton's expectation of her own death. She begins with reference to
"a great and dangerous sickness" which overcame her "upon the occasion of a sudden grief and terror" and continues from expression of
"affliction," through outrage, to descriptions of faintings and collapse in
bed. Extremes of emotion that take Thornton to moments of near self-
dissolution recur. There are references to "a most great and sad excess of
weeping," "lamentable sorrow," "faintings," "the break," and "over-
flow," all of which are precipitated not only by anxiety over her husband's health, but by her "bosom's friend[s]" treacherous exposure of
Thornton's plans for the arrangement of her daughter's marriage. The
emotional heightening of the passage, arising from this multiple threat
to Thornton's identity, leads not only to Thornton's physical collapse,
but equally to a discursive collapse in the language which describes it.
The account is written in an atypically incoherent manner. At one level
the writing here is driven by an emotional, imperative: Thornton
attempts to express her grief and rage at what she perceives as her
friend's betrayal. Yet simultaneously she seeks to vindicate herself from
her friend's accusations by giving her own account of her innocent
motives and actions. Since, however, it is precisely the threat to the
"secrecy" or containment of her plans that has brought her into a state
of destabilizing fury and grief, she is led into a further form of secrecy—
the obscuring of her desires, purposes, and agency behind a syntax that
is complex and ambiguous, as the following brief extract demonstrates:

> Whilst I am in this vale of tears and shadow of death I must not
> expect no more comforts than will preserve me from sinking. Nor
> will I repine at the great Lord of heaven and earth's most infi-
> nitely wise disposition, for he knows how to propose and intermix
> crosses with comforts, smiles with frowns, to his servants here,
> as shall be the best for them, not as they shall think fit which are
> but of yesterday, but himself who sees not as man sees, but has all
> things in his omnipresent and omnipotent power and shall tend
> most to his own glory. No sooner was my strength in part
> recruited again after my dear aunt's departure home, and having

been so weak that I kept my bed above a week, so beginning to rejoice at my deliverance from the late illness both of the plague of slanderous tongues and the faintings abated something, but the first day that I did arise out of my bed, I had the news of my dear husband's falling sick at Malton brought to me by a letter to my brother Denton, which did so suddenly surprise my spirit that I fell to tremble exceedingly with great grief and fears upon me for his safety and life. (pp. 160–61)

Among the notable features of this passage is the description of Thornton's betrayal and slander by Mary Breaks as a "plague of slanderous tongues," a phrase made more forceful than a mere passing metaphor by its presence in a list of physical "illness." The dread of the disclosure of her secrets is, it seems, as life-threatening as the faintings and other bodily sufferings. In the context of the perceived importance of privacy, of the keeping of actions of the self undisclosed or within the safe-keeping of trusted confidants, slander is a potent danger. It comprises the wrong speaking of the subject by an other—the potential destruction of "that most valued jewel," her "good name" (p. 158)—an act which breaks down the boundaries of the self and threatens a loss of control over her own discourse of the self. It involves, thus, a formidable threat to self and self-story in its combined challenge to reputation (most urgently to be preserved at near-death) and to the formal organization and articulation of the story of the self. Here the configuration of issues of slander and dissolution of the self is especially complex, since the arrangements for the marriage of the daughter (also named Alice Thornton) have been made precisely because of fear of Thornton's and her husband's imminent deaths. The importance of preparation for a good, well-ordered death has been pre-figured in *A Book of Rembrances* by the earlier account of the exemplary deathbed of Thornton's mother, and is established for us by this (as well as by the general cultural values of the period) as necessary to self-definition. For Alice Thornton the preparation and right-ordering of her own and her husband's deaths is a potential moment of power. She has, in her life, been denied control in financial transactions and management of her estates, and she has suffered loss of social status through her marriage. The arrangement of her daughter's marriage offers her some redress, through the person of her daughter, for her sufferings. Crucially, for Thornton, agency is only possible at the moment of her imagined dissolution. It is only when Thornton is nearest to effacement that she becomes powerful.

The thwarting of this moment of redress and control, through slander, uncontrolled disclosure, gossip, and a threat to reputation inevitably produces a physical and discursive collapse that is ultimately more real than her supposed imminent death proves to be. That her loss involves a threat to her daughter's security, to her own reputation, that it is brought about by a rift in her friendship with another woman (and that it is made known to her by a female servant, is not prevented by her niece, and that she is comforted and partially restored by the actions and speech of an aunt) invites us to speculate on a further aspect of secrecy and revelation at play in the text. This is a world where a woman's designated emotional as well as legal allegiance is to her husband, but where women such as Thornton are frequently physically separated from their husbands by the difference of their roles. Thornton inhabited an intensely domestic world, peopled by other women. It seems reasonable to recognize therefore (especially when we take into account the conflicting accounts in the different versions of her autobiography of the degree of happiness she experienced in her marriage), that the rift in her friendship with (the aptly named) Mary Breaks may constitute a loss which is of great emotional significance to Thornton. The break with Breaks disrupts her sense of secure selfhood, but is hard to voice in the absence of a legitimized public form for mourning feminine or domestic suffering of this sort; it is therefore not identified as a specific loss in its own right. The impact of the quarrel with Mary Breaks certainly emerges in the text as blurred with and inseparable from anxiety and fear over Mr. Thornton's mortal illness. There is a curious narrative continuity between the episode dealing with Mary Breaks' slander and the death of Thornton's husband, that can only partially be explained by the temporal proximity of the events. They are linked by Thornton's faintings, tremblings, and collapses into bedridden weakness with "heavy and sad affliction" (p. 160).

Paradoxically, however, it is the death of her husband, described as "the most terrible loss that ever woman lost" (p. 161), and which indeed does offer threat to her identity, not only through emotional grief, but through loss of status as a wife and increased financial insecurity, which restores her to articulacy. In the revelation of her mourning she regains control. It is in the disclosure of this grief which "consummate[s her] sufferings" (p. 162) that she is, in a sense, ultimately vindicated.

Secrecy, disclosure, and control have operated, then, in intricate patterns in *A Book of Rembrances*. Between this and the later version of Thornton's autobiography there are experiments with a variety of modes of selection, and revelation or withholding, of material. These relate to the purpose of writing at different moments, according to differing emotional and pragmatic impulses, and to differences between various available models for writing. But issues of secrecy and revelation are bound up, too, with crises of subjectivity at experiential and textual levels which reveal a complex series of negotiations of the loss of others, and moments of near collapse of the self. These crises in turn yield, in perhaps unexpected ways, moments of faltering and fragility which are equally opportunities for control and articulacy.

"I Confess Myself to be *Beside Myself to God*": The Many Selves in *A Vindication of Anne Wentworth* (1677)

Anne Wentworth's *Vindication* of herself crystallizes many of the recurrent issues generated by the reading of autobiography and, in particular, questions of the authority and authenticity of the textual self in seventeenth-century womens' writing.[6] Are we to believe that the "real," the rebellious, Wentworth, the one who committed the socially-proscribed acts of leaving her husband and justifying her action vigorously to the world in her own words in print, is concealed beneath the plethora of biblical references and the convoluted narrative structure which mark her *Vindication*? Does this "authentic" Wentworth cunningly reveal only the socially acceptable versions of her actions in the text, and is the "secret" Anne Wentworth then only discernible through the lens of twentieth-century feminist criticism? Or does the text deny us the binarism of a concealed/revealed Wentworth, and instead offer us so many versions of Wentworth that, in the end, the notion of an authentic self becomes itself untenable? This would suggest that the text conceals nothing, for the often contradictory multiplicity of selves within the text work together to deny the primacy of any one of them.

Anne Wentworth was a Baptist, writing and publishing in the post-Restoration atmosphere of the 1670s. These details are significant on several counts. First, by 1677, when the text was published, the Baptists, like all remaining sects, were operating in a much more hostile political climate than they had been during the Commonwealth and Protectorate. Several Acts of Parliament restricting non-conformist activity had been passed, with the consequence of increased persecution for those who did not comply with them. This resulted in a turning of attention away from the conversion of those outside their ranks to the stricter imposition of codes of behavior and attitudes within the congregation. For Wentworth, this meant that her text was being received into a community already under threat and on the defensive. Second, the Baptists were committed to a literal reading of the Bible in ways that the other sects were not. This concern with the "letter" of the Bible was the source of their sectarian authority and self-justification. While this had the benefit of lending scriptural authority to their activities, it also tied them to a number of well-known misogynist biblical prescriptions, such as Paul's exhortation to women to keep silent in church and not to "usurp authority over the man, but to be in silence."[7] Clearly, these prescriptions of deference and silence presented problems for a woman leaving her husband and trying to justify her activities in print.

Further, the Baptists had a practice of testification, of standing up before their congregation to bear witness to their faith and to their steadfastness in the face of temptation and doubt. It was partly on the basis of this testification that Baptists were received into congregations and maintained their credentials once there. While there is a very written quality to Wentworth's text, with its embedded scriptural allusions and the denseness of its arguments, there is also an element of this spoken testimony, both in the prolific use of italic print to indicate emphasis, and in its lack of linearity, its circular and self-allusive character. This relationship to oral testimony also suggests that the text shares its function, underlining the status of the *Vindication* as a text of justification, of truth-telling, and of affirmation.

The contradiction here between the woman who is silent and the Baptist who speaks out the truth is mirrored in the textual tension between an assertive and a withdrawn self. The Bible is the authority and guarantor for Wentworth's actions, and at times scriptural references provide a touchstone for the flesh-and-blood, vulnerable, and mortal Anne Wentworth under threat from her violent husband:

> Then did the Lord my God say unto me, "I, even I, am he that comforteth thee; who art thou that thou shouldest be afraid of a man that shall die, and of the son of man which shall be made as grass." [Isaiah 51.12] (p. 193)

This construction of the self seems to rely on a kind of secrecy or concealment: concealment of her own response within the word of God; concealment of her rebelliousness within a quotation that posits an affirmation of the addressee through these words of comfort (for her) and condemnation (of her husband).

Such an analysis, however, suggests a clearly identifiable "real" self, discernible through the veils of biblical allusion. But as the textual selves multiply, it becomes more and more difficult to maintain a sense of a textual and acceptable self (itself hidden in layers of biblical language) concealing a rebellious and unacceptable authentic self. At times, for example, Wentworth becomes one with the saints and apostles, as she makes their words her own utterances in her own narrative. Of God's work through her, she writes:

I am called to wrestle not only against *flesh and blood, but against principalities and powers, against the rulers of the darkness of this world, and against spiritual wickedness in high places.* [Ephesians 6.12] (p. 191; emphasis Wentworth's in all quotations)

This suggests a dimension to Wentworth's struggle beyond the earthly, material, and temporal, into the spiritual. The words, however, are St. Paul's, and this appropriation elevates both her and her work to the heights of the apostle himself. His words, then, on the one hand help to conceal her own vain-glory and immodesty in her assertion that her work and her experience have a national and spiritual significance. On the other hand, they construct a Wentworth whose experiences and significance transcend mundane human time and history.

These two textual selves—the fearful woman in need of comfort, and the wrestler with wickedness in high places—are not the sum of the selves ranged through this text. In one lengthy passage, for example, she responds to her critics' accusation of madness by anticipating and working through the range of arguments they might make and that she might make in return. She does this by constructing a variety of contradictory stances for herself. First, her detractors will withdraw the allegation, for it implicates them as her oppressors, and "oppression makes a wise man mad" (p. 190). Then she anticipates that they will want the allegation upheld, for their sanity is dependent on the proving of her insanity. Next, she cheerfully accepts the allegation of madness, for it confirms her fellowship with the suffering of Christ, who was also accused of madness. Following this, she accepts the charge on yet another count: if it be madness to give up her will to God, then she accepts that she is mad, for "I confess myself to be *beside myself to God*" (p. 190). Finally, she denies that she is mad, asserting that she is only carrying out God's will. Here, then, the text produces a series of selves, variously mad and sane, and all of equal standing, for none is finally privileged above the others. They all remain, cumulatively and contradictorily refuting her detractors' allegations.

These serial selves are, however, all posited on a singular pre-existing (but no longer existing), pretextual self. Wentworth writes of the process whereby she came to understand the nature of the work God was calling her to do, a process which involved the systematic dissolution of any sense of coherent and individuated self:

God . . . has been so many years *emptying* me from vessel to vessel, *breaking* me all to pieces in myself, and making me to become as *nothing* before him, . . . and who having taught me to tremble at his

word has thereby called and commanded me into his work, when
I was a thing that *is not* [I Corinthians 1.18] in my own eyes . . .
(p. 185)

Anne Wentworth's multiple and contradictory selves, then, far from
concealing a real, extra-textual self, on the contrary are predicated on the
loss of such a sense of self. The text asserts that there is nothing to be
concealed or revealed; her secret is that there is, paradoxically, no secret
identity in her autobiographical writing. What remain are the new,
godly, transcendent Anne Wentworths, the textual selves whose various
and contradictory characters inhabit the pages of her *Vindication*. A text
such as Wentworth's, which denies us a sense of the author's single,
authentic individuality, challenges us to seek genuine rather than illusory secrets in the texts of early modern women writers.

"To Some Disguise Submit":
The Secret Codes of Katherine Philips's *Poems* (1667)

Katherine Philips is one of the very few seventeenth-century
women writers whose work has received continuous, if usually condescending, recognition in the main stream. Her posthumous *Poems*
(1667) were prefaced by praises from Abraham Cowley as well as
from less famous figures, and she is known to have been lauded by
many, including Henry Vaughan, Roger Boyle, Earl of Orrery, and
Charles Cotterell, Master of Ceremonies at Charles II's court. Several
of her songs were set to music by Henry Lawes, and her first play,
Pompey, was performed to much applause in Dublin, and possibly
in London, in 1663. Keats later praised her lyrics in a letter to J. H.
Reynolds dated 21 September 1817, and a few of her poems have regularly been published in major anthologies. She might seem a surprising figure, therefore, to feature in a discussion of secrecy; there
can be nothing very secret about the literary activities of a writer so
bold as to have sent a manuscript copy of at least some of her works
to the Duchess of York.[8]

It is strange, then, to learn that Philips—Orinda, as she called herself—has usually been seen as private, even secret, about her writing.
Most commentators, old and new, who refer to her biography, do so in
order to prove her blushing embarrassment at having her artistic
endeavors made public in the printing of an unauthorized edition of her
poetry in 1664. So precise was Philips's management of the appearance
of feminine modesty that her account of her unworthiness and unwill-
ingness to be known in public has been regularly quoted and accepted:

'tis only I who am that unfortunate person that cannot so much as think in private . . . I am so far from expecting applause for anything that I scribble, that I can hardly expect pardon.[9]

Philips has been found praiseworthy, as lady and poetess, in this self-deprecation, and perhaps it has played its part in the decision of editors to anthologize her work when that of her more disreputable sister, Aphra Behn, has been refused.

But secrecy takes many forms, and it is not Katherine Philips's successful manipulation of the appearance of modesty that is of most interest to us here, but a particular investment that her poetry has in concealment. For this, we would argue, is closet lesbian verse, encoding its lesbian desire in ways accessible to those, in her times and in ours, with the eyes to see.[10] In contrast to Anne Wentworth's text with its temptation to us to find what is perhaps an illusion of the hidden real self, Philips's verse appears to employ secrecy as a deliberate strategy to preserve and yet express a secret allegiance. Philips's textual encoding has, it seems, succeeded; it has no doubt aided her (sometimes grudging) acceptance by mainstream criticism, which might prefer good love poetry not to be sexually deviant.

The need for secrecy of various kinds becomes clear enough when the details of Philips's biography are sketched. She was born on 1 January 1632, the daughter of Katherine Fowler (nee Oxenbridge) and her husband John, a wealthy merchant. She was educated at school in London, where she remained until the age of 15 when, in 1646, her widowed and recently-remarried mother called her to her own new home in rural Wales and married her to a 54 year old widower, James Philips. This union created an instant problem and need for strategy, for where Katherine was a royalist, James was a prominent parliamentarian. Part of the way she dealt with this was to write prodigious amounts of poetry, which circulated in manuscript amongst her royalist friends. These writings exhibit "secrecy" in more ways than one: as a woman writer, Philips was required to disguise her unfeminine ambition for acceptance as a poetess by constantly asserting her unworthiness; as a royalist, she had to hide her politics by encoding the virulent royalism of her poetry in the language of pastoral; as a woman who desired other women, she had to conceal her desire even while making it the subject of her verse. By using the conventions of the poem praising an idealized lady, Philips was able to present a self which, while possibly both lesbian and self-glorifying, can be interpreted as modest, chaste, and heterosexual.

This sleight of hand is referred to disingenuously in many of her poems of the 1650s. In "To the truly Noble Mrs. Anne Owen, on my first approaches," for instance, Orinda proclaims that by telling "the

World I was subdu'd by you" she can, like other love poets, be "Secure
of fame to all posterity." Such eulogizing is deliberate—"I have plots
in't" (p. 33). Similarly, in "To the Excellent Mrs. Anne Owen, upon her
receiving the name of Lucasia, and Adoption into our Society, December
28, 1651," she explains that the beloved's mind must, in the poetic rendering of it, "to some disguise submit, / Or we could never worship it"
(pp. 32–33). This tradition of lyric poetry, then, allows a very public
affirmation of love and desire to be read as sexless admiration, the
proper pursuit of the acknowledged poet.

The clearest example of the strategy adopted by Philips is found in
"Orinda to Lucasia parting October 166I, at London." The date and
place in the title make it clear, to those in the know, that the occasion is
a precise one, and it is the very exactness of these life references that
makes this poetry a proper object in the study of autobiographical writings, for all the complicated transformations that literary convention
may introduce. Philips's beloved Lucasia, Anne Owen, the addressee of
much of her finest love poetry, had married, and was moving with her
new husband to Ireland. There was good reason to believe, as this poem
asserts, that this parting would be a final one.

> Adieu dear object of my Love's excess,
> And with thee all my hopes of happiness,
> With the same fervent and unchanged heart
> Which did it's whole self once to thee impart,
> (And which though fortune has so sorely bruised, (5)
> Would suffer more, to be from this excus'd)
> I to resign thy dear Converse submit,
> Since I can neither keep, nor merit it.
> Thou hast too long to me confined been,
> Who ruine am without, passion within. (10)
> My mind is sunk below thy tenderness,
> And my condition does deserve it less;
> I'm so entangl'd and so lost a thing
> By all the shocks my daily sorrow bring,
> That would'st thou for thy old Orinda call (15)
> Thou hardly could'st unravel her at all.
> And should I thy clear fortunes interline
> With the incessant miseries of mine?
> No, no, I never lov'd at such a rate
> To tye thee to the rigours of my fate, (20)
> As from my obligations thou art free,
> Sure thou shalt be so from my Injury,

> Though every other worthiness I miss,
> Yet I'le at least be generous in this . . . (pp. 139–40)

It might seem that the extended lament of these opening lines would demand a homoerotic interpretation, and indeed in 1974 John Broadbent declared, with breathtaking assurance, that "'Orinda to Lucasia parting' is such sincere blackmailing bitchery that we are bound to think of her work as lesbian."[11] No secrecy here, we might conclude. But this is not the case. Philips's modern editor, Patrick Thomas, for instance, sees the poem as a heartfelt apology for her having tried to persuade her friend to marry another man.[12] That such a reading, like other platonic assessments of the poem, is possible, is perhaps due in part to the heterosexist assumptions of most readers, or their fervent desire that the poet not be perverse. But it is also permitted by the language of secrecy that "Orinda to Lucasia parting" draws attention to— so as to enlighten those who wish to see it—even while this language serves to hide the poem's possible homosexual meanings:

> . . . I ask no inconvenient kindness now,
> To move thy passion, or to cloud thy brow;
> And thou wilt satisfie my boldest plea
> By some few soft remembrances of me, (50)
> Which may present thee with this candid thought,
> I meant not all the troubles that I brought.
> Own not what Passion rules, and Fate does crush,
> But wish thou could'st have don't without a blush,
> And that I had been, ere it was too late, (55)
> Either more worthy, or more fortunate.
> Ah, who can love the thing they cannot prize?
> But thou mayst pity though thou dost despise.
> Yet I should think that pity bought too dear,
> If it should cost those precious Eyes a tear. (60)
>   Oh, may no minutes trouble, thee possess,
> But to endear the next hours happiness;
> And maist thou when thou art from me remov'd,
> Be better pleas'd, but never worse belov'd:
> Oh pardon me for pow'ring out my woes (65)
> In Rhime now, that I dare not do't in Prose.
> For I must lose whatever is call'd dear,
> And thy assistance all that loss to bear,
> And have more cause than e'er I had before,
> To fear that I shall never see thee more. (pp. 140–41) (70)

The fascination of this poem lies partly in the fact that the desired secrecy (and the secrecy of desire) is openly referred to: Orinda begs "pardon" for "pow'ring out my woes / In Rhime now, that I dare not do't in Prose." By writing in verse, she makes her lines readable as a poetic avowal of platonic friendship. She "dare not" make such a declaration in prose, for fear that the literary conventions which can offer a desexualized interpretation of lines such as 19–20 or 47–48 would not operate to defuse this intensity in prose.

Having taken cognizance of this systematic secrecy, the reader who is willing to notice such a pattern can see—in the very lines that are interpreted by insistently heterosexual readings as evidence of Orinda's "chastity"—a trace of lesbian encoding. The "innocent . . . Design" of this poetry allows loving a woman to be declared "without a crime," and permits this to be compared favorably with the sinister, "Crown-conquerors mirth" of a bridegroom ("To my Excellent Lucasia, on our Friendship," pp. 51–52). Separation deprives lovers of "Love's fruits and joys," which are "made by this / Useless as Crowns to captiv'd Kings" ("A Dialogue of Absence 'twixt Lucasia and Orinda,'" pp. 25–26). Such examples are easily multiplied, and it is no coincidence that so many of them also invite the reader to an alignment with royalist positions: the second level of the poetry's closetedness, its lesbian erotic, is masked by its first level of encoding, the comparison of the state of the unhappy lover to the fate of the exiled king. Finding the royalism, Cowley and other contemporary readers missed or excused the sexual politics, and sexual positions, of Philips's verse.

What these poems indicate is that secrecy adds another level of problem—and of fascination—to present-day work on autobiography. Not only are there the well-rehearsed, though largely unsolved, theoretical and political problems concerning the use we make of autobiographical works. Everything is made more teasingly difficult by those writers who seem to have set out actively to deceive and to be secret. How far should we, like the beloved in Philips's poems, allow ourselves as readers to submit to some disguise?

"Charged . . . With Great Secresy": *The Meditations of Lady Elizabeth Delaval* (c. 1665)

Elizabeth Delaval's *Meditations*, probably written in the early 1660s, are much less holy than their title implies.[13] They consist partly of self-reflection and prayer, in order both to purge and to urge herself on, but partly of more worldly narrative interludes which explain her spiritual anxieties. The collection meditates less on God than on her self—or, as in the work of Thornton, Wentworth, and Philips, her several selves—and represents a process of pondering her own past in her memory and prose. The text has survived until recently in manuscript form only, but clearly anticipates a reader, a "you" who is expected to read right through the work; towards the end Delaval notes in parenthesis "as I have all ready told you" (p. 166), assuming a continuous and attentive readerly presence. The privacy of this text, then, is not that of the autobiography observed from the voyeur's position, whereby a willed secrecy is betrayed in the reading. In Delaval's case the accidents of history—or, more likely, constraints upon female authorship and publication—have, by preserving the *Meditations* in manuscript rather than published form, simply intensified the intimacy between writer and reader.

This is oddly appropriate, since as an autobiographical record the *Meditations* are obsessed with secrecy. Her friendships—or, her account of them—are marked by the excitement of private confidences, but thus bring with them the responsibilities of secrecy and a constant vulnerability to betrayal. Her definition of true friendship appears to be the willingness to "open" her "heart" (p. 34) to the friend, and later in her life she develops a sense of love as "secret . . . passion" (p. 167), which is in turn thwarted by the "secret reason" of her aunt's opposition to her desired match (p. 166). When subsequently invited by Lord Anesley to marry him "privately," she refuses, but then is surprised to find herself encouraged by other relatives to "steal a maryage" secretly (p. 169). In the end, a marriage is forced upon her and she finds herself longing for the solitude and retirement of her "beloved virgin state of life" (p. 202). There are many degrees of secrecy and its invasion here, closely connected both to the social structures of women's lives and to the strategically guarded secrets of a woman's body.

Delaval's account of her first significant relationship, with one Mistress Carter, an older woman, includes a particularly vivid passage evoking the attractions and dangers of a secret friendship. Delaval was ten years old at the time of the events, but writes from the perspective of maturity, condemning Mrs. Carter for cunning deceit and ultimately betrayal of confidences. (The parallel with Alice Thornton's experience with Mary Breaks, and the similar intensity of loss, is striking.) Delaval's friendship with Mrs. Carter is marked by stealth from the beginning. Their contact is maintained and plans laid by daily letters which are hid in "a place in the mated galary just by my chamber dore" to await collection (p. 30). There is "great joy" in the anticipation of the (obviously forbidden) correspondence, but also a constant threat of discovery: "according to her order's" Delaval placed each letter "in my bosome till I found a good opertunity of burning it" (p. 30). The mechanism of the relationship, thus, was dependent upon hidden and potentially incriminating texts.

However, soon the actual substance of their activities came also to focus on the magic of secrecy. Mrs. Carter began to tell the young Elizabeth Delaval

> tale's of fary's, charged me with great secresy and told me that if she and I cou'd but get out often to walke alone, the queen of that unknown land she us'd to talke to me of (provided that she found I was very secret) wou'd be so graceous as to let me se in private one of her court; which fary wou'd be order'd to bring me a considering cap which when I had wore a while upon the intersestion of Mris. Carter (and still upon condition that I continu'ed very secret), another fary shou'd meet me in the wood's with a far greater present, which was a wishing cap; and as soon as I begun to wear it, what ever I desier'd I shou'd obtaine. All this I firmely beleived and wou'd not have reveal'd the secret of this mater for any consideration in the world. (p. 30)

The recurrence of the words *secret* or *secresy* within this passage is remarkable; the pleasures of conspiracy are insistently repeated, as is its strange "charge"—meaning both a dark responsibility and a buzz of excitement. From a friend whose involvement with her is itself concealed from her own family, Delaval hears secret "tale's" about a fairy queen of an "unknown land" with a hidden or imaginary location, who will offer Delaval special powers "in private" which depend upon her continuing "very secret." The boundaries of real and imagined narratives, whose inter-relation is so fundamental to the process of autobiography, coincide on the very issue of secrecy.

This unusual passage, teeming with enticement, fantasy, and desire, is perhaps an emblem of the secret power of female solidarity and imagination. The young girl is tempted (or "deluded" [p. 30], as she says with the benefit of rather bitter hindsight) by the story-telling of another woman, opening up to her a female world in which the queen and her court have the capacity to fulfill her secret wishes. The passage appears to promise that, with due concealment, a woman could be enabled to think for herself while secretly wearing a "considering cap," almost a parody of the standard modest female head-dress of the period but in this case containing hidden power. For, after a due period of considering, she would then receive a "wishing cap" with even greater powers, allowing her to achieve "what ever" she "desier'd." The passage is disturbingly emblematic of the fact that women's inner thoughts and desires can only find expression in the privacy of fantasy. This passage embodies the imaginings of a woman, Mrs. Carter, who was presumably of fairly low status (judging by her title and the apparent undesirability of her influence over Delaval from her family's point of view), and the expressed hopes and longings of an impressionable girl of ten years old. However, though these may have been the secret dreams of those who by virtue of class, gender and age were powerless, the secret fantasies breed involvement and trust:

> Dayly was I longing for the appearance of my first fary (not doubting but the second wou'd soon folow) and continually was I puszleing my head what it wou'd be best for me to wish for.

> As to that Mris. Carter bid me satisfy my selfe, for the wearing of the first cap wou'd make me so perfectly wise that when I put on the second, I shou'd be in no danger of wishing for any thing but what was most to my advantage. (p. 31)

The young Delaval demonstrates here a further attraction of confidentiality: it breeds the other kind of confidence, that of not doubting either the secret promise or the transforming seriousness of its consequences. The whole interlude, as recalled in its autobiographical framework, provides an opportunity for increased self-confidence and a chance to "satisfy my selfe."

   This account of the tantalizing but eventually unfulfilled promise of fairy powers is swiftly followed in the *Meditations* by a denunciation of Mrs. Carter for leading Delaval from the path of a young woman's proper virtues and education:

> So eagerly bent was I upon these thing's that I thought it alltogether needlesse to pray or to read the holy scriptures, and cou'd with all my heart have tore my governesse in peces when ever she hinder'd Mris. Carter's private walk's and mine . . . (p. 31)

Her one intent at the time, she records, was to escape with Mrs. Carter in secret for a private walk in "some retier'd shade far of from all company" (p. 31) in the hope of being "honour'd with the sight" of the fairies. But when the friendship is finally betrayed and broken by Mrs. Carter, and the delusions of the fairy stories made sadly clear, Elizabeth Delaval not only condemns the maturer woman but blames herself for the secret liaisons with Mrs. Carter and the (hoped for) fairies. Ironically she inflicts upon herself a punishment which is remarkably similar to the crime: she plans to

> make it my choice to live conseal'd and take care to hide all that I do. (p. 43)

"Conseal'd" living, here represented as a positive choice, was thus not only associated with subversive female desire, the fairy "land" where the woman must indeed "take care to hide all that I do." The "retier'd shade far of from all company" (p. 31), as Delaval had described the place where she and Mrs. Carter walked in secret, was also traditionally the place for holy women. Concealment could be, and had been, used to foster the so-called feminine virtues of silence and humility; the "sweet" retired life (p. 132), as Delaval later called it, encouraged the modesty of the hidden face. In predominantly protestant seventeenth-century England the metaphoric veiling and retreating which went on in female domestic life had distinct overtones of the pre-reformation nunnery. But there is still actual secrecy, in words and actions, even in this acceptable "conseal'd" living; as Delaval tellingly observes later in her *Meditations*, in contemplative or sorrowful mood she spends her time pouring out "secret complaints to the God of mercy" (p. 182).

There is a more complex irony in Delaval's recounting of, and then condemning, the secret imaginary episode with the fairies. The ingredients of her narrative of Mrs. Carter, of the secret friendship and the hope of fairy gifts, are those of women's autobiography, too: the promise of a story, the appeal of intimacy, the exploration of an emerging personality and her hidden hopes, and the mystery of memory and imagination. Furthermore, the concealed powers of considering and wishing, promised in the fairy caps, are the very basis of the autobiographical instinct with which they are recalled. The *Meditations* function precisely to consider—to recall past events, relive and reconstruct them in writing, analyze and contemplate them in retrospect—and then to wish, whether imaginatively, wistfully, or prayerfully in the texts interspersed by Delaval between the narrative passages. However orthodox the framework of this and many other seventeenth-century women's autobiographical writings may be, the matter originates in the two secret stages of self-contemplation and desire "in private" (p. 31).

We may conclude by observing, then, the fascinating convergence of required or approved secrecy, and subversive imaginative secrecy, both in the writing of Delaval's autobiographical text and in the life of this seventeenth-century Englishwoman. To be hidden was to be both excluded from the wider world, and to be liberated from it, at least in the "court" (p. 31) of the imagination. That which Katherine Mansfield referred to 250 years later as "the secret self" was already in the mid-seventeenth century the uncertain heroine of her own text.[14]

The writings of Alice Thornton, Anne Wentworth, Katherine Philips and Elizabeth Delaval demonstrate a remarkable range of auto-biographical secrecy, in what they "pondered" in their "hearts," how they did so, and why. We have seen secrecy as illusory or real, as a necessity or a pleasure, as rhetoric or fantasy. Methods of concealment vary hugely, too, from the apparent anonymity of the biblical text to the blurring of real and imagined narratives. The influences leading to such secrecy, of course, shift and vary in relation to each individual text. Among the contributory factors are the exploratory and uncertain decades of political and religious history during which these women were writing; the transitional moment in the development of women's subject positions, particularly in the family and the churches; and the early stage in the evolution of confessional codes in autobiographical prose and verse. The key to this phenomenon of secrecy perhaps lies in the convergence of these three elements of period, gender, and genre, all in a critical state of flux. Each of these major factors has been seen, in our accumulated examples, to encourage hiddenness: the social and religious context of the century, the ideology of femininity, and the emerging modes of autobiographical writing.

On the other hand, we could argue that the most predominant of these factors is indeed gender, since the secrecy of, say, private devotion or autobiographical writing is intensified when combined with the gender-specific constraints on seventeenth-century women's lives. Pepys, for example, was preoccupied with secrecy, even resorting to writing his Restoration diary in elaborate code, but this was an individual obsession rather than one which could be said to be in tune with the expected life of a male in 1660s London. Delaval's fascination with secrecy, on the other hand, may be seen simply as an extreme version of the conventionally constrained life, loves and writings of seventeenth-century women. The need for layers of both secrecy and self-revelation in the autobiographical writings of Anne Wentworth and Katherine Philips is linked directly to society's prescription of the possibilities for women's verbal or bodily self-expression. The ironies of autobiography as a genre—concerned with self-promotion (even through self-criticism) while maintaining its modesty of form, and gaining its public authority from the privacy of subjective experience—

are all the more intensely felt in the autobiographical writings of a woman such as Alice Thornton. The very process of pondering one's own life events in one's heart, which is the beginning of the autobiographical instinct, is shot through with gendered associations of discretion and modesty as soon as it is "her" heart where the secret contemplation is taking place. This stereotype is, however, nicely undermined by the completion of the autobiographical process, in which the woman's ponderings are set free from the secrecy of the author's heart in the processes of being written and read. Is the autobiographer, once her autobiographical act is complete, less "feminine" than before? (Would the Virgin Mary ever release the contemplations of her own heart?) The female autobiographer can, of course, never win, and a secret can only remain as such when not disclosed. The double-edged nature of the secret force of autobiography is, finally, concisely expressed in Delaval's account. Having explained her clandestine experiences to us, she adds ironically—while disclosing it before our very eyes—that she "would not have reveal'd the secret of this mater for any consideration in the world" (p. 30).

Notes

1. In the original presentation of this material, responsibility was shared out as follows: (1—Alice Thornton) Elspeth Graham; (2—Anne Wentworth), Hilary Hinds; (3—Katherine Philips), Elaine Hobby; (4—Elizabeth Delaval), Helen Wilcox. The chapter was prepared for publication by Helen Wilcox.

2. See *Her Own Life: Autobiographical Writings by Seventeenth-Century Englishwomen*, edited by Elspeth Graham, Hilary Hinds, Elaine Hobby, and Helen Wilcox (London: Routledge, 1989), pp. 6–16; Catherine Belsey, *The Subject of Tragedy: Identity and Difference in Renaissance Drama* (London: Methuen, 1985), 152–60; Helen Wilcox, "Private Writing and Public Function: Autobiographical Texts by Renaissance Englishwomen," in *Gloriana's Face: Women, Public and Private, in the English Renaissance*, edited by S. P. Cerasano and Marion Wynne-Davies (New York and London: Harvester, 1992), pp. 47–62.

3. Luke 2.19.

4. *Her Own Life*, pp. 147–64. (Since the texts in *Her own Life* are modernized, Thornton's work is referred to there as *A Book of Remembrances*.)

5. See Suzanne Trill, *"Patterns of Piety and Faith": The Role of the Psalms in the Construction of the Exemplary Renaissance Woman* (Liverpool: unpublished PhD thesis, University of Liverpool, 1992), pp. 174–79.

6. *Her Own Life*, pp. 180–96.

7. I Corinthians 14.34–5, I Timothy 2.12.

8. See Elaine Hobby, *Virtue of Necessity: English Women's Writing 1649–1688* (London: Virago, 1988), pp. 128–42.

9. *Poems By the most Deservedly Admired Mrs. Katherine Philips The Matchless Orinda* (London: Henry Herringman, 1667), Av–A2.

10. See *What Lesbians Do In Books*, edited by Elaine Hobby and Chris White (London: The Women's Press, 1991), pp. 183–204.

11. *Poets of the Seventeenth Century*, edited by John Broadbent (New York: Signet Classics, 1974), volume 2, p. 317.

12. *The Collected Works of Katherine Philips*, edited by Patrick Thomas (Stump Cross: Stump Cross Press, 1990), p. 381.

13. *The Meditations of Elizabeth Delaval*, edited by Douglas G. Greene (Gateshead: Northumberland Press, 1978), Surtees Society volume CXC.

14. Katherine Mansfield, letter to Dorothy Brett, 1921, cited in *The Secret Self: Short Stories by Women*, edited by Hermione Lee (London and Melbourne: Dent, 1985), p. xv.

4

Striking Rock: The Letters of Ray Strachey to Her Family, 1929–1935

Johanna Alberti

I first encountered the letters of Ray Strachey when tracing the activities of prewar suffragists into the interwar period.[1] I wanted to know what happened to politically-active women in the interwar period when it seemed as if feminism was dispersed and fragmented. The letters provided bountiful material about one such woman. Ray Strachey was an active feminist from her days as a student at Cambridge before 1910 until her death at the age of fifty-three in 1940. The letters I will refer to were written to her mother Mary (of the American Quaker family, the Pearsall Smiths) who had run away with Bernard Berenson, the art historian, when Ray was four and lived in Italy. The letters were also written to her daughter Barbara who was born in 1912, and her son Christopher, born in 1916. I was delighted and astonished by the sheer volume of the letters: the Pearsall Smiths were a family of letter writers, and Ray was a faithful and prolific correspondent, writing at least once a week to each absent member of the family. The representation of her life is therefore detailed and serial. Addressing people she knew intimately, Ray wrote the letters at high speed, apparently without pausing for thought. Much of the content of the letters is mundane: she was quite consciously unreflective most of the time. My narrative here draws on those passages where she responds more self-consciously than usual to private and public events, although my interpretation is based on a reading of the letters as a whole.

The letters have not been published, which means that my position as their interpreter is crucial. In this chapter I do not address the current theoretical debate about whether we can "resurrect voices from texts" in a straightforward way. Margaretta Jolly, in her chapter in this volume, has suggested a strategy for releasing the reading of letters from deconstruction's "attack on the self," and of avoiding the conflation of history and ideology. She calls attention to the temporality in the narrative of letters, and to the possibility of reading them for what they can "tell us about real struggles that are other than or extra-textual." My reading of Ray Strachey's letters, rather than emphasizing their linguistic structure, asserts that we can deduce from them—in Jolly's phrase—a sense of a "self-in-history." This raises another problem: what "history" might be outside the expressions of consciousness by individuals is ultimately elusive, and can never be satisfactorily captured in the statements of historians. Nevertheless, as a reader I want to be given a context for the reading of texts, however difficult I recognize the boundary between text and context is to maintain. The version I offer here contributes to my evolving interpretation of the politics of feminism in the interwar period. I have set Ray Strachey's private letters beside a selected few of the more public writings of other feminists who were her contemporaries, in order to give some sense of the feminist discourses available to her.

I have chosen the particular years 1929 to 1935 because they were a time of crisis both in Ray Strachey's private life and in European politics. The history of feminism in the early 1930s is a complex one, and as yet little explored by historians.[2] The achievement of female suffrage in 1928 immediately preceded the financial crisis initiated by the Wall Street Crash. The ensuing slump fostered the growth of Fascist ideas throughout Europe. Fascism contained a particular threat to women, a threat arguably masked by Fascism's violent struggle with the political Left, and in Germany by its vicious racism. The political climate of the early thirties which bred Fascist ideas contained within it a more general reaction to the changes which in Britain had given women full citizenship and the theoretical right to become Members of Parliament. Feminists themselves were not immune to that reaction, and it is possible to see links between the ideas of the New Feminism with its emphasis on the needs of women as mothers, and the "cult of the cradle" which was part of the attraction of Fascism for women.[3]

The women's movement was dispersed, but Ray Strachey did not relinquish her identity as a feminist, nor her faith in the efficacy of political activity. Her letters give representation to the experience of suffering, of surviving, and at times of flourishing within a difficult and often hostile political and personal landscape. Judy Giles has suggested that "it is timely to revisit domesticity and to reconstruct the history of women's relationship to the domestic, both as cultural expression and as social institution."[4] What I seek to do here is to reconstruct Ray Strachey's relationship with the domestic within the public worlds in which she was active: I see these worlds as interdependent.

On September 28th, 1934, Ray wrote to her son Christopher:

> I have been, in fact, obsessed & knocked flat inwardly for the last week. But I think my head is coming up above water. It has jolly well got to—for I am aware of the fact that at present, as far as B. [Barbara] is concerned, I am the only solid rock on the horizon. So I have got to solidify.

Ray's relationship to her letters' recipients is apparent in her writing: to some extent she was constructing different identities in response to them, to what she understood to be their need of her. I will argue that each of these identities contains the image of the rock as a symbol. She chose the image because it represented how she felt within her family context and because that was how she wished to be seen and to feel: strong, stable, reliable. But the word rock in English has a different meaning as a verb. In a talk, *The Leaning Tower*, read to the Worker's Educational Association in Brighton in May, 1940 (two months before Ray's death) Virginia Woolf said: "When everything is rocking round one, the only person who remains comparatively stable is oneself." Ray Strachey's world did rock around her in the 1930s. In her persona as daughter, mother, and active political feminist much was demanded of her. Her mother was ill and sometimes suicidal; her daughter was struggling with the contrary pressures of university entrance, deciding on a career, and her relationships with her contemporaries. Ray's best known book, *The Cause*, a classic narrative of the women's movement from the publication of Mary Wollstonecraft's *Vindication* to the achievement of the vote, was published in 1928: over the next seven years, she was to write three more books and work on a fourth which remained unfinished and unpublished. She continued to give time to the National Union of Societies for Equal Citizenship (formerly the National Union of Women's Suffrage Societies) and to its paper, *The Woman's Leader*, but her main feminist commitment was to the London Society for Women's Service. The LSWS had developed from the London Society for Women's Suffrage, and the direction of its work in the interwar period grew out of Ray and her sister-in-law Pippa Strachey's commitment to the issue of women's employment. In this role Ray gave extensive evidence to the Royal Commissions on the Civil Service in 1930, and on the Foreign Office in 1934, members of which were openly hostile to the feminist point of view she presented. In 1933–34, she played a key role in the difficult process of establishing the Women's Employment Federation, designed to promote and facilitate the training and employment of "educated women."[5] She earned money by writing articles and giving talks on the BBC. Because of a drop in her inherited income in the crisis at the end of 1931, she accepted a paid post with Lady Astor, a volatile although sympathetic employer, and continued to work for her until the end of 1934.

I want first to consider the way Ray described herself within her family: in what terms she constructed that sense of solidity which she so valued in herself. Ray's stability was grounded in physical strength and well-being. She and her husband Oliver rented a house in Westminster, but Ray spent as many weekends as possible at "The Mud House," a cottage in Sussex where she had helped dig out a swimming pool. From there, she wrote to her mother, Mary Berenson, on June 6th, 1933:

> I've been having *the most heavenly swims*, in a state of nature, all by myself . . . When not too hot I go & dig on the foundations of the new cottage. Its queer but true, that my passion for digging is unabated, even though Sat. was my 46th birthday. However I feel *so well*, & indeed am so well that I might be 18 (except to look at!) Its a very considerable achievement.

Ray's well-being was perhaps consciously asserted in the face of her mother's frequent health problems. Mary lived with Bernard Berenson at I Tatti, near Florence, coming to England each summer to visit her brother and her sister Alys Russell, her two daughters, and their four children. Ray wrote to her mother at least once a week, struggling sometimes to offer the necessary and constant sympathy:

> I am so much distressed to get another miserable account of your progress. It is *too* beastly for you. I wish there was anything at all that I could do. But even if one is on the spot there is practically nothing, & from a distance the thing is impossible. Only I wish I could. However I suppose the attempt to amuse you with news is all I have open to me. (12 Nov. 1931)

Ray never allowed herself to dwell on pain because complaining about it "doesn't give me any comfort, but only makes it worse! It seems to be a matter of more importance when mentioned somehow, so I say as little as I must" (to M. B., 6 Dec. 1930). Indeed, she sought to separate herself from her body's pain: "What a bore bodies are: the division between mind & body *seems* very real to normal people. But I've no doubt its less clear cut than we suppose . . ." (to M. B., 3 Feb. 1931). However, Ray's letters to her daughter while Barbara was a student are witness to the fact that she was well aware of the connection between body and mind.

> I hear that you are in bed with your insides & I'm so sorry. Its simply beastly to have troubles of the mind turning into troubles of the body. But perhaps you may get relief that way—people sometimes do. My sympathy for your struggles is more real than you may suppose—though of course of very little practical use to you. But you may find some comfort in noticing that your hysteria always coincides with your internals, & is a sort of physical symptom. (12 Feb. 1931)

A week later she wrote:

> I'm glad your monthlies are behaving at last too. You'll probably find yourself prone to disturbances mental & emotional at these times, & you'll have to learn to discount it a bit. Its a damned nuisance, but one can adjust oneself.

That "oneself" is personal: Ray coped with years of problems with her own menstruation culminating in an operation for fibroids in the middle of the 1931 crisis. But Barbara's emotional traumas could not always be put down to PMT:

> Your *vast* volumes arrived yesterday (not overweight physically whatever they were emotionally) & I am left staggering under their contents. You may rest in the conviction that I won't take anything you say too seriously. Indeed my danger is that I may not take seriously enough emotions & states of mind so distant from my own. I can understand about half of what you mean, I think . . . (16 Nov. 1929)

The tone of Ray's letters is that of the "modern" woman identified by Alison Light in the literature of the period. Light has suggested that the "modern woman" between the wars was "taking on what had formerly been regarded as distinctly masculine qualities: in particular the ethics of a code of self-control and a language of reticence." Light argues that her "brisk competence and heroic disavowal could all be part of that reaction to the legacy of representations which had seen ladies as the softer and frailer sex."[6] Ray presents herself as just such a modern woman, but her story also throws light on the limitations of this code when placed under pressure. Ray's attempt to distance herself from Barbara's emotional life was not ultimately successful: the consequences were later to shake the foundations of her sense of the world and of herself as solid and rational.

Work was essential to Ray's sense of self as an independent and active woman at a time when the meaning of work for middle-class women was contested as many moved from voluntary to paid employment. At the beginning of the period I am looking at here, Ray's voluntary work involved helping middle-class women to find paid employment. The right of women, and especially married middle-class women to such work needed to be asserted precisely because it was under threat. Moreover, women were still "protected" by legislation, which meant in effect that they were placed in a subordinate position. As E. M. White put it in a letter to *Time & Tide*: "Sub-adult classification means lowered status, and that in turn cripples women's efforts to secure a decent wage" (14 March 1930). Yet the work Ray herself valued most was not the journalism which she did for money, but voluntary political activism and writing books of her own choice: she was finishing a life of Millicent Garrett Fawcett in the early thirties, and planning a history of the slave trade. Then in the crisis of 1931 she herself had to look for paid work beyond her journalistic writing. She became a parliamentary secretary to Lady Astor, a conservative and also a feminist MP. Ray's sense of independence was challenged by the necessity to do regular paid work under the control of someone other than herself, and her regret at what she experienced as a loss of autonomy combined with her determined optimism into an uncomfortable ambivalence. She wrote to her mother:

> The psychology of doing a paid job is interesting. I find myself ready to be much less impatient & much less active than in an unpaid job. The responsibility no longer seems to be mine. I didn't expect this, but greatly enjoy it. (13 Nov. 1931)

And then, again to Mary, two months later:

> I simply carry out orders, & leave the consequences on her shoulders. Its a queer sensation, which I've never experienced before— I mean putting aside my own judgment. And I rather enjoy it in a way. (17 Jan. 1932)

She was aware from the first of the threat the job posed to her sense of agency: "I am seldom in doubt what to do or how to do it & some of it carries the delightful illusion of being of importance" (to M. B., 19 Nov. 1931). Then, less than a week later, she wrote:

> I grow increasingly sceptical about the amount of good result which emerges from all the turmoil. Still I get a salary out of it, which seems like a solid good to someone! (to M. B., 25 Nov. 1931)

At first she had tried to combine doing the job with writing, taking her papers for the book on slavery with her to the office, and maintaining her work for the London Society for Women's Service. But within three weeks of starting she noted:

> My job . . . takes up most of my time, & I see that I shall have to cut off all attempt to be regular or useful on outside committees. I can "keep in touch" as they say; but I can't contribute any-thing much in the way of thought or initiative, because I haven't much capacity left over from the day's work. (to M. B., 29 Nov. 1931)

She never quite gave up the attempt to combine her own writing with her job, and wrote to Barbara to whom she was prepared to confess her own tendency to try to do too much:

> As for me, I am enjoying myself, as I have got back to writing things again. I have 3 books & 2 articles on hand, & greatly enjoy it. But as usual I have bitten off a great deal more than I can chew. (8 Nov. 1932)

In another moment of self-reflection in a letter to her mother she won-dered:

> whether if I didn't have to attend to children & house & all the other distractions, I should enjoy the snatched moments of work so much? It is obvious that I could have more of them; but would they be so precious? Its impossible to tell! (8 May, 1931)

In her sense of identity as both mother and worker Ray had avail-able to her a feminist discourse expressed in the pages of *Time & Tide*, in particular by Cicely Hamilton, who wrote:

We are beginning to realize that in a world of schools, doctors, nurses and small families—motherhood is very much a matter of divided responsibilities, a part-time job, in short. (November 9th, 1928, p. 1065)

But there was another powerful public discourse in the interwar period which placed much more of a moral weight on motherhood. The slaughter of the war and the decline in the birthrate were important components of this discourse, as was the fear that women's political and professional emancipation would divert women from marriage and motherhood. The institution of the family was defended all the more strongly because of feminist challenges to it, but also because the period was felt to be one of change and instability.[7] Women as mothers were still seen as in need of protection, which in practice meant subordination, as a correspondent to *Time & Tide* pointed out:

Men do not wish to see women as human beings, with very much the same instincts, desires and ambitions as themselves. They want to see them as mothers, specialized creatures with one instinct, one desire and one ambition. (11 April, 1930, p. 478)

The demands on women as mothers were not balanced by any corresponding expectation of men as fathers: men like Oliver Strachey remained in the background of their daughter's upbringing. One of the sources of men's ambivalence about their relationship to both their wives and daughters was identified by Stella Benson when she commented in *Time & Tide* on the "flood of letters, books, epigrams, plays and what not, produced by irritated men on the subject of women" and suggested that:

Quite 30% of the men of the generation now over thirty years of age have mothers they despise . . . The average son takes for granted that Poor Dear Mother talks nonsense on any practical subject except possibly housekeeping. (9 July, 1932, p. 763)

Essential to the power of the discourse of the devoted mother was the reality of women's love for their children. Ray's devotion to her children is palpable in her letters: there is no doubt in my mind that the role of mother was central to her sense of self, although her expression of this—in the modern idiom identified by Alison Light—is underplayed. After seeing him off to school at the age of fifteen, she wrote to Christopher:

When I got home yesterday after pushing you off with such effort
& vigour, the house seemed to be lamentably empty & desolate! &
I wished I had my tormentor back again. A similar wild scrim-
mage this morning got B. out of the house & I have been busy
putting things away & tidying up with (metaphorical) tears rolling
down my chin. (16 Jan. 1931)

Christopher did not share the capacity of his female relatives for letter
writing, and Ray found this difficult, confessing that when he did not
write "a little knot of anxiety collects in the very remote corner of my
mind, & though I don't grow haggard & lose my sleep, my thoughts
swivel in that direction at odd moments."
    She then wrote more openly than usual—and apologetically—
about her feelings for him:

I am so ridiculously fond of you that I do want to keep in touch!
Excuse this sort of remark. Its not the ideal form of correspondence between mother & son—& indeed I'm not going to go all
slushy on your hands. But you & I get on so well, & have such fun
out of each other, that I'm anxious to keep it up. And I know that
this needs attention on both sides as you cease to be a boy &
become a man. I shall give it the best attention I've got, so that
you can count on me in every way you wish. (17 Feb. 1934)

The growing orthodoxy in the interwar period was that children
should be allowed much greater freedom.[8] Barbara's story suggests that
the result of this freedom might not be what mothers desired. This narrative was not unique: a friend of Naomi Mitchison's aunt commented
drily in a letter:

I was interested to her about Naomi and her children. It seems to
me impossible to judge the reactions of any system of education.
Bring up children conventionally and they plunge into vagaries of
all kinds; bring them up on the most modern theories and they
clamour to go to Sunday school. (V. Markham to E. Haldane, 4
Aug. 1933; Haldane Papers 6037 f. 141)

The tone of Ray's letters to her daughter, as is already clear, is often
ironic. The anxiety lies below the surface: "Well, my dear & only
daughter, good luck in your struggles & scrabbles. If this *is* the last
letter to reach you, draw from it a somewhat passionate blessing" (12
Sept. 1933).

Ray wanted her daughter to be independent both psychologically and financially, and she believed that in the changing context of the thirties this meant a university education, followed by training for a career. Ray's letters to her when Barbara was studying before and during her time at university, reveal Ray's own struggles to come to terms with the problems of autonomy and dependence. These letters are more direct and less distanced than usual.

> I am not going to tell you that rational mental behaviour will come of itself. I don't believe it will. There comes a point, which I daresay you have already reached, when *effort & will* enter in . . . To that extent I firmly believe in free will. We can make or ruin ourselves from within, & its not *all* a matter of temperament & one's make up. We've got to put our teeth in *ourselves*, so to speak, as well as into subjects. And no one—neither mother nor father confessor—nor even the object of one's grand passion—can enable one to get out of that quandary. (19 Feb. 1930)

A year later she wrote again on the theme of what she understood was the "rather hard unpalateable essence" of adulthood:

> One has to do it oneself or not at all—& though I believe influences & friends count for *something*, the root of it is always oneself. (17 Feb. 1931)

That Barbara did not agree with such a view or found difficulty in behaving in this way is apparent from the following letter, written almost two years later:

> Try not to worry Wolf or Gran or anyone but yourself & me. One has to swallow one's troubles, especially when they come out of one's own character & mental peculiarities, as far as it can be done. I don't mean to say one has to say nothing about them, but one has to keep the responsibility for them in one's own hands. No one else *can* take that anyhow, & its only agony all round to try to make them do so. (22 Dec. 1932)

Meanwhile Ray refrained from passing judgment.

> As to your jilting, I can say nothing. It would only be wrong if I said anything. But you have *a kind* of sympathy from me, though doubtless unwelcome. As you say, life is complicated. (26 Jan. 1931)

Ray listened to, accepted, and refrained from judging the complexities of Barbara's emotional life partly because she knew well, as she wrote to Barbara, "the feeling of being enraged by family correspondence." She served as a buffer between Barbara and Mary Berenson's condemnation:

> I agree with you that Barbara's talk is really rather shocking. But I am sure she is not nearly so beastly as her words imply! . . . I believe quite firmly in her increasing good sense; but I do wish she would learn a little reticence. I suppose its unusual to wish that one's daughter wouldn't confide so much: but there it is. And the fact is that I don't fully believe in her confidences. (to M. B., 4 Jan. 1933)

Ray wrote to Barbara on the same day:

> You seem to be having a most peculiar, but evidently also a most enjoyable time in your shady haunts. I still preserve a decent veil of obscurity over your actual movements, & expect you home next Tuesday night or Wednesday.

An intricate pattern of inter-generational relationships emerges from these letters. Ray's mother had run away with Bernard Berenson when her daughters were very young, but she had strong views on the moral behavior appropriate to adolescents. She was born in the Victorian era and had escaped from her marriage, but remained economically dependent on a man. Ray was brought up by her Victorian Grandmother, yet was given a good deal of freedom, and apparently would have liked to be able to avoid the institution of marriage.[9] She is reticent about her marriage to Oliver Strachey in her letters, but from what she does write it is apparent that it was based on mutual independence and respect. She was never financially dependent on her husband. Ray's daughter was of the new, comparatively-emancipated generation of the middle-class who were able to mix freely with men, and who were expected to have a career, and Barbara's history demonstrates that the discourses of financial independence and sexual and social freedom available to her were at times in conflict. Perhaps because of her own early experience and her Victorian upbringing, Ray was unable to give Barbara precisely the attention she needed when relating her sexual and emotional life. Ray did seek to give support: her letters to both her daughter and her mother consistently express her faith in Barbara. But in the summer of 1934, Barbara's rash marriage led to a crisis which put considerable strain on Ray's rocklike stability. It was in this crisis that she wrote the letter about needing to solidify which I quoted at the beginning.

In early 1934 Barbara, who had travelled to Australia on a wind-jammer in order to recover from a broken relationship, sent a telegram to say that she was marrying a Finn (soon known as Toby), whom she had met on the boat. Ray gave virtually no hint of misgiving to Barbara although to Mary she expressed her belief that Barbara would soon be pregnant. She was right. Ray wrote to her:

> Your letter from the Makura with its very important news has just come, & leaves me distinctly emotional. I don't wish to be either pompous or sentimental, but this really is such a big thing that I must let off somehow. You probably won't agree with me, but in my opinion its almost more far reaching in ones personal life than having a husband—though that is terrific enough!
>
> . . . You *will* find it all so interesting! I expect you'll turn out to be the best mother there ever was: & I hope its twins if not triplets . . .
>
> . . . Well well well. You *are* in for it now, in every way, with all its horrors & its more than compensating pleasures. (19 April 1934)

When Toby and Barbara arrived back in England, it gradually became apparent that Toby's claims to have a private income, expectations of an inheritance, and a good job in the offing were all fabrications. Ray took care of Barbara through the ensuing crisis, which included near-fatal post-puerperal problems. Ray reduced her hours and eventually gave up her paid work. She had to wrestle with the financial implications of her loss of salary in a situation where Barbara and the baby were financially dependent on her. When the baby arrived she was delighted with him. Her delight led her to an awareness of the limits of rationality.

> Its rather irrational to be so pleased with a baby, but I don't know why one should be always so damned rational: & in fact one isn't! (to M. B., 14 May 1935)

Rationality was part of the discourse adopted by the modern woman which Alison Light has identified, and it was available to Ray in both her public and her private life. Like many other suffragists, Ray understood the campaign for the suffrage to mean the assertion of certain capacities and attributes formerly denied in women. The gaining of suffrage was seen as the belated recognition that women were fully adult, rational individuals. Kathryn Dodd has argued convincingly that the story of the suffrage movement told by Ray in *The Cause* "legit-imises the politics of a modern, progressive, rational and civilised fem-inism."[10] Within the context of the rise of Fascism—the apotheosis of irrationality—this liberal humanist discourse was one that feminists were likely to continue to favor. Faced with a backlash when their claims to full recognition as human beings were again under threat, the need to assert their rationality was imperative.[11]

Paradoxically, the assumption of rationality on the part of the practitioners of liberal politics was one which Ray was to challenge in private, if not in public. The attraction as well as the frustration of the job with Lady Astor was its political nature; Ray was fascinated by political activity:

> I think its odd that it should be so easy to put a finger into other people's pies. I'm always doing it, & it seems to go down. No doubt I often put my foot in, as well as my finger, but I'm gener-ally not aware of that, & am left in the comfortable position of feeling that I've been very useful indeed. Its a great thing to have an elephant's hide, a violent energy & a blind optimism, when one leads the sort of life I do. (to M. B., 3 Dec. 1933)

But she was also well aware of the threat which that activity posed to her sense of the world as a rational place and herself as an agent for change within it:

> I had in the course of my grindstone work to interview an elderly lady & drag out of her her memories of the past. Not much drag-ging was needed I may say. Well, they were almost all highly charged with emotion: indeed at one point she wept copiously. It was largely a record of throbbing hearts with many mostly imag-inary or at any rate highly exaggerated troubles, & storms: jeal-ousies, agonies of unrequited love & what not. I found myself unable to believe 2/3 of what she said. It was of course clear that she herself had gone through all the stories she described. But I think she first invented & then staged them, & then suffered from them & now looked back and wept over them. I found this job rather embarrassing at times, though interesting too. But it gave me a very bad headache. (to Barbara, 26 Jan. 1930)

The urge to "put a finger into other people's pies" was a strong one. In the 1920s Ray had stood three times for Parliament unsuccess-fully, yet she seems never to have been wholehearted about her desire to enter Parliament. Part of this ambivalence was the result of her distaste for the existing political parties. Other feminists exposed to the political world in the interwar period were uncertain whether to be shocked or amused by the behavior of supposedly rational politicians.[12] In Westminster women came up against a world of public school boys: Ray noted, but did not analyze, her own awareness of this world:

> C. [Christopher, then aged 13] brought out a young friend on Sunday, & they behaved like two puppies most of the time, rolling over & over on the floor, & then knocking each other's hats off etc. It is a very curious thing to realize that this is the normal preparation for those who are to administer the Empire! (to M. B., 4 Nov. 1929)

She shared with Eleanor Rathbone, who succeeded in being elected as an Independent MP in 1929, a sense that women's interests and contribution were still not fully recognized within party structures. Ray's attitude is evident in the 1929 election when she canvassed for both Philip Noel Baker, who was standing for Labour, and Lady Astor, a Conservative. She found the results of the election "quite satisfactory— better than if they had a large majority" (to M. B., 7 June 1929). This distancing of herself from party politics is apparent in the 1931 crisis, when she wrote of MPs:

> They are all in a perfect *turmoil*, & change their opinions from hour to hour—& they all seem *much* more excited over election prospects than anyone was or is over the real crisis. I don't think politicians are showing up very well just now. And I must say I am thankful not to be in the House myself. (to M. B., 30 Sept. 1931)

Ray's sense of her own stability and self-control were essential to her response to the collapse of the European stock markets in 1931. The family's financial position had been rocked but Ray's letters at this time are studiously calm; she presents herself as coping without strain. She wrote to Christopher about the sale of some land:

> I hope that will go through without further trouble, in time for me to pay your school bills! Otherwise bankruptcy stares me in the face. But I daresay we shall wriggle along till the whole country crashes to ruin: & then nothing financial will matter. So, as you would say, "no harm." (20 Sept. 1931)

And a week later she wrote to him again:

> Its all a beastly bore. But at least your scholarship & your insur-
> ance will keep you at school! And we have Fernhurst in which to
> retreat & live on rabbits & potatoes! (26 Sept. 1931)

Writing on the same day to Mary Berenson she does not admit to any
doubts about the future:

> Your letters sound very desperate, & as if there was a serious panic
> in your circles. I don't think its as bad as all that—but even if it is,
> its no use getting upset. (26 Sept. 1931)

And in the same spirit she wrote again to Mary two days later that she
fully expected "to get as enjoyable a life out of not having cash as I
have had so far . . . So *do stop* worrying about us. There is no occasion
to . . ." (28 Sept. 1931).

  That mention of capital reveals that she was protected from the
worst consequences of the slump. Ray was fully aware that her personal independence, her ability to choose what she did with her time,
her "liberty of spirit" was made possible by private income (to Bernard
Berenson, 11 Feb. 1930). Nor did she seek to challenge the economic
and political system which hade made this freedom possible. In her letters to Christopher her assessment of the deteriorating international
situation was increasingly bleak:

> The other public news is all as black as ink. I daresay you don't
> read the papers—but its all going from bad to worse—no set-
> tled Government either in France or Germany, & consequently
> no possibility of getting on with the vital international confer-
> ences on debts, reparations & armaments. It doesn't seem possi-
> ble for things to muddle on—but I suppose they will. I don't
> seriously expect the grand crash you are looking for. (2 June
> 1932)

She developed strategies for coping which focused strongly on work:

> Its very queer how the world is collapsing piecemeal. Security
> has quite gone, & your generation may have the most startling
> things to face . . .
>   But that will be your problem. All I can do for the moment is
> to go on tinkering with the present political machine & it generally

seems to be worth while to do so. Now & then a sort of chasm opens up, & the whole thing turns futile. But mostly I'm too busy to notice it! (13 Nov. 1933)

Ray's confidence, her ability to survive both psychologically and financially when under pressure was partly a product of her class. Regenia Gagnier has argued that middle-class women accepted a liberal definition of identity which led them to see "rational behaviour as commensurate with the maximisation of individual utility," and Ray's sense of identity as expressed in her letters bears out this view.[13] Gagnier goes on to argue that working-class women, in contrast, saw self-actualization as successful survival of the family unit. I have suggested that Ray Strachey valued her identity as a rational, independent individual, but that she also positioned that self within a wider network.[14] Her communal role extended beyond that of mother and daughter. She gave support to her sister, her nieces, and her friends. This sort of role was not one she presented as easy or necessarily welcome to her. As she wrote to Mary: "Life sometimes appears to me little more than inching along sideways through a tangle of temperaments . . ." (11 Feb. 1930). It was her reaction to family crises which rocked Ray's world most. She wrote to Christopher about Oliver's niece:

Ursula is completely knocked out & I don't know *what* to do with her . . . And as for myself I can hardly bear it. (23 Jan. 1934)

His offer to come home to look after Ursula gave rise to this revealing reply:

. . . that letter of yours is really the first time I can remember in my whole life when anyone has suggested doing something intensely troublesome to themselves in order to assist me—and you can imagine its value to my feelings. (24 Jan. 1934)

It is clear that Ray did not find it easy to achieve a balance between individuality and communality. I believe that it was her commitment to other women and to feminism which enabled her to do so. Her letters throughout the interwar period are witness to the strength of her commitment to the feminist issues which she saw as important, in particular the employment of women.

I am engaged in a violent wrangle with Winston Churchill on the question of equal pay for men and women in the Civil Service. As the women now enter by open competition, and do interchangeable work with the men, the present system is indefensible. Churchill is clinging to it on economy ground, & we are threatening him with the new voters, & it is rather a fine fight. But of course it eats up my days. However we beat the Treasury 9 years ago over equal entry, & we shall beat them now over equal pay if we stick to it; & so I am sticking. (7 Feb. 1929)

That letter was written to her mother at a time of political and personal buoyancy. There then followed years of private and public turmoil, a "period of reaction" identified by Winifred Holtby in an article in *Time & Tide*:

Talk about "a period of reaction" has become a platitude of journalism: yet it is clearly true that a large number of people are uneasy about the present, and apprehensive about the future. Our happy confidence in the march of civilization . . . has been shaken, and those who had found themselves most satisfied with things as they were are not unnaturally clinging now with increasing fervour to accepted institutions, and disliking with increasing intensity all forms of challenge and criticism. (5 November, 1932, p. 1207)

The effect of these years on the issue of equal pay is apparent in a letter Ray wrote to Christopher in 1934:

This morning I went to give evidence to a Foreign Office Co. on the opening of the Consular and Diplomatic Service to women. We had a lot of evidence, & I knew my case, so that the cross examination was entertaining rather than alarming; but it is perfectly clear that the Co. are a set of complete dead heads, stuck in their prejudices, & entirely unaware of what has been going on recently in the world. (16 March 1934)

Yet she did not lose faith:

the grand equal pay debate . . . took place in the House today & is the climax of 15 years agitation. It all went off splendidly so far as interest & attendance & speaking went, but the Government attitude was frightful. However we now have a new jumping off ground for our campaigns. (7 June 1935)

Ray's work for feminism was a collective enterprise in which she worked alongside women. Molly Hamilton described her as "an organiser of dynamic power, who never asked of others half the work she asked of herself, but always got a co-operation that was warmed by affectionate loyalty."[15] The strength she drew from collaboration with other women had a private as well as a public dimension. In a letter to Christopher in 1934 she wrote:

> For my own comfort I have got Molly down for the weekend, established in Marjorie's house, which gives me a refuge & a chance to have a change of atmosphere.
> My book gets on all too slowly in the midst of this. I think the baby is bound to arrive before I can finish it. (26 Oct. 1934)

This letter for me contains the essence of the process by which Ray Strachey was able to maintain her sense of stability and agency. The book she was writing was on women's employment. The reference to Molly Hamilton is also significant. In the autumn of 1933 Ray spent a holiday in Greece with Molly which she had described to Mary as "more heavenly than I thought possible," and to Barbara as "a fading out process" when "Everything faded out of my head . . ." (12 Sept. 1933). Ray's friendships with women among them Molly Hamilton, Elinor Rendel, her sister Karin, and her Strachey sisters-in-law, especially Pippa, were essential to her.

During the thirties Ray's communal role was extended by the birth of Barbara's son. Being a grandmother was a role which Ray rapidly fitted into her life and the baby became part of her communal responsibility. Not that she absolved Barbara of her responsibility. The process of encouraging Barbara towards financial independence had already been a strong theme in Ray's efforts before the marriage: now Ray was concerned to make sure that Barbara divorced Toby and found herself a satisfying job which would enable her to support herself and the child. For Ray there was no contradiction between independence and motherhood, and her own role within the family was a crucial part of her life as a feminist. For some women the powerful discourse of domesticity in the interwar period may have been destructive, for Ray I believe it was not. Judy Giles has developed Alison Light's argument and suggested that "the dominant discourses of femininity between the wars stressing home-making, cheerful stoicism, common sense and emotional restraint offered opportunities for self definition which challenged the conventional view of working-class women."[16] It was the strength Ray drew from her communal role which enabled her to develop qualities of durability and flexibility which helped her to survive when the world rocked around her in the early thirties. Her "blind optimism" became less blinkered, her "elephant's hide" less thick, and she conserved her "violent energy" for the purposes of survival.

Ray Strachey's correspondence testifies to the importance of letter writing as a practice and letters as a genre. Her letters offer multiple perspectives: they help us to see how one interwar feminist, through the process of letter writing, constructed a sense of self rooted within the family, and moving out from there, contributed to her work for and with women. Through this engagement Ray maintained—although not without difficulty—a sense of personal agency.

Notes

1. Ray Strachey's letters are held in the Smith, H.W. mss., Manuscripts Department, Lilly Library, Indiana University, Bloomington, Indiana. I am grateful to the Lilly Library for permission to quote from the letters. Unless it is clear from the text to whom the letter is written, "To M. B." indicates that the letter is addressed to her mother, and when they are the recipients, her children's names are noted in full. I have punctuated the letters as they appear in manuscript.

2. Exceptions to this general neglect are to be found in some of the articles in Harold Smith, ed., *British Feminism in the Twentieth Century* (Aldershot: Edward Elgar, 1990); and in Martin Pugh, *Women and the Women's Movement in Britain, 1914–1959* (Basingstoke: Macmillan, 1992) which addresses the issues of "The Cult of Domesticity in the 1930s" and "The New Feminism and The Decline of the Women's Movement in the 1930s." Susan Kingsley Kent does not do justice to the thirties in *Making Peace: The Reconstruction of Gender in Interwar Britain* (Princeton, N.J.: Princeton University Press, 1993).

3. Women in Germany were blamed by some for the success of Nazism at the polls: see, for example, "Women in Hitler's Germany," an article written by a German socialist refugee in Britain for *Labour Woman*, June 1934.

Winifred Holtby touched on the attractions of rituals and military pageants for women in *Women and a Changing Civilisation* (London: John Lane, 1934), pp. 102–3. She also attacked the "cult of the cradle" when "Every brand of saccarine sentiment is poured over motherhood and infancy," yet "little done to encourage willing and successful maternity . . ." (p. 168). The New Feminists advocated "endowment" for mothers, and easily available birth control advice, in order to achieve "willing and successful maternity." In concentrating on issues which were understood to be central to the experience of women, but not men, they were in danger of appearing to confine, in Holtby's words, "women's interests to the function of motherhood alone" (*Women*, pp. 168–69). Holtby also quoted the following words from a letter in the *Manchester Guardian* from a "German apologist of her government's policy," who wrote: "Woman has again been recognised as the centre of family life and to-day it has again become a pleasure and an honour to be a woman." The pressures which pushed and the desires which pulled women towards support for the New Feminism were not easily separable from the attractions of Fascist ideas on women. Holtby, like other feminists in the thirties, was well aware of the dangers and alert to the vital distinctions between Fascism and the New Feminism. See Johanna Alberti, "Some British Feminists' anti-Fascism" in (ed.) S. Oldfield, *This Working-Day World* (London: Taylor & Francis, 1994).

4. Judy Giles, "A Home of One's Own: Women and Domesticity in England 1918–1950," *Women's Studies International Forum*, 16.3 (1993): 239–53.

5. For the Women's Employment Federation, see papers in the Fawcett Library.

6. Alison Light, *Forever England: Femininity, Literature and Conservatism Between the Wars* (London: Routledge, 1991), p. 210.

7. Carol Dyhouse, *Feminism and the Family in England, 1880–1930* (Oxford: Blackwell, 1989).

In 1932 Naomi Mitchison edited a book entitled *Outline for Boys and Girls and Their Parents* (Victor Gollancz) which provoked a letter in the press signed by eighteen men "of important standing," as Lady Rhondda put it when she defended the book in *Time & Tide* (15 Oct. 1932), pp. 1096–97. The central complaint of the signators was that Mitchison was advocating the destruction of family life.

8. Amber Blanco White, described in her obituary notice in *The Times* as "collaborator for a time of H. G. Wells in his campaign to break the taboos of Victorian and Edwardian morality (6 January, 1982)," identified the new demands placed on the wife and mother of the interwar period, among which she placed emphasis on "the hitherto unfelt responsibility for our children's characters," *Worry in Women* (London: Gollanz, 1941).

9. Letter from Mary Berenson to Alys Russell and Logan Pearsall Smith, 17 October 1911, quoted in Barbara Strachey & Jayne Samuels, ed., *Mary Berenson: A Self-Portrait from Her Letters and Diaries* (London: Hamish Hamilton, 1983). Ray's reticence was developed during a childhood when she moved regularly from her Quaker and feminist Grandmother's influence to visits to her mother at Berenson's famous villa in Florence, I Tatti. She was immediately attracted to the individuality and idiosyncratic behavior of the entire Strachey family. Oliver Strachey was divorced with a thirteen-year-old daughter in his care, and had just returned from India. Ray's sister Karin believed that he was "bewildered by the niceness of English girls and cannot decide among them." Ray's mother, conveying this information to her husband, added: "Ray, with her direct methods, may bring him down with her little arrow . . ." (letter of 15 May 1911, quoted in ibid.). She was right. They lived amicably together, sharing enjoyment of their children, but moving in separate circles of friendship. Naomi Mitchison, *All Change Here: Girlhood and Marriage* (London: Bodley Head, 1975).

10. Kathryn Dodd, "Cultural Politics and Women's Historical Writing: The Case of Ray Strachey's *The Cause*," *Women's Studies International Forum* 13.1–2, pp. 129–37.

In "The Patriarchal Welfare State," Carole Pateman has pointed out that: "The patriarchal understanding of citizenship means that . . . either women become (like) men, and so full citizens; or they continue at women's work, which is of no value for citizenship . . . Theoretically and historically, the central criterion of citizenship has been 'independence,' and the elements encompassed under the heading of independence have been based on masculine attributes and abilities," *The Disorder of Women* (Cambridge: Polity Press, 1989), pp. 179–204.

11. It seemed particularly necessary for women to assert their rationality when the press focused primarily on the appearance of women in public, commenting on their clothes and on their "femininity"—or otherwise. The compulsion to include a woman's appearance as part of a description of her political presentation has not, of course, died away—even among historians, apparently: "If she had bothered with her clothes, Ray could have displayed her pleasant blue eyes and ample figure to striking effect," Brian Harrison, *Prudent Revolutionaries* (Oxford: Clarendon Press, 1987), p. 168.

12. Winifred Holtby and E. M. Delafield were especially sharp in their humorous representation of the world of patriarchal politics in their writings in *Time & Tide*.

13. Regenia Gagnier, "The literary standard, working-class lifewriting, and gender," *Textual Practice*, 3.1 (1989), pp. 36–53.

14. Liz Stanley, "Moments of Writing: Is There a Feminist Auto-biography?," *Gender & History* 2, Spring 1990: pp. 58–67.

15. Mrs. Mary Agnes Hamilton, *Mrs. Strachey*, broadcast on the Home Service at 1.55 p.m. on Thursday, July 25, 1940. Typescript in the Fawcett Library.

16. Giles, p. 252.

PART II
Selves and Others

INTRODUCTION

Early feminist theorists of the autobiography (1980 is the inaugurative moment here) carved out a space for critical discussion of women's self-representation by celebrating the non-autonomous, other-directed, and communal female selves they encountered in a range of ignominiously neglected works.[1] This strategy had the effect of bringing out into the open and challenging the masculinist aesthetics implicit in existing autobiographical criticism, which sought out and found, in a mutually reinforcing chain, attributes such as individuality, coherence, and self-consciousness. It also opened the way for a revaluation of women's self-representation in terms other than absence or failure.

More recently this preliminary formulation has been usefully questioned and complicated. Poststructuralist and Lacanian theorists have pointed out the mediation of language in the construction of selfhood, and have offered new ways of thinking about the relationship between "self" and "other." At the same time, the idea that women's self-constructions might be distinguished or distinguishable solely, or even mainly, on the basis of sexual difference—as the "other" of some putative universal "man"—has been challenged as reifying and essentialist. In different ways the essays in this section ask whether it makes sense to talk, not of auto/biography, but of "alterbiography": the Life-writing of the other.

For one thing, as Griffin reminds us, the notion of isolate selfhood may itself be "an illusion, a discursive construct operating within particular ideological frameworks" and hence "inapplicable not only to women but to all others." In particular, the ideal autonomous self, seemingly unmarked by gender, race, or class, may be a product of distinct historical conditions: may be contingent upon its difference from—and therefore constituted by—an emphatically gendered and raced "other" whose unrepresentability is the trope that anchors its meaning. Hence, Khanna develops the insights of Gayatri Spivak to show that the concept of a self shoring itself up in the face of the unknown—a concept central to autobiographical narratives of exploration, adventure, and discovery—is based on a hypothetical other being: the "dark continent" or racially other woman against whose assumed silence and opacity the self is defined.[2] Khanna extends this finding to psychoanalytic theorizing itself, arguing that contemporary understandings of the "I," of consciousness and the unconscious, are likewise constructed upon the same homogenized, disenfranchised other. Broughton meanwhile suggests that individual male selves—in this instance Sir Leslie Stephen's—are indebted for their self-construction to a network of subjectivities whose economic and discursive interdependence is never entirely erased. Broughton draws on Mary Poovey's work to suggest that some of the givens of mainstream autobiography, such as its story of development, self-mastery, and success, may have an inbuilt gender as well as the more obvious class dimension. The gendering of autobiography, according to this argument, rests not simply in the fact that men's Lives are more patently stories of self-advancement, but in the fact that the story of struggle and advancement which "one woman inaugurates and another rewards" is itself an ideological trope for the experience of alienation under patriarchal capitalism.

Seeing the clusters of texts addressed in this section as in negotiation with each other, rather than as mainstream or marginal, enables us to explore the possibility that the auto/biographical master-narratives of a culture may be as deeply embroiled in the task of managing difference as the more overtly oppositional or hysterical utterances of the powerless. Mustafa Kemal's historic speech to congress after the Turkish War of Independence, Stanley's account of exploration in Africa, Freud's "excavation" of female sexuality, or Leslie Stephen's construction of a repository of "national" biography may be as bound to the dynamics of gender and race as the more visibly contingent "other" narratives they subsume. And just as recognizing the complex and fragile negotiations between self and other in autobiography enables us to demystify the cultural authority of individuals, so identifying the role played by biography and autobiography in the construction of the master-narratives of Western culture—here the narratives of nationalism, modernism, imperialism, and psychoanalysis—can help us understand the role of the micro-politics of the subject in macro-political change.

It is crucial, however, that the effort to contextualize and thereby challenge the autonomy and timelessness of the Western autobiographical self should not degenerate into generalizations about the "death of the subject" per se. As Sidonie Smith and Julia Watson have argued in a recent collection, the bland postmodern assertion that the subject is itself colonized replicates and reinforces Western feminism's tendency to "hypostasize a universally colonized woman universally subjected to 'patriarchal' oppression."[3] Similar dangers attend psychoanalytic accounts of the subject of autobiography. It is commonplace to argue that people become autobiographers rather in the way human beings become selves: like a baby gazing at its image in the mirror the autobiographer imagines a coherent, unified, and individual identity—a self—

at the expense of a contradictory, fragmentary, and undifferentiated experience of being-in-the-world. Like an infant entering language, the autobiographer assumes the first person singular at the expense of all other grammatical positions. According to this way of thinking, the autobiographer buys into the symbolic order by taking up a position in relation to the Law of the Father—the position of subject—and by repressing other kinds of identification. As Toril Moi puts it, "The speaking subject that says 'I am' is in fact saying 'I am he (she) who has lost something'— and the loss suffered is the loss of the imaginary identity with the mother and with the world."[4] Feminist theorists have been drawn to this analogical way of talking about autobiography for a number of reasons, not least for the glimpse it promises of a maternal realm—a feminine alterity—in the interstices of the symbolic order. However, as Ayşe Durakbaşa's essay shows, the analogy needs to be used with caution. Halidé Edib's invocation of a quintessentially Lacanian "mirror" scene does indeed narrate growing up and becoming a subject as wistful analogues of loss: the loss of the mother, of childhood, of irresponsibility. But as the larger context of her Memoirs forcibly reminds us, Edib typically reclaims a feminine childlike self the more roundly to abjure it in the service of a narrative of nation-building. The banishment of an archaic, childlike other—figured in Edib's text as an other self, as her own children, and as the ultimately disenfranchised woman warrior, or female subaltern, in the nationalist struggle—may be the price not just of autobiographical subjecthood, but of political success.

So while all the essays in this section suggest that the autobiographical self, like the psychoanalytic self, is constituted by loss, and is founded upon the incorporation into the I of an other, they share a recognition that metaphorizing that other is not the same as attending to its specificity. The tendency to conflate the two remains one of the besetting sins of feminist autobiographical criticism: its celebration of the female (as) other colludes in the "universalizing agenda of Western theorizing that erases the subject's heterogeneity as well as its agency."[5] The rapid crystallization of a canon of classic—mainly high modernist or postmodern—women's autobiographies suggests that only certain kinds of self, founded on certain re-figurations of the other, fulfill the requirements either of mainstream feminist, or of mainstream poststructuralist aesthetics. As Griffin points out, there could be no more dramatic enactment of otherness than Alice Toklas' *What is Remembered*: a narrative preconditioned by and founded on Gertrude Stein's fictive rendition of her identity as "wife of a genius" in *The Autobiography of Alice B. Toklas*. Yet Toklas' narrative hardly ever figures in autobiographical criticism, much less in its canon of cherished texts.

This kind of critical myopia has serious consequences for the woman who finds herself pre-figured in discourse as the other of a more powerful subject: for the colonized woman who is represented as the White Man's dark continent; for the non-elite woman warrior who finds she does "not fit the actual things" when nationalist victory has been achieved; for the lesbian whose status as significant other to another woman renders her doubly invisible. What is needed, then, is a way of reading the other back into the discourse of the self without reifying or essentializing either. As Khanna puts it, "Autobiography as a genre has to be recoded with values of difference, and understood as both making the 'I' and revealing its inadequacy." This is a complex project, but the following essays suggest possible starting points: awareness of intertext and context; a willingness to weave "catachrestically" back and forth between literal and metaphorical constructions of the self and the other, and above all a patient attention to the cultural specificities, desires, and languages of the other.

Notes

1. See for example Estelle C. Jelinek, ed., *Women's Autobiography: Essays in Criticism* (Bloomington: Indiana University Press, 1980); see also Estelle C. Jelinek, *The Tradition of Women's Autobiography from Antiquity to the Present* (Boston: Twayne, 1986).

2. It would be interesting to extend this radical deconstruction of the "common sense" components of the autobiographical canon to other texts and other conventions: to the confessional mode and the conversion figure, for instance, or to the "seminal" texts of Augustine, Bunyan, Rousseau, Franklin, and so on.

3. Sidonie Smith and Julia Watson, editors' introduction, in *De/Colonizing the Subject: The Politics of Gender in Women's Autobiography* (Minneapolis: University of Minnesota Press, 1992), p. xiv.

4. Toril Moi, *Sexual/Textual Politics* (New York and London: Routledge, 1985), p. 99.

5. Sidonie Smith and Julia Watson, loc. cit.

Further Reading

Barrett, Michèle. "Some Different Meanings of the Concept 'Difference,'" in Elizabeth Meese and Alice Parker, eds., *The Difference Within* (Amsterdam: John Benjamins, 1989), pp. 37–48.

Davies, Carole Boyce. *Black Women, Writing and Identity: Migrations of the Subject* (New York and London: Routledge, 1994).

Fox-Genovese, Elizabeth. "My Statue, My Self: Autobiographical Writings of Afro-American Women," in Shari Benstock, ed., *The Private Self: Theory and Practice of Women's Autobiographical Writings* (London: Routledge, 1988), pp. 63–89.

Lionnet, Françoise. *Autobiographical Voices: Race, Gender, Self-Portraiture* (Ithaca: Cornell University Press, 1989).

Martin, Biddy. "Lesbian Identity and Autobiographical Difference[s]," in Bella Brodzki and Celeste Schenck, eds., *Life/Lines: Theorizing Women's Autobiography* (Ithaca: Cornell University Press, 1988), pp. 77–103.

Miller, Nancy. "Representing Others: Gender and the Subjects of Autobiography," in *differences*, vol. 6, no. 1 (Spring 1991), pp. 1–27.

Pratt, Minnie Bruce. "Identity: Skin Blood Heart," in Elly Bulkin, Minnie Bruce Pratt and Barbara Smith, *Yours in Struggle: Three Feminist Perspectives on Anti-Semitism and Racism* (Brooklyn: Long Haul Press, 1984), pp. 9–63.

Sommer, Doris. "'Not Just a Personal Story': Women's *Testimonios* and the Plural Self," in Bella Brodzki and Celeste Schenck, eds., *Life/Lines: Theorizing Women's Autobiography* (Ithaca: Cornell University Press, 1988), pp. 107–30.

Smith, Sidonie and Watson, Julia, eds. *De/Colonizing the Subject: The Politics of Gender in Women's Autobiography* (Minneapolis: University of Minnesota Press, 1992).

Spivak, Gayatri Chakravorty. "Can the Subaltern Speak? Speculations on Widow Sacrifice," in Cary Nelson and Lawrence Grossberg, eds., *Marxism and the Interpretation of Culture* (Urbana: University of Illinois Press, 1988), pp. 271–313.

Domna Stanton, "Autogynography: Is the Subject Different?," in Stanton, ed., *The Female Autograph: Theory and Practice of Autobiography from the Tenth to the Twentieth Century* (Chicago: University of Chicago Press, 1987), pp. 5–22.

5

In Search of a Voice for Dopdí/Draupadí: Writing the Other Woman's Story Out of the "Dark Continent"

Ranjana Khanna

This article addresses the following questions, (how) can the Other woman speak? (How) can she speak/write her life? And (how) can she speak/write her life in her own political, gendered, and regional language, her own psychic economy, when we are looking at her waiting for her to articulate?[1] How could a figure who has frequently been constructed as metaphor or as an object of research, represent herself autobiographically and/or indeed politically?

This is not to suggest that the literary and the political can be conflated under the ambiguous term "representation." Rather, we will consider the ways in which the various teleological and linguistic frameworks we recognize as representation both reflect and are constituted through autobiography. How, then, does the object of that teleological narrative speak her autobiography in a context in which she has been overdetermined by it? Are agency and subjectivity constituted as impossibilities for the "Other woman?" And beyond these questions lies another: Is the autobiographical even desirable for the Other woman, the (formerly) colonized woman who is not part of the elite of the country in question?

The four sections of this chapter reflect different moments of research on the notion of the Other in relation to Indian mythistory, postcoloniality, and feminism. First, I consider how, in the context of late nineteenth-century British exploration and Viennese psychoanalysis, the colonized woman becomes constructed as Other through metaphorization. I read

Stanley and Freud, looking at the similarities between the archaeological and psychoanalytic discourses which excavate their "dark continents": Africa for Stanley, female sexuality for Freud. I show how autobiography works within their analyses as a way of constituting self through projecting an Other. This Other both defines that self and is constituted by it. Their analyses, whether archaeological or psychoanalytic, are revealed to be both implicitly and explicitly autobiographical. After a brief discussion of Bhabha's theorizations of the postcolonial Other, I consider Mahasweta Devi's story "Draupadi,"[2] analyzing how the violence of interpretation is played out upon the body of the Other. In dialogue with Spivak's ambiguous translator's foreword to the story,[3] I offer a reading of the myth of Draupadi, and ask whether there is a space within it that might be epistemologically emancipatory for woman as subaltern.

Stanley and Freud

The metaphor of the dark continent first came into use in H. M. Stanley's explorer's narrative about Africa: *Through the Dark Continent*.[4] It is also used by Freud in an exploratory narrative, not in relation to Africa, but to female sexuality. In his article "The Question of Lay Analysis," Freud says:

> the sexual life of adult women is a "dark continent" for psychology.[5]

This section draws these two uses of the metaphor together, asking whether it is possible to represent the (over-) metaphorized as a thinking subject.

Stanley opens the chapter of his autobiography called "Through the Dark Continent" with:

> In a camp in the heart of Africa, not far from Lake Bangweolo, David Livingstone, the travelling evangelist, lay dead. . . . Let me see: Livingstone died in endeavouring to solve the problem of the Lualaba River. John Hanning Speke died by a gun-shot wound during a discussion as to whether Lake Victoria was one lake, as he maintained it to be; or whether, as asserted by Captain Burton, James McQueen, and other theorists, it consisted of a cluster of lakes. . . . To know the extent of the worth of that lake would be worth some trouble. Surely, if I can resolve any of these, which such travellers as Dr. Livingstone, Captains Burton, Speke, and Grant, and Sir Samuel Baker left unsettled, people must needs believe that I discovered Livingstone!

A little while after the burial of Livingstone at Westminster, I strolled over to the office of the "Daily Telegraph," and pointed out to the proprietors how much remained shrouded in mystery in Dark Africa . . . Africa includes many dangers from man, beast and climate. . . .[6]

Stanley's trip to the dark continent is inspired by the dead Livingstone. The purpose of his journey is not merely to uncover the truth about the lakes of Africa, but to prove that it was he who found Livingstone. In the guise of a quest for the lake, his real desire is to discover the effect of the lake on the man. The fellow explorer for whom Stanley searched far and wide across Africa had, it seems, been overwhelmed by Dark Africa's shrouded mysteries. Dark Africa, like the Medusa, has turned the living to stone.[7] Stanley must overcome the threat of castration by the terrifying Medusa that is Africa, and stand erect as he who conquered her mysteries. David Livingstone and John Speke call out to Stanley from beyond the grave, urging him on not only to the solving of a mystery, but to immortality. The archaeological narrative is, then, predetermined by an autobiographical myth. Both narratives firmly establish an I, the autobiographical subject, as their organizing principle.

In his use of archaeological and exploratory images, Freud echoes Stanley. Witness two archaeological metaphors, drawn from Stanley and Freud respectively:

Forty years of my life have passed, and this delving into my earliest years appears to me like an exhumation of Pompeii, buried for centuries under the scoriae, lava, and volcanic dust of Vesuvius. To the man of the Nineteenth Century, who paces the recovered streets and byeways of Pompeii, how strange seem the relics of the far distant life! Just so appear to me the little fatherless babe, and the orphaned child.[8]

And from Freud:

There is . . . no better analogy for repression, by which something in the mind is at once made accessible and preserved, than burial of the sort to which Pompeii fell a victim, and from which it could emerge once more through the work of spades.[9]

Freud's reads uncannily like Stanley's; he appears as that man of the nineteenth century of whom Stanley writes. Indeed, it is Freud's own reading about archaeology which drew him to his discoveries in psychoanalytic method. Psychoanalysis as a mode of discursive analysis thus reflects this nineteenth century narrative. Formed of this narrative, it is naturally attuned to it, analyzes it wonderfully.

The metaphor of the dark continent, however, signals something quite different from these archaeological images of Pompeii. The dark continent connotes a great deal, but denotes nothing: it is undefinable. I am unconvinced by David Macey's assertion that Freud "appears to be blissfully ignorant of the political connotations of his metaphor."[10] In his German text, he uses the metaphor in English.

> Vom Geschlechtleben des kleinen Mädchens wissen wir weniger als von dem des Knaben. Wir brauchen uns dieser Differenz nicht zu schämen, ist doch auch das Geschlechtsleben des erwachsenen Weibes ein *dark continent* für die Psychologie.[11]

The relevant, and slightly longer passage in the translation is:

> We know less about the sexual life of little girls than of boys. But we need not feel ashamed of this distinction, after all, the sexual life of adult women is a "dark continent" for psychology. But we have learnt that girls feel deeply their lack of a sexual organ that is equal in value to the male one; they regard themselves on that account as inferior, and this "envy for the penis" is the origin of a whole number of characteristic feminine reactions.[12]

Leaving the metaphor in its original English, Freud grants it a further aura: of colonialism and its projection of a mysterious Africa. The unknown of the self is displaced on to imprecise metaphor: the more it is explored, the more it is shrouded in mystery. It is precisely the "Englishness" of the image which is salient to the Austrian Jewish German speaker. The British explorer lives through Freud's text. Freud transforms the intrepid explorer of far off lands into psychoanalyst exploring analysand. And yet it is the British explorer and Freud identifying with him who emerge as the central mysteries: the dark continent as mystery invokes the figure of the explorer/self, who can then construct an autobiography in the case of Stanley, or psychoanalysis in the case of Freud.

Freud assures us that "we need not feel ashamed" about our lack of knowledge of female sexuality, metaphorizes woman as dark continent, and in this blurring of her specificity, transfers the shame that "we need not feel" about our lack of knowledge, on to her. She ends up with the shame: for her lack of sexual organ; for her inferiority with respect to the male; in short, for her envy of the penis. His lack of knowledge has been replaced with her lack of penis. His phallacious knowledge can understand her body, her sexuality, only in terms of what his is not. Fearing her difference, he makes her other, obliterating the specificity and difference of her body by turning it into a fetishized metaphor of the unknown: dark continent. Fetishized, it is clothed in obscurity and thus cannot pose any threat to his own erection (of himself). This dark continent is defined as lack. The Other of man and of Europe are constructed as inferior versions of this self, becoming self in a castrated form.

Both Freud and Stanley fix their objects of discovery as mysteries which they have explored and on to which they can project their fantasies. Stanley's erection of Livingstone and through this, his erection of himself is not very different from Freud's erection of (himself as) Oedipus. Rita Ransahoff tells the following story:

> . . . the small group of his followers in Vienna gave him a medallion with his profile on one side and a Greek design of Oedipus answering the Sphinx on the other. Around it was the line from Sophocles's *Oedipus Tyrannus*: "Who divined the famed riddle and was a man most mighty." When he was presented with this medallion, Freud turned pale. He explained that as a student in the University, he would stroll around the court looking at the busts of former illustrious professors. He had a fantasy that one day his bust would be there, and on it would be inscribed this line of Sophocles. In 1955, years after this daydream, (Ernest) Jones presented a bust of Freud to the University of Vienna to be placed in the arcade. On it was inscribed the line from Sophocles.[13]

Erected as the solver of the riddle of the Sphinx, of the riddle of femininity, of the pre-Oedipal stage of sexuality that he characterizes as the Minoan-Mycenaean behind the Greek,[14] Freud constructs woman as (mysteriously) castrated. Stanley, although refused burial next to his mentor Livingstone, erects himself as explorer and survivor of Africa.

How can the dark continent articulate itself when it is constructed as this mysterious, dangerous, less than man (castrated), less than white Judaeo-Christian (savage), archaic Other? Where can the apparently signified woman and (colonized) Africa find a space in which s/he can speak, when the metaphor used to describe her constructs her as (fetishized) other? And how can the doubly metaphorized African woman find a voice in this economy? Is her story of self possible when she has been constituted as other—as that against which self is defined?

Reading Freud and Stanley in this way, taking their metaphors, in a sense, too literally, enables us to glimpse how the particularities of such ideological moments unfold, and how these moments are informed by certain teleologies, whether explicitly autobiographical, as in Stanley's case, or implicitly so, as in the case of the psychoanalytic framework.

Bhabha

Homi Bhabha is a theorist concerned with the question of how the other can speak, how the fetish can look back and therefore release herself from the position into which she has been projected. In his essay "Articulating the Archaic,"[15] Bhabha suggests that the moment that the colonizer confronts the object he has colonized—the moment that the object transcends his/her object position—is the moment that the colonizer must attempt to articulate his relation to the colonized other. It is in the attempt to articulate that the colonizer realizes his inability to find the appropriate words. Traversing India and Africa in his quest for the concept of self underpinning British colonialism, Homi Bhabha takes his examples from, (among others) Forster and Conrad.[16] The "ouboum" in the Marabar Caves in Forster's *A Passage to India*, and the cry of "the horror! the horror!" in Conrad's *Heart of Darkness* are moments of the impossibility of articulation. Confronting the colonized, the colonizer is left with signifier alone: the empty sound which signifies no more than its own indeterminacy: "ou-boum!" "the horror! the horror!"

Bhabha sees the moment of the impossibility of articulation as that of the "hymen," as the moment of the "entre," or "between." Derrida suggests that the entre is the hymen between desire and fulfilment, the moment between the oppositions of desire and perpetration, where confusion is sown between a series of opposites.[17] It is this moment "between," which, according to Bhabha, characterizes confrontation between colonizer and colonized: the moment when the authority of the subject is thrown into confusion because it sees the falsity of its position as its other's (superior) opposite. The moment of the impossibility of speech is thus the crisis of "his" representation of "her."

But in the texts Bhabha cites, the effects of the abject moment of non-sense are not promising: Adela can have Aziz accused of rape for assaulting her banal preconceptions. Kurtz cruelly exploits the natives of his heart of darkness, commodifying them by exploiting them through ivory trade. And where the two dark continents, Africa and woman, come together in the figure of the colonized woman, we are left with little more than a fetishized commodity. The mystery and muddle found in the caves (antres) of I, the mysterious riddle of femininity, the dark mysteries of Africa—all blurring conceptually in their metaphorization of each other—leave little space for these muddles to conceive of themselves other than as "muddle." So, how can this dark continent, the colonized woman, articulate itself, or be represented?

For the feminist, postcolonial moment to release itself from a monolithic discourse of the same—a discourse which allows the other to speak only in terms of unspeakability by the self who constitutes it—we need to dramatize movements between the many different discourses which enable the other woman's subjectivity.

Dopdi and Draupadi

Mahasweta Devi's Bengali short story "Draupadi" is about a woman in the Naxalite movement, an underground political movement in West Bengal in India. Her name is Dopdi, and she is from the Santal tribe, and, as a non-caste, non-Hindu aboriginal, she bears very little similarity to the Sanskritic mythical princess Draupadi for whom the story is named. Dopdi's husband has been killed by the police for his involvement in the movement, and now the police force is pursuing her. The army officer who is in charge of the pursuit is very familiar with the underground movement. He has researched it carefully, knows its demands, can predict its changes and its members' movements. Finally, Dopdi is tracked and caught. The object of the search is raped and mutilated, will not speak, and refuses clothing. This is where the story ends.

In her helpful translator's preface to this short story, Gayatri Spivak reads the story as an analogue of the "First-World scholar looking to the Third-World."[18] Like Bhabha, she addresses the problem of articulation, asking whether it is possible for the Other woman to speak. The over-metaphorized object of search, she suggests, cannot be heard behind the analysis of the first-world scholar, or indeed, behind the figure of Senanayak, the army officer.

Extending Spivak's analysis, we can read this as an instance of the impossibility of self-representation for Dopdi, both in the political sense of the word, and in the figurative or literary sense. The story dramatizes the way in which some autobiographical narratives—(police) investigation, or (literary) analysis—gain precedence over others. The possibility of the others' narrative, autobiographical or otherwise, does not exist. This is not, however, to suggest that a figure such as Dopdi, whom I have cited as the other woman, should simply have a space in which she can speak or, assuming literacy, can write her autobiography. This would not necessarily allow her to represent herself politically: speaking from a particular location is emphatically not the same as politically representing the needs of that location.[19]

Spivak interprets the figure of Senanayak, the army officer, whose name actually translates as "leader of the army," as a "pluralist aesthete."[20] She honors him with this name because of his fascination with the figure whom he tries to capture, Dopdi, and with the underground movement she represents for him. Spivak identifies Senanayak with first-world scholarship, and herself with him: not only because she is an academic in the First World, and as such is directly complicit with its exploitative machinery which works against the Third World, but also because she inherits its elitist scholarly techniques. In this case, she means the way information is gathered, stored, and deployed to constitute Dopdi as what she calls herself: "the object of your search." Senanayak can predict her movements, understand her political sympathies, and can create files and dossiers about her. Dopdi is a figure with a history so carefully documented that she can do and be nothing unpredictable. Senanayak knows what he needs to know in order to own her and to name her as his own. On capturing her, he orders her repeated rape and mutilation. His sympathy with her extends only to knowledge of her. He is complicit with the institution which humiliates and degrades her, fixing her as an object to be known, interrogated, and, finally, assimilated.

Spivak helps us beyond this brutal impasse by situating the story in the context of her mythical namesake, Draupadi, the heroine of the *Mahabharata*. She summarizes Draupadi's story usefully:

> (Draupadi) is married to the five sons of the impotent Pandu. She provides the occasion for a violent transaction between men. . . . Her eldest husband is about to lose her in a game of dice. . . . The enemy chief begins to pull at Draupadi's *sari*. Draupadi silently prays to the incarnate Krishna. . . . The Idea of Sustaining Law (Dharma) materializes itself as clothing, and as the king pulls and pulls at her *sari*, there seems to be more and more of it. Draupadi is infinitely clothed and cannot be publicly stripped. . . .[21]

The counterpoint of this with the last section of the Mahasweta Devi's story interests me here. Having been gang raped and cruelly mutilated, her breasts bitten and torn, her pubic hair matted with blood, Dopdi, unlike her mythical namesake from the *Mahabharata*, refuses clothing. Rather, she confronts Senanayak with the power of his knowledge. Her difference has been obliterated by his way of knowing, the all-powerful Father has named her as lacking, both literally and metaphorically. She is the tribal woman who will not comply with the dominant politics, the communist rule of the state, because she has not been politically represented by it. She lacks financially, and, as she confronts Senanayak, she lacks clothing. He has seen her as a wound in the political economy, and, with his knowledge, he has wounded her.[22] As the object of his search, she has been constrained by his actions. Now he is confronted with an abjection of his own creating: here is a terrifying Medusa, who demands that the horror done to her be seen by its perpetrator. She can now exist only as mutilated, as wounded, as less-than: a horror he has created by seeing her as object-to-be-known. His power is that of naming, and he is the metaphorical father of the police force that sanctions the abuse of its prisoners, those that are not duped by the name of this father, and are therefore lacking in its terms.[23] As namer, he, in a sense, can name himself: his own name reflects his control over definition. He is his profession: Senanayak, as we have seen, means army officer. The linguistic economy, in this sense, represents him in the most literal denotation.

Is this moment of confrontation, this moment when, like the fetish challenging the fetishist for recognition, the "object of . . . search" looks back, a useful and a revolutionary one? Is Dopdi truly an agent here?

> . . . Once Dopdi enters, in the final section of the story, the postscript area of lunar flux and sexual difference, she is in a place where she will finally act *for* herself in *not* "acting," in challenging the man to (en)counter her as unrecorded or misrecorded objective historical monument. The army officer is shown as unable to ask the authoritative question, What is this? . . .[24]

It seems to me unlikely that this is a moment of revolutionary transformation. The confrontation between the symbolic father and the abjection he has created still remains within an economy of lack: his economy where he can name her as other, obliterating her difference. This confrontation still works in an exchange of glances in which he is advantaged, and in which the validity of his logic goes unquestioned. The shock of being confronted with abjection may well force the lawgiver to question his own sense of self, but will it necessarily result in giving up his power as namer? The moment of confrontation may well be a disruption, but it is not necessarily therefore a solution in the story.[25]

But surely woman does not exist only at that juncture where her gaze refracts man's, nor yet does she exist solely in the terms through which man can understand her—those terms that have created her suppression and oppression? The disruption of Senanayak's role as "pluralist aesthete" comes only at the point of confrontation. This point of refraction is not autonomy: it is a sense of autonomy in which Dopdi must rely on the presence of Senanayak. He might have heard her when she was speaking, not with the aim of knowing her finally, but with the aim of learning her languages, her different economies, and the way that she is compromised by the specific discourses with which she must contend. That way, he will not seek out the final truth, the bare body which can be known. Instead, as history confirms, the army officer Senanayak can ignore her cry for Aboriginal rights and tribal self-determination. Senanayak is ultimately a pawn of bureaucrats who speak as part of a highly-centralized government, and who can give out orders from Delhi. He does not have to listen to her voice protesting against the expropriation of tribal land by Bengali-speaking caste-Hindus and urban-based forest developers. The communist government of West Bengal has cast a blind eye on the system of bonded labor, so Senanayak can as well.

We can learn from the mythical Draupadi of the *Mahabharata*, stretching the meaning of Mahasweta Devi's story and Gayatri Spivak's interpretation so as to make a different kind of theoretical intervention. Draupadi's five husbands, the brothers Pandava, are involved in a feud with their one hundred fraternal cousins, the Kaurava. The main story of the *Mahabharata* is based on this feud. In the *Mahabharata*, at the moment when one of her husbands, the eldest of the brothers, loses her in the game of dice to the Kaurava, Draupadi, striving to achieve autonomy from her husbands, points out to him that he has already sold himself, and poses as a riddle the question of whether or not he can, therefore, sell her. No one is able to answer the question adequately, and everyone is left puzzled as to whether she can be gambled away or not. At the moment where the Kaurava try publicly to strip her, naming her whore because of her many husbands, she prays to Krishna, and her *sari* becomes infinite.[26]

Popular rewritings of the story include the prayer to Krishna. In other versions the prayer is absent, and Draupadi is referred to at this moment by another of her names, Krishnaa, meaning "dark." However, as Spivak has pointed out, the infinite *sari* represents the idea of Sustaining Law, *Dharma*. In so far as the riddle cannot be answered adequately by any of those present, Draupadi's honor is retained, and *Dharma* is sustained. The solution to Draupadi's riddle exists within a symbolic realm to which the gamblers have no access. Like Dopdi's song, Draupadi's *sari* is infinite and inaccessible to those who want to commodify her.

The traditional patriarchal Hindu reading of this story might be as follows. The stripping of Draupadi will dishonor the brothers Pandava. Their wife will be put on display. They will be dishonored not only because their wife will be naked, but also because she is dragged from her quarters in an "impure" state. She is menstruating, and because of this, she is not in the main part of the house, is not wearing the clothes and jewelry befitting her status as princess, and is covered only by the cloth worn during menstruation. The god Krishna saves her and her husbands from the dishonor of witnessing her abject impurity.

Alternatively, we might give this story a more feminist gloss. Draupadi has always been associated with the god Krishna. In fact, as I have said, one of her names is Krishnaa, meaning dark. She is dark precisely because she did not have a usual birth, she was not of woman born, but was created by and born of fire. Her invocation of Krishna might be read as an address to and reappropriation of her mythical origin, where she inhabits his name Krishna, with her, Krishnaa. She can thus save herself in a way which does not simply preserve her husbands from the shame of her "impurity." She can allow the texture of her sari, and the textuality of her words, to rise to a different level of conversational exchange, exempt from the brothers' transactions, and also free of a construction of herself as impure. She cannot be bartered with, as her languages, the texts of the weave in her menstrual cloth, speak a language in which she cannot be commodified.[27] Just as Senanayak's role is represented absolutely in his name, demonstrating how his autobiography is both generated by and reflected within his epistemological and linguistic economy, so Krishnaa moves to a different level of discourse in which her mythical namesake becomes literalized as *Dharma* in cloth.

At this moment Draupadi/Krishnaa belongs to no one, and the transaction cannot be completed in the terms of the two sets of brothers. She cannot be reduced to the flesh they use as currency; she cannot be named, she cannot be the means of exchange between men, she cannot be humiliated. She hides that which would wound their visual economy, but not hers. Her protection of her menstruating body with infinite clothing, which contrasts so poignantly with Dopdi's display of bleeding wounds, affirms her control of her reproductive function: neither she, nor any potential children, can be named. The tribal Dopdi cannot step out of her wounded, humiliated, and mutilated status because the words of Senanayak, the army officer, have controlled her. The mythical Draupadi/Krishnaa cannot be named, finally, because she refuses to be the object of search: her body belongs to no one. Whilst *Dharma* sustains her, no one present can adequately answer the question she poses:

no one can see beyond their own "law of the father," beyond the "economy of the same" to comprehend the register in which the question is posed.

How can we avoid being Senanayak, creating and mutilating objects of investigation? How can we listen to the multiple traces and infinity of discourses which emerge from the different economy into which Draupadi/Krishnaa steps? She defies being locked into the economy of exchange: she uses her *sari* not to confront the subject, but to step outside its exchanges. As she stands between the dealers in a transaction who use her as currency, she defies them, drawing in the different discourses, the different weaves which make her up as subject, in ways the two sets of brothers cannot even begin to understand.

Pedagogical and Performative

Of course, there is a profound irony in my reading of Mahasweta Devi's story. I have, in a sense, rejected the empirical (or literal) tribal Dopdi in favor of a metaphor: Draupadi of *The Mahabharata*, a Sanskritized myth of pan-Indian Aryanization. In the process of seeking out the literalness repressed beneath the myth of the dark continent, I have, in my allegorical reading of "Draupadi," metaphorized the political into the mythical in a rhetorical move known as "catachresis": the abuse of a trope. What is the political repressed beneath the mythical?

Hitherto I have read *against* names and naming in a number of ways: in the case of the dark continent; in the case of Senenayak the army officer, whose power to control through language is reflected in the literalizing of his profession in his name; and in that of Krishnaa, who invokes her own origins and not the god Krishna when she utters the name. In contrast, Dopdi, the fallen, abject tribal woman, has seemed to remain simply a catachresis for Draupadi, the mythological Aryan princess of whose name Dopdi's is a cruel parody. However, by reversing the process and bringing Dopdi to bear on Draupadi, we can, in turn, recuperate the Sanskritic Draupadi as a catachresis for a mythic, pre-Sanskritic, tribal Dropdi.

The mythical Draupadi's darkness, connoted both by her name Krishnaa (meaning dark) and by her lack of Aryan blood (she is fire-born), can be read as a euphemism for a transformation she undergoes: the indigene, her tribalism repressed, becomes Aryan in myth. Draupadi's polyandry, as Spivak points out, is the only Sanskritic example of such a marriage arrangement,[28] though polyandry is much more common among some aboriginal tribes in India.[29] Draupadi can, then, be seen as a signifier of the transformation of the tribal into the

Aryan. According to this reading, her designation as Aryan is itself a catachresis.

My move between the literalizing of the sign at the beginning of this chapter, and the allegorization of the story of Draupadi, represents a shift in my conceptualization of the other, and therefore also a shift in my conceptualization of self. The interpretive move the First-World scholar (Senenayak) needs to make to release Dopdi from imprisonment as an object of (re)search is a move from what Homi Bhabha has called pedagogy to performance. The apparently pedagogical concept underlying the designation of dark continent as mysterious is dramatized as performative in my reading, so that the explorers' autobiographical and archaeological narratives disclose the submerged connections between their senses of self, and the ascription of mystery to the dark continent. Spivak's analysis of the performance of the various discourses informing Mahasweta Devi's story and her own allegorical reading of it, erases the literal tribal both from the story and from the myth. The pedagogical has been erased in favor of the performance. But catachresis, the abuse of metaphor, is a product of both the literal and the metaphorical, the pedagogical and the performative, and thus represents a moment when the binary opposition between these categories breaks down.

It is the pedagogical moment of the literal, where a concept of self can be assumed without analysis of how that self is constituted in performance, which gives rise to the inquiry with which I began: can the other woman speak? The question represents a moment in which the other is projected by the self. While it is indeed necessary to ask how the other woman can speak from the impossible subject position afforded to her by discourses in which she is preconstituted as metaphor, it is also necessary to explore the performance of her difference: the multiple discourses within which she exists as discursive formation. Senanayak, who reduces Dopdi to object, does not see the performance of her difference. Draupadi, who apparently prays to Krishna, is not understood as the dark tribal counterpart, Krishnaa. By reading Dopdi as catachresis, by retrieving the literal beneath the metaphorical, we find what has been repressed. Only from this position can we begin to understand the figurative, and the performance of difference, which allow Dopdi/Draupadi to speak.

Conclusion

Reading Dopdi's speech, the researcher cannot presume that she can represent herself politically: articulation from a particular position does not necessarily mean articulation of that position. However her speech may reveal both her political demands and political interests.

In a more recent essay, Spivak writes:

> Current postcolonial claims to the names that are the legacy of the European enlightenment (sovereignty, constitutionality, self-determination, nationhood, citizenship, even culturalism) are catachrestical claims, their strategy a displacing and seizing of a coding of value.[30]

The question, then, is not simply: how, as a postcolonial subject, does one construct oneself as belonging to a country with its own history, for that "oneself" is a catachrestical concept. The question is, rather, how does one speak in a voice which incorporates the "infinity of traces"[31] which exist between discourses in the varied and various inherited languages?

The question of whether the other woman, pre-constituted by colonial discourses, can speak, suggests an identifiable voice, a voice of dissent whose oppositionality reflects nothing but the violence done to her by a self who seeks to discover, to know, to teach. Much in the same way that writing of nation in the postcolonial context always betrays the differences suppressed by the pre-Independence nationalist urge, so the representation in writing of the postcolonial woman exceeds the bounds of what Bhabha has called the "continuist accumulative"[32] sense of I developed in and through autobiographical representations of the self.

For this reason, at the moment the postcolonial self performs life-writing, the concept of self implicit in autobiography needs to be renegotiated. Autobiography as a genre has to be recoded with values of difference, and understood as both making the I and revealing its inadequacy. Writing the other, creating agency out of those very discourses of self which create the other as dark continent, requires a kind of mimicry which belies the possibility of the pedagogical. This "I" cannot simply tell:

> The subject is graspable only in the passage between telling/told, between "here" and "somewhere else," and in this double scene the very condition of cultural knowledge is the alienation of the subject.[33]

With the displacement of the pedagogical which inevitably occurs once its performativity is analyzed, comes a displacement of the self against which the other woman of my original inquiry was conceived.

The postcolonial context highlights the catachresis at the heart of self. This begs the question: how does one teach (or indeed research) post-coloniality if the pedagogical is undermined at the very moment of its articulation? And how does one teach autobiography—of any period or context—once notions of self as autonomous, self-directed agent have come under fire? Perhaps it is in the classroom, where the performance of multiple readings is made possible by differences of background, political sympathy, and interest, that the pedagogical reading of other-ness can be most successfully challenged. Through this process, auto-biography is revealed as text, and text as performance, rather than rev-elation, of self. This shift between pedagogy and performance allows us to acknowledge the lack of singularity in any subject position; to chal-lenge the appeal for a voice or an autobiographical self; and to prob-lematize the terms of the question: can the other woman speak?

As I hope I have shown, one way to let the other speak is to flesh out the different discourses by which it is constituted: in this instance those of the tribal, of Aboriginal rights, of national languages and lin-guistic specificities, of resistance, of communist politics, mythical ori-gins, repressive religions, and rural strife. Moving, catachrestically, back and forth between discontinuous registers of literalness and metaphor, we can weave a new tapestry: a productive Derridean "between" exempt from the imperious discourses of exchange. The autobiogra-phy, as a discourse of postcolonial selfhood, can emerge not in the oppo-sition of self, or in the quest for other. Rather, it can exist in the space, the "infinity of traces," between.

Notes

Thanks to Srinivas Aravamudan, Trev Broughton, Misha Kavka, Laura Mulvey and Nicole Ward Jouve.

1. These questions are prompted by Gayatri Chakravorty Spivak's arti-cle, "Can the subaltern speak?" *Marxism and the Interpretation of Culture*, eds. Cary Nelson and Lawrence Grossberg (Basingstoke and London: Macmillan Education Ltd., 1988), pp. 271–313.

2. Mahasweta Devi, "Draupadi," *In Other Worlds*, trans. Gayatri Chakravorty Spivak, pp. 187–96.

3. Spivak, "Translator's Foreword," *In Other Worlds*, pp. 179–87.

4. Henry Morton Stanley, *Through the Dark Continent* (New York: Harper and Brothers, 1878).

5. Sigmund Freud, *The Standard Edition of the Complete Psychological Works of Sigmund Freud*, 24 Vols., trans. & ed. James Strachey (London: The Hogarth Press & The Institute of Psychoanalysis, 1953–74), (referred to hereafter as *S.E.*). Sigmund Freud, "The Question of Lay Analysis," *S.E.* (1926), XX: p. 212.

6. Henry Morton Stanley, "Through the Dark Continent," *The Autobiography of Henry M. Stanley*, ed. Dorothy Stanley (Boston and New York: Houghton Mifflin Co., 1909), pp. 296–97.

7. I allude here to Freud's analysis of the figure of Medusa. See Sigmund Freud, "Medusa's Head," *S.E.* (Published posthumously: 1940c [1922]), XVIII: pp. 273–74.

8. Stanley, *The Autobiography*, 6.

9. Sigmund Freud, "Delusions and Dreams in Jensen's *Gradiva*," *S.E.* (1906 [1907]), IX:40; see also "Notes Upon a Case of Obsessional Neurosis," *S.E.* (1909), X:176–77; and "Case History of Fräulein Elisabeth von R," *S.E.* (1892–93), II: p. 34.

10. David Macey, in *Lacan in Contexts*, writes of Freud's use of the metaphor of the dark continent, saying:

> In keeping with a rationalist ideology of enlightenment, he frequently applies metaphors of darkness—often drawn from archaeology and exploration—to areas of ignorance . . . (Freud) appears to be blissfully ignorant of the political connotations of his metaphor (the dark continent). Within the discourse of late-nineteenth-century colonialism, Africa is moist, dark, unknown. It is, however, amenable to penetration, providing that the appropriate degree of force is used.

David Macey, *Lacan in Contexts* (London and New York: Verso, 1988), pp. 178–79.

11. Sigmund Freud, "Die Frage der Laienanalyse," *Gesammelte Werke*, 14, Vols. (1926), (London: Imago Publishing Co., 1948), XIV: p. 241.

12. Freud, "The Question of Lay Analysis," p. 212.

13. Rita Ransohoff in *Bergasse 19: Sigmund Freud's Home and Offices, Vienna 1938*, ed. Edmund Engelman (New York: Basic Books Inc., 1976), 59. Also, Ernest Jones, *The Life and Work of Sigmund Freud*, 3 Vols. (New York: Basic Books, 1953–57), 2: p. 14.

14. Our insight into this early, pre-Oedipus, phase in little girls comes to us as a surprise, like the discovery, in another field, of the Minoan-Mycenaean civilisation behind the civilisation of Greece. Sigmund Freud, "Female sexuality," *S.E.* (1931), XXI: p. 226.

15. Homi K. Bhabha, "Articulating the Archaic," *Literary Theory Today*, eds. Peter Collier & Helga Geyer-Ryan (Ithaca, N.Y.: Cornell University Press, 1990), pp. 203–18.

16. E. M. Forster, *A Passage to India* (1924: Harmondsworth: Penguin, 1979); and Joseph Conrad, *Heart of Darkness* (1902; Harmondsworth: Penguin, 1973). Interestingly, Bhabha picks on works which lend themselves very readily to interpretation as metaphors of the ambivalent "other" country as woman and unconscious.

17. Jacques Derrida, *Dissemination*, trans. Barbara Johnson (Chicago: Chicago University Press, 1981), pp. 212–13.

18. Spivak, "Translator's Foreword," p. 179.

19. I am thinking here of Spivak's analysis of Marx's concepts of *vertreten* and *darstellen* in relation to the work of Foucault and Deleuze. See Spivak, "Can the Subaltern Speak?"

20. Spivak, "Translator's Foreword," p. 179.

21. Spivak, "Translator's Foreword," p. 183.

22. Her "difference" is therefore reduced to "castration" in Senanayak's projection.

23. I am alluding here to Lacan's concept of language, the Symbolic, as the "law of the father." *Le nom du père*, will hold things in their stride when they wander (errare) from their prescribed course. She who will not accept "le nom du pere" as "gospel truth," who cannot hear his "non," who is "non dupe" by his word, will err (erre) in his language, and will be repressed by it. Lacan entitles his unpublished Seminaire XXI "Les non dupent errent" (1973–74). Jacqueline Rose discusses this title in her introduction to Jacques Lacan, *Feminine Sexuality: Jacques Lacan and the Ecole Freudienne*, eds. Juliet Mitchell and Jacqueline Rose trans. Jacqueline Rose (London and Basingstoke: Macmillan, 1982) 39. The concepts of *le nom du père* and *les non dupes errent* are discussed in his seminar of the following year entitled "R.S.I." See especially *Ornicar?* 4 (1975): pp. 91–106; and 5 (1975): pp. 15–66, where the relevant sections of "R.S.I" have been transcribed.

24. Spivak, "Translator's Foreword," p. 184.

25. Spivak ends her comments on this story at this moment of confrontation. She does not give the story a psychoanalytic gloss as I have done here, and she does not continue with a reading of the myth of Draupadi after explaining how the peasant woman Dopdi's refusal of clothing contrasts to the Sanskritic mythical Draupadi who can call on Gods to assist her. Of course, such luxuries and opportunities are not open to most!

26. For more on Draupadi's relationship to Krishna, see Alf Hiltebeitel, *The Ritual of Battle: Krishna in the Mahabharata* (Ithaca, New York: Cornell University Press, 1976). For information on the cult of Draupadi, see Alf Hiltebeitel, *The Cult of Draupadi 1: Mythologies: From Gingee to Kurukshetra* (Chicago and London: University of Chicago Press, 1988).

27. Purnima Mankekar notes "the semiotic excess surrounding the figure of Draupadi as she gets disrobed in front of her family." Purnima Mankekar, "Television Tales and a Woman's Rage: A Nationalist Recasting of Draupadi's 'Disrobing,'" *Public Culture*, 5 (1993), p. 488. Mankekar also notes the various uses of the myth through the nationalist struggle for Independence for India, to the recent television series of the *Mahabharata* and its relation to the idea of "Indian Womanhood."

28. Spivak, "Translator's Foreword," p. 183.

29. In *The Heroic Age of India*, N. K. Sidhanta speculates on the tribal roots of Draupadi's polyandrous marriage to the Pandavas, suggesting that the Pandavas were non-Aryans. N. K. Sidhanta, *The Heroic Age of India* (London: Kegan, Paul, Trench, Trubner and Co., Ltd., 1929).

30. Spivak, "Postcoloniality and Value," *Literary Theory Today*, p. 229.

30. Antonio Gramsci, *Selections from Prison Notebooks*, trans. Quintin Hoare and Geoffrey Nowell Smith (New York: International Publishers, 1971), p. 324. Of course, I am taking huge liberties in shifting the phrase from the context of humanist Marxism to anti-humanist deconstruction.

32. Bhabha, "DissemiNation," p. 297.

33. Bhabha, "DissemiNation," p. 301.

6

Leslie Stephen, Anny Thackeray Ritchie, and the Sexual Politics of Genre: Missing Her

Trev Lynn Broughton

I wish to write mainly about your mother. But I find that in order to speak intelligibly it will be best to begin by saying something about myself.[1]

The recovery of women as autobiographers—as authors as well as objects of the discourses of selfhood—has had far reaching conse-quences for many disciplines. One largely unexplored consequence is that men's modes of self-representation, and hence masculinities, can be seen in a new, feminist light. Acknowledging the existence of women as autobiographers permits us to consider the possibility that, far from being a male domain to which women have had no or restricted access, autobiography as a genre has been contested terrain. In Victorian Britain, at least, debates over the nature and value of autobiography as a recognizable genre were of a piece with struggles over the construc-tion of gender—which is no more than to say that identities and repre-sentations are theoretically inseparable. A feminist reading of a man's autobiography will be attuned to this possibility, and will look beyond the images of men and images of women present in the text to the strategies of representation deployed to manage difference: difference within as well as between genders; within as well as between genres. I would suggest, furthermore, that a feminist reading of a man's memoir can help us understand the conditions and the limits of his rhetorical power.

Sir Leslie Stephen's *Mausoleum Book* is addressed to his children in the darkest hours of his grief over the death of his second wife, Julia Duckworth Stephen. It is generally accepted that, far from being a simple outpouring of emotion, the *Mausoleum Book* is a very complex document. Explicitly or obliquely, it partakes of a number of literary genres: hagiography, letter, elegy, biography, confession, apologia, mémoire d'outre tombe, anti-conversion narrative, reminiscence. In one sense the generic mix is intentional: the *Mausoleum Book* is Stephen's letter to Julia's children commemorating their mother, and is to serve as a gloss on the correspondence between himself and Julia he has been re-reading and organizing since her death. Evidently this does not fully account for the book's generic confusion. Some readers attribute its sliding between apparently incompatible forms to Stephen's agnosticism and to his reluctance, in the face of mortality, to do without some vestige of a redemption narrative. Less sympathetic biographers have ascribed the generic bumpiness to the twists and turns of Stephen's conscience as he reviews what has been politely called his domestic exigence—his history of moodiness, especially about money matters. Stephen himself points to another possible reason. He is deeply insecure in his profession, and because of this is unable to write in an unliterary way, even in an avowedly private, personal document.[2] I would not wish to dispute any of these interpretations as far as they go. The *Mausoleum Book* is indeed a painful and sometimes embarrassing testament to violent love and grief, spiritual unease, writerly anxiety, and guilt. What is not generally admitted is that these facets of the text are linked.

I want to trace some of the *Mausoleum Book*'s submerged patterns of association; to map connections between professional, sexual, and generic issues as they figure in Stephen's self-representation, and to argue that it is in these taut and often brittle links that we can begin to perceive the gender of Victorian Eminence in its latter days. The character and intricacy of these connections, and their relationship to the social construction of literary masculinity at the turn of the century, can only be glimpsed intertextually: not only because texts in the broadest sense are our sole aperture on the distant past, but because the late Victorian literary patriarch, the hero as Man of Letters, was in many ways a self-consciously textual construction. My subdivision of this study into different strands of context is thus a matter of emphasis—a way of highlighting my main themes—rather than a setting of boundaries between literary and nonliterary issues. For instance, what I have called personal contexts—in this instance Stephen's relationships with his family—were very often textually mediated at the time, through letters or within an ever-expanding cottage industry of biography, mem-oirs, and reviews. On the other hand, literary contexts, such as contem-porary debates about matters of biographical etiquette, were one of the media within which Stephen forged both his own identity and the terms of his domestic authority. The division is useful, I hope, because it brings into focus Stephen's efforts to manage the inseparability of tex-tuality and gender by appealing to a sexual division of (literary) labor. For what I want to ask in this essay is how issues of gender and genre are interrelated in the *Mausoleum Book*. To begin to address this I will ask a more limited question: how and why does a document claiming to be mainly about Julia Stephen contrive to be mainly about other people—about Stephen's first wife, her sister, his in-laws, his friends, and most of all, himself?

Personal Contexts (I): Families

I want simply to talk to you about your mother. (p. 3)

Biographers of both Stephen and his daughter Virginia Woolf have noted that the Julia of the *Mausoleum Book* is a distinctly unreal person-age. Almost unapproachable in her purity and perfection, she is the Angel in the House of Victorian domestic ideology: a pedestalled saint to be reverenced rather than cherished. Straining to capture her quali-ties, Stephen hazards a series of extravagant comparisons. Julia is at one moment a "sister of mercy . . . most tender, skilful and judicious," while at the next her attraction is the uncanny allure of a great work of art: the Sistine Madonna, a masterpiece of Greek sculpture, Wordsworth's "phantom of delight." What makes Julia so compelling a subject, and yet so elusive to description, is that her beauty implied her spiritual qualities without—and Stephen labors to make his point—excluding bodily or material beauty. Her appeal was that she embodied (and temporarily resolved) the contradiction at the heart of domestic femininity: the sexiness of the sexless Angel.[3] She represents for Stephen "the complete reconciliation and fulfilment of all conditions of femi-nine beauty" (pp. 30–37). It is on this vision of a woman at once seduc-tive and virtuous, at once spiritual and emphatically corporeal, that Stephen wants his children to focus their gaze:

Ah! my darlings, try to fix her picture in your minds. To see her as she was is to me to feel all that is holy and all that is endearing in human affection. (p. 33)

Mary Poovey has drawn attention to what she calls the "self-consistency" of the "Angel in the House" image. By this she means her
essential selflessness and hence her exemption from the strife of the
public world of market relations. The domestic Angel's freedom from
internal conflict or doubt was necessary to a "binarized" sexual division
of labor, rights, and duties (the so-called "separate spheres"). It was
also integral to a model of male identity whereby the contradictions
inherent in the capitalist mode of production were recast as an internal
drama of alienation and self-mastery through work: a narrative "which
one woman inaugurated and another rewarded."[4] The image of the
Angel in the House and the master-narrative of male development were
thus mutually constitutive tropes within bourgeois culture. Poovey has
also noted the persistence at the heart of the domestic ideal of a seemingly incompatible image of woman: woman as fleshly desire, as the
residual other half of Enlightenment man's divided self. In the Victorian
period this "loose" woman was only partially displaced on to the figure
of the prostitute or the exotic racial other, and she surfaces in cultural
debates much closer to the middle-class home: in anxieties about gov-
ernesses or about surplus single women, for instance. These were what
Poovey calls "border cases" in the functioning of mid-Victorian ideology: debates which blurred in some way the sexual opposition upon
which all other oppositions were supposed to be based, because they
"threatened to relocate difference—either to move it from the sexual to
some other, cultural division (such as class) or to uncover it *in* woman,
the very subject upon whose self-consistency the ideology rested."[5]

There are signs throughout the *Mausoleum Book* that such anxieties are invading the Angel's House, and are fracturing the self-consistency of the Angel herself. One reason seems to be that Julia fell in
love and married not once but twice. Surveying Julia's letters to Herbert
Duckworth and to himself, Stephen confronts the possibility that
women might change, and that heterosexual desire—supposed to
secure difference by guaranteeing the complementarity of the sexes at
all levels of society—might actually imply a more slippery, dialectical
kind of otherness. Of Julia's letters to Herbert, for instance, he admits
that "there is often something alarming in the sight of a noble and pure
minded young woman accepting a husband with complete confidence[. . .] One might read such language used by a thoughtless or
impulsive girl, and fear that it might turn out to be the prologue to a
tragedy." Such a reading would, of course, be incompatible with the
Julia myth; yet the alternative is equally disconcerting: "What I seemed
to read in her letters is the opposite of this. The strength of her passion
seems to be a guarantee not only for its purity but for its thorough

insight" (p. 37). One of the uncanny elements of Stephen's account of Julia is the sensation that she is reading him rather than he her.

Further misgivings arise from Stephen's understanding of the nature of authority, and of the relative efficacy of domestic and literary influence. Comparing his own achievements as a writer and thinker with Julia's legacy as a woman, Stephen finds his own life wanting. For where his work will have made "no perceptible difference to the world," Julia's life has been "the outpouring of a most noble and loving nature, knitting together our little circle, spreading its influence to others, making one little fragment of the race happier and better and aware of a nobler ideal." Had Stephen succeeded in all his ambitions as a writer (which he insists he has not), his books would have merely "expressed a little better than other books thoughts which were fermenting in the minds of thousands" and would have survived at most a generation before becoming "obsolete" and "superfluous" (pp. 95–96). Julia, on the other hand, had only to be herself, a pure-minded Englishwoman, to express the best desires and aspirations of a whole culture. Despite all this, it is Julia, the "beloved angel," who alone drives Stephen back to his losing battle as a professional writer: he is left with a memory "that will, I can even now hope, encourage me in time to work for you" (p. 97). The paradox embodied in the image of Julia—that she is the pretext for and an indictment of his efforts as a writer—is never far from the surface of the text. Her very perfections seem to imply a criticism of him, and he is haunted by "Hideous morbid fancies . . . which I know to be utterly baseless, and which I am yet unable to disperse by an effort of will. I must live them down" (pp. 57–58).

So the simple task of fixing Julia in her children's memories, and hence of installing a narrative of redemption based on human affection rather than on, say, divine intervention, founders on an image of domestic perfection that is already *unheimlich*. Gradually the process of writing about Julia threatens to dislocate difference from its secure moorings in heterosexual marriage and to relocate it within Julia, within writing, and even, critically, within the autobiographer himself. An enterprise more fraught with ideological pitfalls would be hard to imagine, and the tension shows everywhere—in the digressive structure, in startling asides, in petty semantic quibbling, as well as in strings of tortuous disavowals. That Stephen should risk exposing the cracks in the mausoleum would seem foolhardy, were it not for his ulterior rhetorical motive, which is to invite sympathy and secure support from his children. In the face of the death of his wife and so many of his contemporaries,[6] Stephen risks reopening the narrative of his life so as to claim his children—or rather Julia's children—as the consolation prize of his old age.[7]

Personal Contexts (II): Fathers-in-Law

   Puzzling over Julia's father's unobtrusive personality, Stephen comments that "Somehow he did not seem to count—as fathers generally count in their families" (p. 26). For Leslie Stephen in 1895 the problem of whether—and how—a father should count is an urgent one. As a newly-widowed father it is necessary for him to establish claims on his children's energy, time, and affection. In practice this means appealing to different constituencies in slightly different terms: his own children, his step-children, his sons and daughters. (The "you" of the *Mausoleum Book* slides between these overlapping groups.) Most importantly for his own comfort and well-being, it means securing the attention of his eldest daughter Stella, who he hopes will take her mother's place in the family home. The effort he devotes to this end suggests that this is not a sacrifice that can be taken for granted in the 1890s. Proclaiming himself—now—worthy of Stella is a complicated maneuver, for it involves admitting the possibility of insufficiency (that is, difference) in their former relationship. He executes this maneuver by constructing a new narrative of stepfatherhood:

> I used to think it rather strange that, young as you were at the time of our marriage, the instinct of fatherhood did not become fully developed. I was sensible of a something different in our relations. And yet, my dear ones, I love you now like a father. . . . (p. 66)

   If the narrative of becoming a father is likely to unleash even more unmanageable contradictions than that of becoming a husband, it has, at least, a potential dividend. His peace of mind depends on his success in reasserting his role as paterfamilias in relation to his daughters generally, and, more tendentiously, in relation to their future husbands. Working with some fairly unpromising materials, Stephen struggles to construct a genealogy for his own story in which fathers of daughters count. He does this by drawing on another, much older story of fatherhood: the story of the exchange of daughters between fathers and husbands that Gayle Rubin has called the "political economy of sex."[8] He links his own predicament—his need to question or even renegotiate the terms of his domestic authority with his daughters and their spouses— with the fate of his two fathers-in-law: with Minny's father, William Makepeace Thackeray, whose wife was left in a lifelong state of "dreamlike incapacity" by a bout of puerperal fever, and with Julia's father, Dr. Jackson, who, as we have seen, seemed to Stephen "something of an outsider" in an otherwise closeknit family.

Stephen goes to some trouble to establish ties, however tenuous, of filiality and loyalty between himself and these dispossessed fathers-in-law. In each case he launches into one of the *Mausoleum Book*'s complex digressions, each of which belongs in different ways to the prehistory of Stephen's household. The anecdote concerning Dr. Jackson is relatively straightforward. Dr. Jackson and his wife spent the early years of their marriage in Calcutta, where Mrs. Jackson, falling ill, was successfully treated by a medical colleague called Rankin. Dr. Rankin declined to accept payment from a fellow medic's wife, so Mrs. Jackson made him the present of a watch. The two doctors subsequently disagreed over Rankin's "grotesque" attempts to convert the staunchly Anglican Jackson to agnosticism, and, by way of "symbolically shaking the dust off his shoes," Rankin returned the gift of the watch. Matters were eventually put on a more satisfactory footing when, years later, Rankin returned to London "very poor and very ill," and was "soothed" through his last days by his old adversary Dr. Jackson and by Stephen himself.

Mrs. Jackson, whose body, after all, is the story's point of departure, rapidly becomes incidental to the main plot, which is about one good turn (curing Dr. Jackson's wife) deserving another (forgiving and nurturing Dr. Rankin). Debts of honor are paid off, professional dignity is restored, and reasonable relations between the two are re-established. By the same token, Jackson the life-long believer and Stephen the convinced agnostic are conjoined in their sympathy for "poor old Rankin" who is portrayed as socially marginal and naive. The shift in perspective from one homosocial friendship to another is accomplished by Stephen's conclusion to the story: "[Rankin] died very soon afterwards, and is buried at Kensal Green, just outside consecrated ground, with a queer inscription on his tombstone—I often look at it—saying that he was 'neither theist nor atheist.'" Only the watch, kept "in a kind of limbo of suspense" during the intervening years, and handed over by Mrs. Jackson to Stephen on Rankin's death, betrays that anything in the story remains unresolved. Stephen firmly dispenses with any uncomfortable or superstitious associations that might cleave to it: "When I am dead, let it go to the one who is most in want of a watch" (pp. 27–28).

Stephen's transaction with his first father-in-law, the novelist Thackeray, is yet more oblique—necessarily so as Thackeray died in 1863, twenty-four hours before Stephen was due to be introduced to him at Trinity, and some time before he (Stephen) became part of Minny's social circle. The story concerns the proper circulation of cash, a subject about which Stephen admits he is chronically anxious and to which he returns several times, despite priding himself on his reticence (pp. 90, 24). On his marriage to Minny, Leslie found himself having to deal, not with his father-in-law, but with Minny's elder sister Anny. Anny is reckless with money, over-spending both her private income and her earnings from writing ("As soon as money came into her purse it flowed out"), and even after her sister's marriage Anny continues to dissipate both her own and Minny's money. The result of this is that Minny's income from her father's estate—her dowry in effect—regularly evaporates before it reaches her husband. (This seems less unreasonable when one realizes that Leslie had moved in with the sisters rather than the other way round). Stephen recounts how he gained the financial upper hand by diverting Minny's income to himself, in return for which he takes initial responsibility for the household expenses. This means of course that the spendthrift Anny is now regularly in debt to him: a situation he compounds much later by helping her buy her own marital home. Stephen's self-construction as creditor is a characteristic piece of sophistry: he boasts—his word—of his self-imposed silence about these debts, and proclaims to his children his intention to write them off. They are to refuse any repayment that might be offered in the future ("which, I confess, strikes me as improbable"). All in all, Stephen is satisfied that despite her profligacy, he has "no cause of regret for any of [his] pecuniary relations with Anny" (pp. 24, 25).

Having pecuniary relations with Anny, however, is a poor substitute for the legal, economic, and above all symbolic transaction between a bride's father and her husband. A footnote added three years later (1898) affords a more complete resolution to the story. Having protested he would never countenance repayment from Anny, Stephen admits he has accepted £400 from her, as Minny's portion of the £4000 Anny has earned by using their joint property (Thackeray's unpublished papers) as the basis for Prefaces to a new edition of her father's complete Works. By this convoluted means, Leslie Stephen, in his old age, is able at last to establish symbolic relations with a father-in-law who died a quarter of a century before.

To clinch his deal with the future, Stephen supplements his histories of becoming a husband and becoming a father with dark hints of an ancient patriarchal trope: social life as the exchange of women between men. At stake in both the father-in-law anecdotes, beyond their testimony to Stephen's good humor and reasonableness, is women's ability to give and receive property in their own right; or, to put it another way, women's right to symbolize rather than always to be symbolized. The resolution of the stories depends on this ability having been short-circuited or bypassed. The narrative of the *Mausoleum Book* ends with

Stephen's birthday gifts to Julia's eldest daughters on May 30 1995: for Stella, a chain he had given to her mother on their marriage; to Vanessa a photograph of Julia by Mrs. Cameron. The bargain is sealed. "We will cling to each other" (p. 97).

Literary Contexts (I): Anny and Leslie as Writers

Within and between the many narratives of Stephen's masculine selfhood—the bourgeois narrative of redemption by heterosexual marriage; the patriarchal story of the exchange of women; the story of developing fatherly instincts, to name but three—ironies and inconsistencies proliferate as difference migrates from one site to another. Tug at any loose end and the pattern dissolves. In the rest of this article I will disentangle one of these threads to show that, in 1895, border issues of gender and sexuality are interwoven with questions of autobiography.

One of the *Mausoleum Book*'s most telling ironies concerns Stephen's token settlement with the Thackeray estate. Until the 1890s no biography of Thackeray had been authorized because Anny had adhered faithfully to her father's command: "When I drop, there is to be no life written of me; *mind this* and consider it as my last testament and desire."[9] This portentous embargo was part of a Thackeray mythology Anny herself had helped to construct and perpetuate; deferring to it may have allowed her to annex her literary patrimony—her father's papers—to her own memories of him in profitable ways. While Leslie was writing the *Mausoleum Book*, Anny had been using the format of Biographical Introductions to dodge this prohibition on biography, and to earn money to repay her debts. These Introductions or Prefaces were short essays situating each of her father's works in the context of what she knew or remembered of his life. Cumulatively they constituted a critical biography. Whether Anny's auto/biographical efforts represented a conscious circumvention of her father's will or a circumlocution in the face of social convention, it seems probable that Stephen's assumption of the name, and law, of the father, was in this instance contingent on Anny's own subversion of it. That Stephen's own settling of accounts should depend on Anny's conversion of her father's last testament into her own *magnum opus* neatly illustrates how closely Stephen's self-construction as a man was implicated in the self-representation of his significant others, and of Anny in particular.[10] And depending on Anny, as Stephen never ceased to remind his readers, was a risky business.

As a living woman, and as part of Stephen's kinship network, Anny was supposed to anchor the epistemological structure of the

Mausoleum Book. She was at one end of a complicated chain of associations supposed to fix their mother in the minds of Julia's children. As we have seen, Stephen thinks he must "say something about himself" in order to write about Julia. This involves speaking of his own domestic history with Minny; and to describe Minny, whom none of them knew, he must first describe her sister Anny, whom they all know (pp. 4,8,12). This patterning of associations is not fanciful either on my part or on Stephen's: as Gillian Beer has pointed out, such associational thinking was fundamental to Stephen's enlightenment scepticism, foregrounding the perceptor (Stephen, and through him his children) as the provisional guarantor of meaning.[11]

Independently of—but in tension with—this associative chain, Anny has an interjacent, more thematic role in the *Mausoleum Book*, which derives from her frequent appearance in Stephen's correspondence with his wives, and which has to do with her refusal to be one of Stephen's Angels:

> I have digressed a little: partly, perhaps, because, as I find from my letters, when Anny lived with me, I was constantly framing theories to account for her. You see the result, but it is also true, as I said, that anything I can say of Minny must start by reference to Anny. (p. 7)

Why this need to frame theories to account for Anny? Why return to her again and again? She is, as we have seen, the other against whom Stephen measures his own prudence, sagacity, and self-restraint, not just in matters of domestic economy but in professional terms as well. This double role is crucial. Partly as a rival for his wives' attention, but also as a competitor for literary reputation, Anny is pivotal within Stephen's self-justifying rhetoric. For in her dual aspect as woman and writer we see colliding the two carefully separated assertions I have charted in the *Mausoleum Book*—what we might call its agnostic and apologetic axes, and gloss as "Life will have meaning if we all fix our eyes on perfect femininity" and " I have a right to be cared for because of who I am."

And because she effectively functions as a hinge between these incommensurate claims, Anny continually sends Stephen's prose off at unpredictable tangents, launching him into the dangerous territories of difference he is at such pains to avoid:

> Now you know Anny and I think that I can best tell you what I care to tell about Minny by first speaking of Anny. Her influence

upon my life, too, was great enough to require some notice of her.
Anny inherited no small share of her father's genius, but with differences which I attribute, or think attributable, to her Irish blood.
She is still, she was, I think, still more obviously when I first knew
her, the most sympathetic person I ever knew. [. . .] Some of the
prejudices, fancies and so forth which she had accepted, as it were,
by reflection from other minds faded when the object was no
longer in front of the mirror. (p. 12)

The identical qualities Stephen prizes in Julia—the instincts that put to
shame his "ratiocinations" (p. 95)—seem in Anny to lead in the direction
of discord and contention. Where Julia's compassion yields a benefi-
cial, redeeming influence, in Anny it is symptomatic of mercurial thinking and results in unreliability. Stephen's half-hearted attempt to code
Anny's excess of sympathy as Irish only partly camouflages its femininity: a potential genius on her father's side, she is Irish on her
mother's, and her mother, as we know, spent fifty-three years in a state
of "dreamlike incapacity" (p. 19).

Clearly, Anny's combination of "her father's genius" and her
mother's "sympathy" puts at risk the *Mausoleum Book*'s implicit claims
both about the heterosexual division of labor and the political economy of gender. For this reason, she figures as a disruptive presence in
the *Mausoleum Book*'s domestic idyll.[12] It is mainly as a writer, though,
that she discomposes Stephen. In a long and seemingly unnecessary
passage, Stephen rehearses his objections to her work and working
methods. Because of her habit of pinning together fragments of ideas as
they occur to her ("with literal not metaphorical pins"), her manuscripts, like her personality, are a "chaotic jumble, maddening to print-
ers." "Once," he claims, in an aside typical for its tone of exasperated
affection, "when a story of hers was published in Australia, the last
chapter got into the middle and nobody found it out" (pp. 13–15).[13] In
contrast Stephen stresses the laboriousness of his own literary life, its
regularity, meticulousness, craftsmanship, and sheer, crushing volume.
In this way he establishes his credentials as a writer, even as he affects to
deprecate his place (a footnote? a paragraph?) in the history of nineteenth-century English thought.

The comparison turns out to be neither neat nor conclusive, however. At intervals throughout the *Mausoleum Book* Stephen becomes dis-
tracted by the way Anny's unsystematic, confused, absurd, muddled,
vague, unfocused, contradictory, and intricate methods of thinking and
writing (he uses all these epithets and more in quick succession) generally enable her to "work round" to "sound conclusions" and "sound

opinions" (p. 14).[14] Anny's apparent ability to get away with it—to flout literary convention, to make work look like leisure (or more accurately to make professional work look like domestic work)—is profoundly troubling to Stephen. If Anny can work round to sound conclusions by such haphazard means without sacrificing her impact, or income, as a writer, then the vocation of letters is effectively deskilled and devalued. Anny, in other words, poses in an especially forceful way the issues of class and gender difference supposed to be resolved by Stephen's own narrative of self-mastery.

Literary Contexts (II): Leslie and Anny as Auto/Biographers

As well as being something of a loose cannon in Stephen's rhetorical arsenal, however, Anny is part of Stephen's literary context in a more general way. Her career as a writer, like Stephen's, got under way in the 1860s, and by the last decades of the century, she was sharing with him a need to mark the passing of an era. In obituaries and dictionary entries, in biographies and reminiscences, they commemorated and mourned the deaths of Tennyson, the Brownings, Thomas Carlyle, George Eliot, and a multitude of other eminent acquaintances. For all its painful intimacy, the *Mausoleum Book* was part of this much wider project of reappraising and reaffirming the Victorian achievement at the end of the century.

Debates about biography, autobiography, and the relations between them were central to this process, and by the late 1880s Stephen, as literary critic, biographer of his friend Fawcett and editor of the *Dictionary of National Biography*, had established himself as an authority on such matters. As a more or less professional biographer, Stephen had a considerable ideological and material interest in doing so. Potential contributors to the DNB were sent Stephen's entry on Addison as a pattern to follow, and the consensus held that "if [a man's] biography was worth writing . . . let Mr. Leslie Stephen survive him."[15] In 1891, exhausted by the strain of enforcing brevity, punctuality, and accuracy on his unruly hordes of contributors, he had handed over editorial responsibility for the *DNB* to his assistant Sidney Lee in order to devote himself to "more congenial subjects, and at my own time"—only to have his time hijacked by the task of writing a biography of his brother Fitzjames. Of this book he complained to his friend Charles Eliot Norton, in a letter of 23 December 1894, "it is the stiffest piece of work I ever undertook. It will, however, have the merit of shortness. Lives are really becoming overpowering."[16]

How and where (not, of course, whether) to erect a barrier between private and public discourses; how to draw the line between writing self and biographical subject, how to filter out the significant and representative from the ephemeral and accidental: Stephen's power to arbitrate on such questions defined him as professional biographer, while his reminders that any solution must be arbitrary defined him, residually, as philosopher.[17] Questions of biographical expedience, propriety, and adequacy are never far from the surface of the *Mausoleum Book*, whether in fleeting allusions to *causes célèbres* such as Froude's handling of Carlyle, or Lockhart's of Scott (pp. 89, 102), or in bouts of textual self-reflection.[18]

At the same time that Stephen had been absorbed in "doing dictionary," Anny had been experimenting with the genre. In biographical fiction and essays, in introductions to and biographies of women writers, in reminiscences of famous acquaintances and, as one of the relatively few women contributors, in work for the *DNB*, Anny had been engaged with many of the same philosophical and literary issues as Stephen, though in a characteristically lighthearted way.[19] Inevitably, her approach was one Stephen found unsettling. Witness his response in 1885 to her draft of an entry on Elizabeth Browning for the *DNB*. While twice conceding the piece to be "very well done," Stephen allows himself some "savage criticisms." Anny should avoid phrases such as "little maiden," should steer away from compliments to the living (to the works of Tennyson in particular, which, however "pretty," are "maudlin," "sickening" and of a "keepsake flavour"); she should omit any reference to Browning's "'spiritisms'—damn it—" and, p.s., "What on earth is a 'mutual grandmother?'" In case we had missed the gender subtext, Stephen concedes that Anny has made the best of a bad job. "After all I can't believe much in Mrs. B. She shrieks too much." In other words, Elizabeth Browning was lucky to be in the *Dictionary* at all. It appears that the business of managing women as contributors and as subjects by casting them as slippery feminine other was feeding into Stephen's representation of his editorial self as orderly, objective, and precise: "Too much sentimental reflection looks terribly out of place in our dismal work."[20] The desire vested in, and shored up by, the idea of a Dictionary of National Biography—the desire to forge links between ways of knowing, strategies of representation, and national identity—is openly expressed in gender (and implicitly in class) terms. Professional biography, he implies, must result from, and in, masculine alienation in the face of a sexual division of literary labor.

Nothing could be further from the dismal world of the *DNB* than Anny's *Chapters from Some Memoirs*, her most overt experiment in auto/biography and her preparation for the *magnum opus* of the Biographical Prefaces. First appearing at intervals in *Macmillan's*

Magazine, Chapters was published in book form in 1894, only months before Julia's death and Stephen's writing of the *Mausoleum Book.* Bouncing back from the trauma of her mother's death in January 1894, Anny embarked on a series of "Notes on family history" for the next generation, and watched the appearance of *Chapters* with undisguised relish: "I love my recollections, and I now understand why everybody writes them. One begins to dance again, and lark, and frisk, and thrill, and do all the things one can hardly believe one ever did."[21] It is easy to see why Anny in her late fifties rubbed Stephen up the wrong way.

Chapters recalls a childhood and youth spent migrating between her father's literary London and the genteel émigré world of her grand-parents' Paris. The text picks its way between two taboos—Thackeray's forbidden Life and his wife's mental illness—by blurring the bound-aries between memory and fiction and between the trivial and the sig-nificant. In other words, Anny turns the problems of biography into its poetics: a strategy which lends the narrative its curiously familiar, modernist air. "How odd," she remarks, "those mysterious moments are when nothing seems to be happening, but which nevertheless go on all the rest of one's life."[22] In her approach to time past ("that very dis-proportion which passing impressions most happily take for us, and which they often retain, notwithstanding the experience of years") and to time present ("that present which is quite apart from time and dates") she joyfully eschews the chronological and the cumulative mode of biography, offering us instead a "witch's caldron" of memory, consisting of "heterogeneous scraps" (pp. 87, 93, 67). Her sense of sig-nificance is equally anarchic: she delights in the fact that things strike children "oddly, partially, and for unexpected reasons" (p. 1). Her childhood landscape may have been full of eminent men, but, surreally enough, "they were men walking as trees before us, without names or histories" (p. 14). She remembers a fleeting image of Trelawny scowling at his reflection in the looking glass; the soles of Gladstone's boots seen from the ventilator of the House of Commons. Her memories are of "odds and ends happily harmless enough . . . the back of one great man's head, the hat and umbrella of another" (p. 67). She celebrates the quirkiness of the child's-eye view, preferring to the disembodied, panoptical height of the Arc de Triomphe the view from the curbstone below, "where much more human impressions are to be found" (p. 33). And to eke out the pleasure of her reminiscences, she supplements her half-memories of half-heard music and momentary glimpses of someone who may or may not have been George Sand by turning to her collaborator in nostalgia and "faithful confidante"—the *Biographie Générale* (p. 4).

Conclusion

Poovey's concept of border cases is relevant to Stephen's auto/biographical enterprise in several ways. Just as, in the 1840s and 50s, the debate about writing as viable professional work for men had been a test case of the limits of middle-class ideology, in the 1890s a great deal was at stake in the delineation of biography as productive work. Situated on the boundary between proper biographical labor and homely pottering-about, auto/biography as a genre seems, in 1895,to have become a site of anxiety. Stephen's own *Mausoleum Book* polices, even as it exposes the arbitrariness of, the border between middle-class work and non-work, professional and domestic life, the public and the private, the masculine and the feminine.[23] Anxiety suffuses the text at a structural level, and persists at the level of content in a tissue of coded messages about issues apparently far removed from the book's object of writing about Julia: about the nature of fatherly authority, for instance, and about the role of independent women, especially women as writers. These in turn are connected to a crisis of representation—a crisis over the very "narrative of personal development" upon which the bourgeois subject is so precariously balanced.

Stephen had taken it upon himself to train a generation of scholars, some of them women, in the discipline of biography. His reputation depended on his ability to enforce probity, exactness, and self-effacement in his contributors, and to make them take seriously, as a matter of national responsibility, the dignity of individual Lives. The irreverence or lacksadaisical approach of a single contributor, an Anny Thackeray Ritchie for instance, could jeopardize the whole edifice. In her way of life, in her methods of work and in her approach to life-writing Anny played fast and loose with many of Stephen's assumptions about what it meant to be a professional Man of Letters. Her presence in the *Mausoleum Book* is symptomatic of the kinds of unreconciled contradictions I have pointed to within Stephen's portrayal of himself. She is, in effect, one of the links I alluded to between the text's divergent concerns with gender, genre, and identity.

As autobiographer, in particular, Anny represented competing solutions to the epistemological and literary problems that were Stephen's professional turf. The task of delimiting and regulating written lives became more absorbing for him the more his reputation—and income—depended on the genre. At the same time, the more strenuously he attempted to frame theories to account for Anny, the more his own writing, while not exactly frisky, tended to reproduce her digressive, fragmentary style. *Chapters from Some Memoirs*, with its "apparently structureless narratives," has been accurately described as a kind of "refracted Autobiography" which "at once establishes and denies a centre."[24] Ironically, this is a fair description of the *Mausoleum Book* itself.

My examination of the *Mausoleum Book* encourages me to suggest three lines for future enquiry. The first is a kind of health warning over the mythology of Anny Thackeray. The insistence with which commentators on Anny during her life and subsequently have returned to the same anecdotes of her vagueness, her sympathy for others, and her disorganization leads me to suspect that she has an ideological function in the historiography of Victorian letters.[25] Her work, both in its weaknesses and in its strengths, was and is appraised almost exclusively in terms of these qualities of unreliability and woolliness: indeed the ease with which her personality and writing can be collapsed together seems to be part of her cultural resonance. For Stephen, evidently, Anny represented not just other ways of being and working, but other kinds of stories and other ways of thinking—or not thinking—about genre.

Having advised caution in handling the Anny story, I would add that feminist reappraisals of life-writing allow us to see it as a contested genre, rather than one over which some men had unproblematic control. On 29 January 1898, Stephen wrote to George Smith, proprietor of the *DNB*, that his entry on William Makepeace Thackeray "was written under difficulties because I cannot speak freely, writing as I do under Anny's authority. I had therefore to be dry and cramped for fear of making it too effusive."[26] If thoughts of Anny could tie Stephen up in knots, they could also precipitate a reshuffle in the division of biographical responsibility. Two months later he wrote to Norton that:

> My greatest helper has been and is [Anny] Ritchie—the most sympathetic and sociable of beings that ever lived, as I often think. She is bringing out a new edition of her father's works and certain "biographical prefaces" [. . .] really, as I think, very interesting. I have written a Life of him for the Dictionary, which is as dry as I can make it, but intended to serve as a kind of table of contents to her quasi-biography; and I hope to keep her dates and facts a bit straight . . .[27]

My final point has to do with literary history. In the *Mausoleum Book* issues of gender and genre are reciprocally at stake in ways that reflect—and constitute—a crisis of literary masculinity. This crisis, while in important ways specific to the Stephen family and its circumstances, was part of a wider shift in literary sexual politics in the 1890s in England. The last decade of the nineteenth century was not just the era of the *DNB*: in and through the massive press coverage of the Oscar Wilde trials, the "New Woman" and the so-called Marriage Question, it also witnessed the crystallization of gender identities around what we now recognize as the hetero/homosexual divide.[28] The tensions and anxieties expressed in the *Mausoleum Book* anticipated, and may even be said to have precipitated, the experiments with gender and genre we associated with modernism, and with Virginia Woolf in particular.

In this essay I have deliberately avoided reading Stephen from the point of view of Woolf's literary development. My purpose has been to examine the operation of gender in the male text rather than the other way round. It is worth remembering, however, that Virginia's rewriting of the Victorian age owes as much to Anny's as to her father's style of being and writing, or rather, as her obituary to Anny made clear, her aunt provided her with a way of looking at, by seeing round, the frock-coats and frowns of the Victorian Mausoleum.

> Very likely the great man has said nothing memorable, perhaps he has not even spoken; occasionally her memory is not of seeing him but of missing him; never mind—there was an ink-pot, perhaps a chair, he stood in this way, he held his hat just so, and miraculously and indubitably there he is before our eyes. Again and again it has happened to us to trace down our conception of one of the great figures of the past not to the stout official biography consecrated to him, but to some little hint or fact or fancy dropped lightly by Lady Ritchie in passing, as a bird alights on a branch, picks off the fruit and leaves the husk for another.[29]

Notes

I would like to thank Ruth Symes and Hermione Lee for their perceptive comments on this essay.

1. Alan Bell (ed.), *Sir Leslie Stephen's Mausoleum Book* (Oxford: Clarendon Press, 1977), p. 4. Page references are henceforth given in the text.

2. All these interpretations are touched on in Alan Bell's introduction to the text. In *Leslie Stephen: The Godless Victorian* (London: Wiedenfeld and Nicolson, 1984), Noel Annan has argued that the *Mausoleum Book* is an "electuary of sentimentalism" and that the sentimentalism "concealed [Stephen's] fear—that people would blame him for Julia's death or put it about that he had brought her unhappiness." He concludes that, in terms of his future reputation, "Stephen had signed the warrant for his arrest in the book he wrote for his children" (p. 127).

3. I am indebted to Hermione Lee for reminding me that Edward Burne-Jones painted Julia as the Virgin in his *Annunciation* (1879), where she appears both sexy and chaste, positioned beside the featheriest of angels.

4. As Poovey puts it,

> The paradox of individualism defused the potentially pernicious effects of competition, not only by foregrounding its role in establishing a national identity while implicitly limiting who could compete, but also by rewriting competition as an integral part of the individual—as one of the forces behind personal development.

Mary Poovey, *Uneven Developments: The Ideological Work of Gender in Mid-Victorian England* (London: Virago Press, 1988), p. 114. As the origin, instigator, and goal of this narrative of personal development, or story of self-mastery, the figure of the loving mother/perfect wife played a key role in the "ideological work" of bourgeois individualism (p. 9).

5. Poovey, p. 12.

6. The narrative is punctuated by the "painful milestones" of death, and degenerates ultimately into a "series of obituary notices" (pp. 66, 101).

7. The *Mausoleum Book* is addressed to Julia's children only: George, Stella and Gerald Duckworth, and Vanessa, Thoby, Virginia, and Adrian Stephen. By this time, Laura, Stephen's daughter by his first marriage who was understood to be backward, had been placed in an asylum.

8. Gayle Rubin, "The Traffic in Women: Notes on the 'Political Economy' of Sex" in *Toward an Anthropology of Women*, ed. R. R. Reiter (New York: Monthly Review Press, 1975).

9. Anne's Journal is quoted in H. T. Fuller and V. Hammersley, *Thackeray's Daughter: Some Recollections of Anne Thackeray Ritchie* (Dublin: Euphorion, 1957), p. 94. Of course, several unauthorized works on Thackeray had appeared, much to the disgust of both Anny and Leslie. In what follows I shall adopt Leslie's affectionate use of Thackeray Ritchie's nickname Anny.

10. For the Biographical Prefaces as Anny's *magnum opus*, see Winifred Gérin, *Anne Thackeray Ritchie: A Biography* (Oxford: Oxford University Press, 1981), p. 232.

11. Gillian Beer, "Hume, Stephen and Elegy in *To the Lighthouse*" in *Mrs. Dalloway and To the Lighthouse*, ed. Su Reid (London: Macmillan, 1993), pp. 71–86. Su Reid, in her introduction to Beer's essay, glosses the philosophical debate thus: "whether individuals, and things, exist permanently in themselves and so continue to exist whether anyone is thinking about them or not, or whether that is an illusion and everything exists as it is perceived" (p. 9). The theoretical debate leads into "a series of questions about the identity of the

writer or thinker, his reputation and its survival, and his independence of thought or his dependence on humbler men."

12 Stephen goes so far as to drag in his mother-in-law to testify that "Anny was always the aggressor and could not keep silence" (p. 23).

13. The description of Anny and her work can be found pp. 13–15. The same tone can be heard in many of Leslie's letters to Julia. In a letter of 18 July 1877, quoted in Annan, op. cit. p. 119, he had (briefly) defended the idea of education for women on the grounds that "If (but don't breathe a whisper of this) Anny had been educated at all, so as to have some rudimentary perceptions of what is meant by systems or by thinking, she might have done something incomparably more telling than she can ever do now." Ten years later, on 4 October 1987, he wrote, again to Julia, "I must say that Anny's audacity in sewing together a lot of descriptions of scenery and calling it a story rather amuses me. But she certainly has or had a 'gift' as they call it." Letter quoted in Carol Hanbery MacKay "The Thackeray Connection: Virginia Woolf's Aunt Anny" in Jane Marcus (ed.) *Virginia Woolf and Bloomsbury: A Centenary Celebration* (London: Macmillan Press, 1987), p. 69.

14. In effect, Stephen is to Anny as his hero Hume, in Stephen's *History of English Thought in the Eighteenth Century*, appeared in relation to the "thousands of inferior thinkers" who were dealing with the same problems as Hume and, though with far less acuteness or logical consistency, arriving at similar conclusions." In *To the Lighthouse*,Virginia Woolf was to spoof this relationship as Mr. Ramsay's irritated consciousness of the interdependence between the great man and the "lift man in the Tube." See Gillian Beer, "Hume, Stephen, and Elegy," *passim*.

15. Speech given by Maunde Thompson in praise of Leslie Stephen, reported in the pamphlet *Dictionary of National Biography: Dinner to Mr. George Smith, from the reports of the Times, Standard, Daily News and Daily Chronicle of June 7 1894*, p. 10.

16. Frederic William Maitland, *The Life and Letters of Leslie Stephen* (London: Duckworth, 1906), pp. 403, 420. The episode is also recounted in Gillian Fenwick's excellent *Leslie Stephen's Life in Letters: A Bibliographical Study* (Aldershot, Hants: Scolar Press, 1993), p. 121.

17. Gillian Beer, op.cit. p. 79, notes that "Stephen, with Hume, affirms chance and custom rather than order and reason as the basis of perception." The dividing line between subject and object was, for Stephen, a "fiction."

18. The so-called Froude-Carlyle controversy, a literary scandal revolving around Thomas Carlyle's posthumous publication of his marital unhappiness and remorse, is one of the key literary contexts for the *Mausoleum Book*. Another is the hushing-up of John Addington Symonds' *Memoirs*.

19. In her early journalism she had remarked that "Where a book ends
and the reader begins is as hard to determine as any other of those objective and
subjective problems which are sometimes set." See "Maids-of-all-work and
Blue Books" in *Toilers and Spinsters and Other Essays* (London: Smith, Elder, 1890
[first published in book form 1873]), p. 52. Even in her late teens, in a journal
entry during the Crimean War, she had mused:

> What a queer thing it is to think that I care more if my father's finger
> aches than if the whole Imperial family be extinguished. That to me
> everything happens only to make part of *my* existence. [. . .] Perhaps these
> times appear differently to me, to what they do to every other mind?
> Perhaps Minny sees the trees blue not green, and Amy thinks them red.

Quoted in *Letters of Anne Thackeray Ritchie*, ed. Hester Ritchie (London: John
Murray, 1924), pp. 64–65.

20. Letter from Leslie Stephen to Anny Thackeray Ritchie quoted in Fuller
and Hammersley, p. 157. Cf. *Mausoleum Book*, p. 13: "Fitzjames and I in those
days called [Anny] a 'sentimentalist,' a name which in our mouths implied
some blame." Towards the end of his life Stephen was to define sentimentalism
as "Indulgence in emotion for its own sake." See Maitland, p. 437.

21. I am indebted for this quotation, and for clues as to the publication history of *Chapters* to Carol Hanbery MacKay "Biography as reflected autobiography: The self-creation of Anne Thackeray Ritchie" in *Revealing Lives:
Autobiography, Biography and Gender*, ed. Susan G. Bell and Marilyn Yalom
(Albany, NY: SUNY Press, 1990), p. 65.

22. Anny Thackeray Ritchie, *Chapters from Some Memoirs* (London:
Macmillan, 1894), p. 166. Page references are given henceforth in the text.

23. "I do not feel equal to taking up my old tasks again. Yet [. . .] I am
strong enough for some little employment . . ." (p. 3).

24. MacKay, "Biography as Reflected Autobiography," pp. 66, 76.

25. This is not to suggest that the historical Anny was not infuriatingly
scatty. By all accounts she was!

26. Fenwick, op. cit., p. 244.

27. Maitland, p. 449.

28. See for instance, Eve Kosofsky Sedgwick, *Epistemology of the Closet*
(Harvester Wheatsheaf: Hemel Hempstead, 1991); Ed Cohen, *Talk on the Wilde
Side: Toward a Genealogy of a Discourse on Male Sexualities* (New York and London:
Routledge, 1993); Lucy Bland, "The Married Woman, the 'New Woman' and the
Feminist: Sexual Politics of the 1890s," in *Equal or Different: Women's Politics
1800–1914*, ed. Jane Rendall (Oxford: Basil Blackwell, 1987).

29. Woolf's Obituary of her aunt, first published in the *Times Literary Supplement* 4 March 1919, is appended to Winifred Gérin's *Anne Thackeray Ritchie: A Biography* (Oxford, etc.: Oxford University Press, 1981), pp. 279–84. Another important literary outcome of the negotiations over auto/biography between Anny and Leslie is, of course, Woolf's delineation of Mrs. Hilbery as biographer in *Night and Day*.

7

What Is [Not] Remembered: The Autobiography of Alice B. Toklas

Gabriele Griffin

Alice B. Toklas' *What is Remembered* and Gertrude Stein's *The Autobiography of Alice B. Toklas*[1] pose a direct challenge to definitions of autobiography such as Philippe Lejeune's: "[a] retrospective prose narrative written by a real person concerning his own existence, where the focus is his individual life, in particular the story of his personality."[2] Toklas and Stein present a female protagonist focusing on an other as opposed to a self as their primary concern. Lejeune goes on to assert that autobiography assumes an identity of name between author, narrator, and character. To the extent that these texts resist such conflations and closures, they raise questions about women's construction of narrative selves, opening gaps between signifier, signified, and referent. I want to argue that these gaps are suggestive of the kinds of discursive mobility investigated by Judith Butler in her essay "Imitation and Gender Insubordination."[3]

The story of Toklas' writings is a particular one, determined by her association with Gertrude Stein. This means that whatever she might have been independently of Gertrude Stein, as a public persona she is defined as a relational being rather than as a separate individual. Her textual existence was determined, indeed created, in *The Autobiography of Alice B. Toklas*: a text by an other who, as the agent in this process, occupied the position of subject. This view of Toklas' dependency on Stein for her being(-in-print), which accords Stein primary and Toklas secondary status, is reinforced by indexes such as the *MLA International Bibliography*: virtually every year someone finds something to say about *The Autobiography of Alice B. Toklas*, while perhaps one year in ten someone has something to say about Alice B. Toklas' autobiography.[4] The critical reception of Toklas' work thus reproduces her secondary status *vis à vis* Stein's.

One of the few texts addressing the work of Alice B. Toklas is Catherine Stimpson's "Gertrice/Altrude: Stein, Toklas, and the paradox of the happy marriage" which appeared in 1984 in a book entitled—significantly it seems to me—*Mothering the Mind: Twelve Studies of Writers and their* Silent *Partners* (my emphasis).[5] What was/is this silence about? Or, to put it another way, what does this sign signify?

Adrienne Rich: I write this   not for you
who fight to write your own
words   fighting up the falls
but for another woman   dumb
with loneliness   dust   seeping plastic bags
with children   in a house
where language floats and spins
abortion   in
the bowl[6]

Toklas received her first, and it would seem abiding public definition of self in Stein's *The Autobiography of Alice B. Toklas*. Here the creating subject, Stein herself, appears to use Alice as the mirror in which she finds her own aggrandized reflection.[7] This process is not unlike the one ascribed by Virginia Woolf in *A Room of One's Own* to men for whom "women have served all these centuries as looking-glasses possessing the magic and delicious power of reflecting the figure of man at twice its natural size."[8] Twice its size, perhaps, because the looker, in the present instance Stein, occupies both the position of subject and that of object.[9]

Anne Sexton: And this was the cave of the mirror,
that double woman who stares
at herself, as if she were petrified
in time—two ladies sitting in umber chairs.[10]

The definition ascribed to Toklas in *The Autobiography of Alice B. Toklas*, that of "wife of a genius," was a relational definition of self which did not, on the surface at least, appear to accord equal status to Toklas, but rather resulted in the notion (discussed by Stimpson in "Gertrice/Altrude" for example) that Toklas and Stein's relationship was modeled on a Victorian marriage, with Stein commandeering the public front and Toklas occupying the private sphere—a kind of women's room. As Stein wrote famously in *The Autobiography of Alice B. Toklas*, "The geniuses came and talked to Gertrude Stein and the wives sat with me" (p. 95).

Being cast in the role of Victorian wife seems to be equal to being perceived as a non-person, as having no subject status, or indeed any status at all.[11]

Emily Dickinson: I'm Nobody! Who are you?[12]

No doubt—and there are a number of Victorian texts which would support this—many Victorian wives suffered from being constructed as nobodies.[13] But seeing Toklas in such terms can be a way of making her "still," of silencing her.[14] It is too easily assumed that the Victorian wife—if, indeed, such a unitary category can be meaningfully employed—invariably lacked the subject status we too readily associate with having a public voice. Such discursive insistence can be read as reproducing a particular, textually-constructed formation which, through its reiteration, is simply affirmed and promotes the status quo. It is important, as Butler reminds us, "to recognize the ways in which heterosexual norms reappear within gay identities, to affirm that gay and lesbian identities are not only structured in part by dominant heterosexual frames, but that they are *not* for that reason *determined* by them" (p. 23). Smith proposes more specifically that "however much 'Alice' might play the role of wife, there is no wife there because the regulatory practices of compulsory heterosexuality have not successfully produced 'Alice' as a wife . . . And however much 'Gertrude Stein' might play the husband, that husband is indeed a woman."[15]

The non-subject status apparently conferred upon Toklas by Stein's "autobiography" of her has been reinforced by the fact that Toklas herself was an extremely reluctant self-publicist[16] who offered no alternative public voice to Stein's during the latter's lifetime. Only after Stein's death in 1946 did Toklas begin to project her own voice, and her letters, two books on cookery, and her autobiography were then published.[17] But this projection of voice on Toklas' part was not predicated upon the desire to acquire the subjecthood and consequent status of an author. Rather, she seems to have written the cookbooks as a result of impecunity, whilst the publication of her autobiography and letters was initiated by others.[18]

But there is another way of thinking about this, based on Butler's theory as to how the self comes into being:

. . . the self only becomes a self on the condition that it has suffered a separation . . . a loss which is suspended and provisionally resolved through a melancholic incorporation of some "Other." That "Other" installed in the self thus establishes the permanent incapacity of that "self" to achieve self-identity; it is as it were always already disrupted by that Other; the disruption of the Other at the heart of the self is the very condition of that self's possibility. (p. 27)

One might argue that Toklas was ushered into articulation and thus into a kind of self by the loss of Stein. She resolved this loss by incorporating a construction of Stein into her work. This very incorporation signals Toklas' inability to achieve self-identity in her work—self-identity here referring to Lejeune's conflation of the identities of author, narrator, and character. The disruption of Toklas' sense of self occasioned by Stein's death served as a precondition for Toklas' entering writing and thus constructing a self through and within a form of public discourse which also suspended the loss she had to confront.

Toklas' resistance to becoming an authoring subject in her own right is evident in the title of her autobiography, *What Is Remembered*. The relative pronoun with which it begins, its use of the passive voice, and its implicit according of object status to the remembering subject who remains unnamed, indeed unrecorded, all serve to create a sense of indeterminacy. Compare Toklas' title with that of her contemporary Eleanor Roosevelt's autobiography: *This I Remember*.[19] Where Roosevelt uses a demonstrative pronoun and the first person to reduce ambivalence and to specify the direct connection between the remembering subject and the remembered material, Toklas' *What Is Remembered* seems to deny the presence of Toklas as the writing subject and as the central concern of her own text.

Indeed, *What Is Remembered* was initially conceived as a joint project between Toklas and Max White to promote Stein and her work. As Toklas wrote to Carl Van Vechten about this collaborative effort: "[Max White and I] are agreed that the reminiscences should be centered on Baby and her work. That mine be discarded—possibly to throw light on her method. You agree—don't you?"[20] Through such deliberate self-effacement Toklas actively collaborated in the construction of the public persona of "Alice B. Toklas" as "*wife* to the genius Stein." This image was further fostered by the obliteration of much of the written evidence concerning those areas of Toklas' life that were independent of Stein. Thus Edward Burns wrote, in his introduction to *Staying On Alone*:

Initially, I wanted to include [letters] from all periods of her life but abandoned the idea. Miss Toklas' letters to her father, written with regularity from 1907 to his death in 1922, could not be found. Her letters to her friend Claire Moore de Gruchy were all destroyed by Mrs. de Gruchy shortly before her own death. In the late 1920's

Annette Rosenshine, another childhood friend, destroyed all of Alice's early letters to her. Alice's closest friend, Louise Taylor, lost most of the pre-1946 letters when her valise was stolen from a train during World War II.[21]

In the absence of this material, Toklas' image has remained, in literary critical terms at least, that of appendage to Stein without independent subject status.

Adrienne Rich: *But we have different voices, even in sleep,*
and our bodies, so alike, are yet so different
and the past echoing through our bloodstreams
is freighted with different language, different
meanings—
though in any chronicle of the world we share
it could be written with new meaning,
we were two lovers of one gender,
we were two women of one generation.[22]

"Could be written" but is not. On the surface, in her own work, Toklas does not appear—to borrow a phrase from Jane Marcus[23]—to re/sign herself as a subject, to construct a self which might deconstruct her role as "wife to the genius of Stein." Rather, she seems to underwrite her known status, reinforcing the public image created for her by Stein in *The Autobiography of Alice B. Toklas.* In *What I Remembered* Toklas, instead of re/signing—producing a new image of—herself distinct from the one given her by Stein, appears to sign—concur with—her public persona as Stein's "wife." This is consistent with Toklas' sense of privacy. Though delighting in gossip (but only with close friends), Toklas was invariably dismayed when privacy around personal relationships was violated by public display.[24]

But, and this is crucial, Toklas' endorsing of the definition of self she had received in *The Autobiography of Alice B. Toklas* does not imply, as is frequently assumed, that she lacked a sense of an independent self. The easy and erroneous equation made between being a wife and being a non-person is not borne out by Toklas' writings. Both her autobiography and her letters indicate that she was an agent in her own life, making deliberate and considered choices in the light of an understanding that "two women together is work / nothing in civilization has made simple, / two people together is a work / heroic in its ordinariness."[25] The subjecthood Toklas constructs for her self in her writings both mirrors and contradicts Stein's autobiography of her.

H. D.:   *This search for historical parallels,*
              research into psychic affinities,

              has been done to death before,
              will be done again;

              no comment can alter spiritual realities
              (you say) or again,
              what new light can you possibly
              throw upon them?[26]

Toklas, like Stein, provides neither analytical nor interpretive comments on the incidents she describes in *What Is Remembered*. Instead, the reader is offered an associative perspective on Toklas and her relationships, which she is then left to interpret for herself. Typically, Toklas writes:

> It was Roger Fry who had brought Clive Bell and Mrs. Bell to see Gertrude Stein in Paris. Mrs. Bell was the very plain sister of the very beautiful Virginia Woolf. They were the daughters of Sir Leslie Stephen. The two sisters, impersonating Indian princesses, had once been received by an admiral on a man-of-war and cannon had been fired in their honour. A typical English prank. (pp. 88–89)

Here Toklas seems to follow what she remembers (the associative element) without articulating the reason why she chooses to talk about these specific things. This absence of causality is signalled by the lack of subordinating conjunctions and other grammatical indicators of relationship between the points made. Toklas does not write about what remembering these details about the Bells/Woolfs means to her; she does not "psychologize" the incident described but seems to stay with the surface. She tells us how Virginia and her sister looked and an anecdote she knows about them, though it is left unclear whether or not Toklas was told that anecdote at that meeting or heard of it in a different context. The overall effect of this technique is to suggest that she puts down what she remembers as she remembers it, in no particular order (other than a vaguely chronological one) and to no particular end. The reader is thus invited to decide what what is remembered, and what Toklas' technique of writing, mean.

      What Is Remembered seems to redress the (im)balance(s) created by Stein's autobiography of Toklas. For although both texts present roughly the same material, the emphasis and encoding in each autobiography is different: a perfect instance of Stein's assertion that "there is no such thing as repetition," only insistence, and that "we all insist varying the emphasizing."[27] Thus one interesting example of the difference between Stein's and Toklas' autobiographies concerns the textual treatment of Harriet Levy, the woman with whom Toklas came to Paris in September 1907 and with whom she lived until 1910. Levy was a source of annoyance and tension between Toklas and Stein: the "obstacle" which, in the initial stages of their relationship, prevented Toklas from joining Stein at 27, rue de Fleurus. Where, in *The Autobiography of Alice B. Toklas*, Stein deals with Levy by not mentioning her at all as far as possible, or by referring to her, in the persona of Toklas, in terms of the anonymous "my friend," Toklas restores Levy to her original importance in her life by giving her her name. Toklas also, rather comically, describes an occasion when Stein, obviously disenchanted with Levy, told the latter in so many words to drop dead. "One afternoon [Toklas writes] Gertrude told Harriet there was nothing for her, Harriet, to do but to kill herself. This upset me more than it did Harriet, who merely retired into a deep silence" (p. 36). The night after this conversation Harriet apparently had a vision of God, and when Toklas related this to Stein, her response, as reported by Toklas, was as follows: "Gertrude let out a large laugh. Harriet preferred seeing God to killing herself. What am I to do with her. We will have to find someone who will undertake a solution of her experience" (p. 37). Toklas records how she finally managed to get rid of Levy so as to be free to move in with Stein (p. 61). The differential treatment of the figure of Harriet Levy in *The Autobiography of Alice B. Toklas* and *What Is Remembered* thus provides a measure of Stein's desire to efface Toklas' previous attachments, and Toklas' sense of having her own story independent of Stein.

Butler's insistence on the provisionality of categorizations of identity is important in this context. In "Imitation and Gender Insubordination" she writes:

> To claim that this is what I *am* is to suggest a provisional totalization of this "I." But if the I can so determine itself, then that which it excludes in order to make that determination remains constitutive of the determination itself . . . its signification is always to some degree out of one's control . . . its *specificity* can only be demarcated by exclusions that return to disrupt its claim to coherence. (p. 15)

Only by reading both texts—Stein's and Toklas'—and becoming aware of their differential presentation of the same events, can one recognize the provisionality and specificity of each, and how each disrupts the other. This process of re-reading serves to question the fixing of identity which would relegate Toklas to the position of object. It also implicates the reader in the destabilizing of such provisional totalizations—to borrow Butler's phrase—as the category "wife." The issue raised by Toklas' autobiography (though not by Stein's text) which is most immediately relevant to any discussion of the two women as relational and relating beings, is Toklas' fascination with Stein's "theory of dependent independent and independent dependent natures" (p. 41). Toklas quotes Stein:

> There are two kinds of men and women, those who have dependent independent nature in them, those who have independent dependent nature in them. The ones of the first kind of them always somehow own the ones they need to love them, the second kind have it in them to have power in them over others only when these others have begun already a little to love them, others loving them give to such of them strength in domination. (p. 42)

Reading Toklas' writings it becomes clear that Stein and Toklas were in a complementary and equal relationship in which Toklas might be cast as the dependent independent one and Stein as the independent dependent one, a difference and complementarity based on Toklas' and Stein's respective needs —however those needs developed. When the last dog they had co-owned died five years after Stein's death, Toklas lamented, "it is the beginning of living for the rest of my days without anyone who is dependent upon me for anything."[28] Toklas needed to be needed, and Stein needed her in ways encoded in their nicknames "Baby" and "Mama Woojums."[29]

Adrienne Rich: The daughters were never
             true brides of the father

             the daughters were to begin with
             brides of the mother

             then brides of each other
             under a different law[30]

It seems to me that, in contrast to what especially male critics such as Georges Wickes[31] and others seeking to comment on the power structures of the Toklas/Stein relationship have maintained, there was a balance and an equality in that relationship, chosen and fully endorsed by both women. It is much more strikingly portrayed in Toklas' writings than in Stein's, and it is easily lost if we treat Toklas as "nothing but the memory of [Stein]."[32] Toklas, for example, describes their early meetings in much greater detail than Stein, conveying in those descriptions a sense of independent selfhood. Thus Toklas reports that she responded to Stein's familiarity in calling her by her first name with "But I did not propose to reciprocate the familiarity" (p. 28). Toklas' style of writing also suggests a much greater sense of subject status than Stein's *Autobiography* would allow. Typically, in the first sections of her autobiography Toklas writes in simple tenses and in the indicative, projecting a first-person narrator who regularly attributes direct actions to herself. Later in the text that first-person singular is frequently and unselfconsciously supplanted by the first-person plural ("We fell madly in love with Granada" [p. 83], and so on), revealing a sense of commonality rather than of being subsumed by Stein. At the same time, Toklas continues to portray herself as active, making and implementing decisions ("Gertrude had a serious attack of colitis. I was frightened and took her hurriedly to Gibraltar, where she happily recovered" [p. 82]). Almost despite its title, *What Is Remembered* offers numerous instances of Toklas' and Stein's equal agency within their relationship.

One might expect a re-appraisal of *What Is Remembered* to be possible in the context of recent feminist readings of autobiography which have offered a critique of the emphasis male theoreticians place on the autobiographical self as an autonomous, unified individual constructing himself in opposition to all others. As Susan Stanford Friedman states, such "individualistic paradigms of the self ignore the role of collective and relational identities in the individuation process of women and minorities." Friedman goes on to say that "The concept of isolate selfhood is inapplicable to women."[33] One might want to argue, further, that this concept is inapplicable not only to women but to all others; that the idea of "isolate selfhood" is an illusion, a discursive construct operating within particular ideological frameworks and in no way reflective of the material conditions in which we exist. Given Toklas' profile as a relational being, her autobiography ought to attract the interest of women writing on autobiography. But this has not so far been the case. Feminists such as Shari Benstock have chosen to cite *The Autobiography of Alice B. Toklas* rather than *What Is Remembered*.[34] Why? I would suggest that Toklas' work poses a dilemma for feminist writers concerning the conceptualization of the subject in autobiography.

Adrienne Rich: *No one lives in this room*
            without confronting the whiteness of the wall
            behind the poems, planks of books,

> *photographs of dead heroines.*
> *Without contemplating last and late*
> *the true nature of poetry. The drive*
> *to connect. The dream of a common language.*[35]

For where does the emphasis fall when we talk of women in their auto-biographies constructing their experiences in relational rather than in autonomous terms? We still, it seems to me, tend to place the emphasis on the self. In analyzing autobiography, our concept of self continues to be based on the phallic I, the shadow of which so disturbed Virginia Woolf.[36] A quick glance at a collection of essays such as Benstock's *The Private Self: Theory and Practice of Women's Autobiographical Writings* confirms this. Many of the essays focus on the single writing woman, single here not meaning unmarried but singular in all senses of the word: Mary Wollstonecraft, Jane Austen, Dorothy Wordsworth, Emily Dickinson, Simone de Beauvoir. Even feminist critics working on auto-biography seem to consider the self rather than the relational self the proper focus of their work.

Two possible explanations for this phenomenon come to mind. (1) All assertions to the contrary notwithstanding,[37] the self who defines herself in relational terms—the "wife" for instance—is likely to have little socioeconomic status in her own right in Western society and thus becomes "invisible" as a result of her relationally based self-definition. (2) Autobiography is supposed to be the story of the narrating self. Autobiography is not *alter*biography or the story of the relationship between one self and another. And insofar as this definition underlies critical analysis of autobiography, this emphasis on self turns the narrative into the text of the phallic I. It seems very difficult, even when we talk of women's autobiographical selves as relational, to avoid concentrating on one self instead of on the dynamics of relationship. It may be that auto-biography is fundamentally and inescapably a narcissistic form: that it ultimately refers us back to the self rather than to the relational. Perhaps there is a kind of writing which has not yet emerged which foregrounds the relational element, replacing the phallic I with self-in-relation.

Adrienne Rich: two women, eye to eye
> *measuring each other's spirit, each other's*
> *limitless desire,*
>> *a whole new poetry beginning here.*[38]

A final point: it seems significant to me that critics who have tried to analyze the relational self in Toklas' writings have been women like Catherine Stimpson, an "out" lesbian critic.[39] It may be—and I'm merely speculating here—that in contrast to a reading primarily interested in Stein or in the modernist period, a lesbian reading of *What Is Remembered* might bring to the text a perspective more strongly focused on the relational. The word lesbian itself, since it denotes a woman's emotional and sexual preference for women, supposes a relational stance. A lesbian reader, then, herself defined relationally, may be more open to reading *What Is Remembered* for its portrayal of Toklas as a relational and equal being.

Alice B. Toklas: It was Gertrude Stein who held my complete attention, as she did for all the many years I knew her until her death, and all these empty years since then. She was a golden presence, burned by the Tuscan sun and with a golden glint in her warm brown hair. She was dressed in a warm brown corduroy suit. She wore a large round coral brooch and when she talked, very little, or laughed, a good deal, I thought her voice came from this brooch. It was unlike anyone else's voice—deep, full, velvety like a great contralto's, like two voices. (p. 23)

Notes

1. References to Alice B. Toklas, *What Is Remembered*, reprint (London: Granada, 1983), and to Gertrude Stein, *The Autobiography of Alice B. Toklas*, reprint (Harmondsworth: Penguin, 1966), will be given in the text hereafter.

2. Philippe Lejeune, *On Autobiography* (Minneapolis: University of Minnesota Press, 1989), pp. 4, 12.

3. Judith Butler, "Imitation and Gender Insubordination," in *Inside/Out: Lesbian Theories, Gay Theories*, ed. Diana Fuss (London: Routledge, 1991), pp. 13–31. Page references will hereafter appear in the text.

4. See, for example, Sidonie Smith, *Subjectivity, Identity and the Body: Women's Autobiographical Practices in the Twentieth Century* (Bloomington and Indianapolis: Indiana University Press, 1993), pp. 64–82; Leigh Gilmore, "A Signature of Lesbian Autobiography: 'Gertrice/Altrude,'" in *Autobiography and Questions of Gender*, ed. Shirley Neuman (London: Frank Cass, 1991), pp. 56–75; Sabine Vanacker, "Stein, Richardson and H. D.: Women Modernists and Autobiography," *Bête Noir* 6 (Winter 1989), pp. 111–23; Cynthia Merrill,

"Mirrored Image: Gertrude Stein and Autobiography," *Pacific Coast Philology* 20/1–2 (November 1985), pp. 11–17.

5. Catherine Stimpson, *Mothering the Mind: Twelve Studies of Writers and their Silent Partners* (New York: Holmes and Meier, 1984), pp. 122–39.

6. From *The Dream of a Common Language: Poems 1974–1977* (New York: W. W. Norton, 1978), p. 15.

7. See Cynthia Merrill, "Mirrored Image," p. 15.

8. Virginia Woolf, *A Room of One's Own*, reprint (London: Granada, 1983), p. 35. Commentators such as Sidonie Smith (*Subjectivity*, pp. 74–78) have highlighted Stein's identification with masculine positions.

9. This is, in a way, a double *mis*recognition, as discussed by Jacques Lacan in "The Mirror Stage as Formative of the Function of the I," in that the dual distortion of self-as-other (i.e. man as woman) and self-as-magnified, presents an image of the I based on *Verneinung*, the negation of the I before the mirror. See *Écrits: A Selection* (London: Tavistock Publications, 1980), pp. 1–7.

10. From *The Complete Poems* (Boston: Houghton Mifflin, 1981), p. 41.

11. John Stuart Mill's argument in *The Subjection of Women*, reprint (London: Virago, 1983), centered on this issue.

12. From *The Complete Poems*, reprint (London: Faber and Faber, 1984), p. 133.

13. See, for example, Harriet Taylor Mill, *Enfranchisement of Women*, reprint (London: Virago, 1983); Leonore Davidoff and Catherine Hall, *Family Fortunes: Men and Women of the English Middle Class, 1780–1850* (London: Hutchinson, 1987), pp. 114–18.

14. In *How to Suppress Women's Writing* (London: Women's Press, 1984), pp. 62–75, Joanna Russ provides an eloquent account of this kind of silencing; see also Tillie Olsen, *Silences* (London: Virago, 1980), pp. 213–23.

15. Smith, *Subjectivity*, p. 82.

16. Toklas was, for example, appalled when she was invited to write the foreword for the Yale edition of Stein's work (*Staying On*, p. 215).

17. They were published as *Staying on Alone: Letters of Alice B. Toklas* (New York: Liveright, 1973); *The Alice B. Toklas Cookbook* (New York: Harper, 1954); *Aromas and Flavours of Past and Present* (New York: Harper, 1958). *What Is Remembered* was first published in 1963.

18. See Toklas, *Staying On*, pp. 185, 257. The autobiographical project seems to have been initiated by Max White, the edition of her letters by Edward Burns.

19. Eleanor Roosevelt, *This I Remember* (New York: Harper, 1949).

20. Toklas, *Staying On*, p. 358.

21. Ibid., p. xix.

22. Rich, *Dream*, pp. 30–31.

23. Marcus uses the term "re/sign" in her essay "Invincible Mediocrity: The Private Selves of Public Women" to discuss the ways in which women of public stature use autobiographical writings to counter their public image with representations of their private selves. See *The Private Self: Theory and Practice of Women's Autobiographical Writings*, ed. Shari Benstock (London: Routledge, 1988), pp. 114–46. Judith Butler, from a materialist deconstructionist perspective, considers the political utility of the possibilities of resignification for women, in her essay "Contingent Foundations: Feminism and the Question of 'Postmodernism.'" See Judith Butler and Joan W. Scott, eds., *Feminists Theorize the Political* (London: Routledge, 1992), pp. 3–21.

24. Her letters to her friends are full of gossip about other people and their affairs. Typical are the references to Picasso's private life in her letters to Thornton Wilder and Donald Gallup. See *Staying On*, pp. 293, 309–10. For her dismay over the publication of personal writings, see pp. 62, 63, 74–75.

25. Rich, *Dream*, p. 35.

26. H. D., *The Collected Poems 1912–1944* (Manchester: Carcanet, 1984), p. 539.

27. Gertrude Stein, *Look At Me Now and Here I Am: Writings and Lectures 1909–1945*, reprint (Harmondsworth: Penguin, 1990), p. 100.

28. Toklas, *Staying On*, p. 268.

29. Ibid., p. 5.

30. Rich, *Dream*, p. 52.

31. George Wickes, *Americans in Paris* (New York: Doubleday, 1969), pp. 49–64.

32. Toklas, *Staying On*, p. 358.

33. Susan Stanford Friedman, "Women's Autobiographical Selves: Theory and Practice" in *The Private Self*, ed. Benstock, pp. 35, 41.

34. *Women of the Left Bank: Paris, 1900–1940* (London: Virago, 1987).

35. Rich, *Dream*, p. 7.

36. In *A Room of One's Own* Woolf writes:

after reading a chapter or two a shadow seemed to lie across the page. It was a straight dark bar, a shadow shaped something like the letter "I."

One began dodging this way and that to catch a glimpse of the landscape behind it . . . Back one was always hailed to the letter "I." One began to be tired of "I." (p. 95)

These comments are extensively discussed by Sidonie Smith (*Subjectivity*, pp. 1–10).

37. Although theorists as diverse as Nancy Chodorow in *The Reproduction of Mothering* (Berkeley: University of California Press, 1987), Carol Gilligan in *In a Different Voice* (Cambridge, Mass.: Harvard University Press, 1982) and Patricia Waugh in *Feminine Fictions* (London: Routledge, 1989) emphasize and celebrate the relational self as primary, woman-centered and socially better-adjusted, such feminist re-visioning does not seem to have led to a parallel shift in cultural perceptions.

38. Rich, *Dream*, p. 76.

39. See, for example *Where The Meanings Are* (London: Routledge, 1989).

8

The Memoirs of Halidé Edib: A Turkish Woman Writer in Exile

Ayşe Durakbaşa

Although virtually unknown in the West, Halidé Edib Adivar (1884–1964) is well-known to the Turkish reader as Corporal Halidé of the Turkish War of Independence.[1] Halidé Edib and her husband, Adnan Adivar, were members of the inner circle of Mustafa Kemal, Commander of the Nationalists and President of the Grand National Assembly. Since, at this time, the Ottoman government in Istanbul was under Allied occupation, this Assembly, convened in April 1920, was in effect the sole legitimate body representing the Turkish nation. Although as a woman Halidé Edib could not officially become a deputy in the Assembly, she participated fully in the revolutionary political milieu and felt herself to be at the center of the nationalist struggle. However, in 1925, two years after the foundation of the Turkish Republic, ideological differences between Halidé and her husband and Mustafa Kemal forced the couple to leave the country. They spent the next fourteen years living in exile in Europe.

From this time, Halidé Edib assumed the role of spokeswoman for the Turkish nation in the making: she went on lecture tours and published a number of books about the cultural and political experience of Westernization and modernization in Turkey.[2] Her two volumes of memoirs, which she wrote in English while living in England, cover the period from 1885 to 1923.[3] Considered solely as pieces of history-writing, they have provided invaluable information to European historians of the Near East. Indeed she orders her autobiographical materials according to the conventional periodization of Turkish history ("Between the Old and the New Turkey, 1885–1908" and "New Turkey in the Making"), and marks the 1908 Constitutional Revolution as a significant event in her own life.

Considered from the point of view of the feminist historian and critic, however, the memoirs take on further significance, since they tell the story of a pioneering woman who perceived her making as an individual, an intellectual, and a writer as inseparable from the birth of a nation: she claimed to write her name *into* history as the writer *of* Turkey's nationalist history. In other words, she never conceived her memoirs as merely personal narrative. In presenting to the world the true history of the nationalist struggle of her people, she saw herself as engaging in the most public form of narration: recounting one of "the greatest epics of modern Europe," as she puts it in the epilogue to the first volume. At the same time, Edib's memoirs are multilayered; they can be read as the memoirs of a participant in and builder of the master-narratives of Turkish Enlightenment and Turkish nationalism; yet they also tell us that story from a woman's point of view. Not only do they shadow the political autobiography with the history of the domestic sphere; they also disclose the private dimensions of the public story itself.

"More Than a Mother":
The Private Self as Soldier

The first volume, *Memoirs of Halidé Edib*, provides a vivid story of life in an Ottoman *konak* or upper class household: the "wisteria-covered house" which belonged to her grandmother and which provided the title for the Turkish version of the memoirs.[4] The first chapter, "This is the Story of a Little Girl," is written in the third person, as the adult Halidé looks back at her childhood self. The narratorial voice is nostalgic, though because her mother died of tuberculosis when Halidé was very young, the nostalgia is shot through with anxiety. Suffused with her grandmother's love, the wisteria-covered house ensures that the child feels peaceful and secure; in contrast, the child's mother is pale, ill, fading away to extinction: "This mother is a thing of mystery and uneasiness to the little girl" (4).

However in the second chapter, "When the Story Becomes Mine," Halidé shifts to the customary first person and launches into a remembered encounter with her own mirror image. The scene is strikingly reminiscent of the Lacanian "mirror phase":

The brown childish orbs, brilliant and troubled in some unfathomable way, looked at me wonderingly. The next moment I had put a small hand over the mirror and covered those painful interrogation-points, leaving visible only the unformed round chin and the patch of red lips of the little girl. I realized then for the first time that this face, which people as a rule considered something unusual and unlike its environment, was mine. (30)

This moment of recognition is also the recognition of herself as alienated, as "other" in the classic Lacanian sense, and the strategy she adopts of shifting between the third and first person at this and other points in the memoirs seems to rehearse the troubled and inherently divided act of self-recognition. Her narrative both dwells minutely on disturbing and highly-personal scenes of recognition in the past and dramatizes them as the scene of writing itself:

> The story of the little girl is my own henceforth. As I go on painting my life at the time as sincerely as I possibly can, I realize that the me inside the almost strange body of mine is giving place to the external me, the flesh and blood me, and I am passing gradually out of that early inward consciousness into the common reality of life. I am no longer so distinct from other people. I am part of the huge congregation of human beings, and am doing as they do. So I may as well transfer the story entirely to the first person. (32)

The "I" of these accounts seems intent on sealing up fractures in the self even as she prises them open in the act of analyzing her feelings. Her narrative is dominated by a language of self-making, a confident sense of having overcome her childish longing for love to become a fully developed person. Yet at certain points in her life-story she readmits the timid, feminine self which she must transcend in order to take on her many roles and responsibilities as public speaker, journalist, interpreter, and nurse in the nationalist struggle.

As well as enacting an individual crisis of subjectivity, however, the memoirs provide an intimate view of the competition and conflict, grievances and solidarity, experienced among the women of a single household and between the different households of her father's wives. Growing up in multiple households, Halidé Edib observes these dynamics closely. Although her childhood self often feels lost, as if wandering in an unreal landscape and belonging nowhere, in adulthood her basic network of friendship and solidarity is shown to be founded on the extended family she acquired through her father's wives. She has the support of her sisters at times of crisis, and is enabled to pursue her career and her social, political, and intellectual activities by her sister, Mahmure Abla, who is on hand to take care of her two children when she is prevented from doing so herself.[5] The world of sisters, half-sisters, step-sisters, step-mothers and "in-laws" surrounds her like a "naturally" organized sisterhood.

The second volume of Edib's memoirs, *The Turkish Ordeal*, attempts a chronological history of the Turkish War of Independence, while simultaneously telling her own story. It describes her experience of being based with the commanders at their headquarters where, from her study, she pursued her regular writing, as well as working as an interpreter and a journalist, and keeping up a diary.[6] As the following passage reveals, her determination to write a personal account of the nationalist struggle had originally been prompted by a crucial moment of conflict with her leader, Mustafa Kemal Pasha. Confronted with the probability that his official version of events would concentrate exclusively on war, strategy, victory, and political achievement, she became convinced of the need to resist his account by opposing it with her own "human document."[7] Moreover, her capacity for resistance would be enhanced by her ability to write her account in English, which, as a foreign language, would afford her the possibility both of a larger audience, and also, perhaps, of a sense of distance from a milieu of personal stress:

> I would try to recreate that period of Turkish history by preserving a faithful record of my experiences during that great ordeal. I would try to tell the story of Turkey as simply and honestly as a child, that the world might some day read it—not as a historical record nor as a political treatise, but *as a human document* about men and women alive during my own lifetime; and I would write it in a language far better fitted to reach the world than my own. It was that very night, as I lay in bed after the scene with Mustafa Kemal Pasha, that I determined to write my Memoirs and to write them in English. (Volume II, 190, my emphasis)

This one of the rare instances when Edib acknowledges a repressed inner self, a lost child usually censored in gestures of self-abnegation and in a rhetoric of sacrifice in the interest of a greater good: the political goal of national salvation. Halidé's own children, her two sons by her first marriage, had been sent to the United States for their high-school education when she and her second husband, Adnan Adivar, left for Ankara to join the Nationalists. In the memoirs it is only at moments of emotional tension such as this that we are allowed a glimpse of the intensity of her feelings for her children. As the narrative progresses, we begin to see the connection between her determination to write her own name into history and the pain of the ordeal of losing her children. She must forgo motherhood for the sake of becoming a wise mother to her nation:

> I set to work on a new program. I took an old wooden table to one of the empty rooms at the back of the farm and there began to write the story of my own life. . . . I thought of it as an attempt to touch people whom I had never met, and would never meet—an attempt to reach distant firesides where human hearts are yearning for true contacts with other human beings who are too far away for them to meet in the flesh. But *in reality it was to be written above all for the little folk who were just setting out to cross the Atlantic.* I did not allow myself to visualize them or to dwell on the thousand and one memories ever ready to arise: the time had not yet come for me to permit myself the luxury of tears. Nor did I allow myself to face the fact that there was only one chance in a million that I would ever see or touch them again. But *I wanted them to have an account of me.* I wanted them to understand how circumstances and my too large and greedy heart had led me to be more than a mother. (Volume II, 191, my emphases)

What begins to emerge here, and what needs to be stressed in the context of a discussion of women's relationship to war, is that Edib's account of her experience as a woman soldier in a nationalist struggle is not restricted to its painful consequences: her narrative has a heroic as well as an elegiac dimension. In the person of the young soldiers whom she embraces as "more than a mother" she achieves direct contact with the very "simple Anatolian Turk" upon whose traits the Turkish character will come to be based. In this way she attributes to herself a role, albeit an indirect one, in the formation of the national character itself. Hence the metaphor of motherhood—as the prerogative of social control over the young—becomes a means of enlarging rather than simply repeating imposed sex roles, a means of expanding her social space.

Furthermore, as we shall see, she relished her sense of significance within the male military order and hierarchy, as well as the thrill of insignificance of being subsumed into the military design. She describes a liminal state, to borrow Victor Turner's term, in which she feels dispossessed of her previous social status and enjoys a new freedom and energy.[8] She recounts how , in the face of conflict, her "curious way of identifying [her]self with [her] nation" now took its highest and strongest form:

I meant to be among the strugglers who might prevent the imminent disaster or die in the effort. I did not mind how insignificant
and absolutely small my part might be. It was a gigantic picture of
an unparalleled struggle: let me be the most insignificant detail.
(Volume II, 283)

Now that I was a soldier I was acting like a soldier; consciously, even subconsciously, I seemed to have ceased to be an
individual. I was a number in those military designs which moved
hither and thither, a mere drop in the gathering human torrent in
the wastes of Anatolia. And we drove on. A silent and yellow
bareness, occasional rises of land in the distance, solitary horsemen whose horses' hoofs awakened echoes in the silence at intervals. (Volume II, 285)

Such descriptions of geography, space, and movement from the
point of view of the "voyeur of landscape" have been found to be commonplace in women's accounts of war. Clare Tylee's study of women's
autobiographies of the Great War has shown that women tend to fictionalize war and the armies of men as heroic, even though they may
find ways of articulating their inner pain at the destructiveness of war.[9]
Ironically, war is a state in which women's familiar sense of invisibility
can be celebrated as a sense of equality—a sense of shared subordination to the process of military mobilization. Moreover the responsibility
of recording military operations may itself lend them a certain glamour,
especially as consciousness of a great military design is often associated with the emotional charge of impending battle or even victory. As
we see here, Halidé Edib's memoirs convey her fascination at being
part of the struggle for Turkish independence:

The corn fields, yellow and ripe, waved on either side; military
transports were in groups here and there, with khaki-colored figures moving among them. We passed by a field hospital, and I
saw one sister in a white apron standing near. The wild ride with
the hoofs echoing amid the booms of artillery stirred something
strange in me, by which I began to know the emotion which takes
hold of the men in fighting. I meant to put it all in a novel; even
the sister whose face I could not distinguish was going to be the
center of a human hurricane.

. . . The hills surrounding the valley at our feet were lively
with the lugubrious intonation of artillery, and the nervous *tac-tac*
of the machine guns. Through the field-glass I was seeing the

game of war as it is played, and the beast in me was enjoying it as much as the rest, forgetting what its results would look like in the hospitals later on. I could see men coming nearer and nearer, and even the fall of the men in the front line, leaving it indented and broken; and the final onslaught with bayonets. (Volume II, 302–3)

Although fascinated by the spectacle of war, and enjoying her sense of inclusion in the war effort, she nevertheless attempts to keep her distance from the euphoria of victory ("I meant to put it all in a novel . . ."). Here again, the metaphor of motherhood plays a part. Recording the ritual aftermath of battle, she takes on the detached wisdom of the universal mother, who feels sympathy for the mothers of the soldiers on both sides, and who is able to look over and beyond the war-game in which the commanders, like little boys, are indulging:

The commanders of Sakaria came one by one to congratulate Ismet Pasha and to receive congratulations. In spite of their subdued and dignified manners, I could not help thinking of my little Hassan when he had worsted the boys of another quarter in a street fight. (Volume II, 305–6)

Through a Padded Screen: Author as Heroine

If Halidé Edib could be said to be aware in a feminine way of the dreadful consequences of war, she also exploits to the full the power invested in her as author, creating for herself the role of heroine. In doing so, as we have seen, she portrays herself as an exceptional woman, one whose life differed fundamentally from that of the majority of women who played no significant part in the fight for national independence and survival. Her novel, *The Shirt of Flame*,[10] likewise draws heavily on her wartime experiences though its protagonist, as she hints in the memoir, is a nurse whose angelic capacity for sympathy gives her insight into the epic strivings of those around her.

As a writer in the canon of nationalist literature in Turkey, Halidé Edib creates heroines who represent a new ideal, forged out of the crisis of gender roles during the period of modernization and Westernization in Ottoman and Republican Turkey at the turn of the century. Unlike many of the male writers of the period, whose response to social and political flux was to associate female sexuality with chaos and cultural disorder, and whose solution was to construct heroines in need of male patronage and control to manage their undisciplined virginal sexuality, Halidé Edib tried to create a new kind of heroine, sexually powerful yet still subject to self-control and to a sexual code.[11] Hence, her autobiography presents a feminine "I" capable of both self-development and self-discipline

From my parallel reading of the English and Turkish versions of her memoirs, I sense that she gained a certain freedom by expressing herself in English. As both a Western and a second language, English helped her distance herself from the female role as it was constructed within Turkish culture, and from the primary duties which it enjoined on her to be a wife and mother. The American College for Girls in Istanbul, of which she was the first Turkish Muslim graduate, had afforded her a network of alliances among American and English missionary circles, and with it a fund of commonplaces of feminine self-presentation which included the vocational.[12] For this reason, writing in English meant she could tell her story according to a different set of assumptions about femininity and about herself. It may also have epitomized for her the specificity and specialness of her own education, and hence may have enhanced her sense of herself as a writer and a pioneering woman in a way the Turkish language could not. Describing an early visit to London, she remarks:

> In the solitude and the discreet half-light of the English atmosphere I worked well. The noise which one may expect of the great traffic of London is so smooth and even, and the life of the great city so softly tuned down to a strange order, as if all passed through a padded screen before it reached you, that it throws one entirely into oneself. No atmosphere is more restful and favorable to creative work than that of London for an unknown and young writer. The isolation is so complete that one is forced to dig into one's inner resources. (Volume I, 331)

On the whole, however, Halidé Edib's life in exile is not included in the autobiography. She prefers to construct her self-image through reference to a particular past self: the Halidé Edib of the War of Independence. Her identity as adult and as literary exile is assimilated into this single persona. The fact that she chooses to voyage back into the past and that her present is virtually absent from the text is perhaps the most interesting feature of her autobiographical act. We do not know and cannot tell from her account where and how she was writing this autobiography; all we know is how her past experiences made her an advocate of Turkish nationalism. She sees her adult self as emerging directly from the Turkish ordeal: a positive outcome of the struggle. The ordeal may have involved conflict and ambivalence, but it has produced a stable self. It is as though the self becomes fixed with the end of the War of Independence. Once having reached a point of fulfilment beyond the need for further development, the self no longer requires a temporal dimension.

In a sense, the absence of any reference to the time of writing shores up her authority: what she is is an author, and nothing more (or less). Paradoxically, the primary importance of the autobiographical act is thereby impressed on the reader at all times. The distancing mechanisms of a foreign language and a fixed perspective both serve to create a distinct space for herself as a writer. In her record of the birth of the Turkish nation, Halidé, the insignificant witness, transforms herself into Halidé Edib Adivar, the writer.

There is a remarkable ease in the way Edib places herself at the center of her story as a notable participant in, and witness of, the building of the new Turkey. Yet in her narrative one can also detect a "hidden tale of doubt" about the value and integrity of the successful self she has so confidently asserted; one can glimpse, to borrow Patricia Spacks' phrase, "selves in hiding."[13] While the success story tells of her life in the early years of the century as one of the well-educated "new women" of the Turkish elite, the hidden tale suggests how insecure and insignificant that new woman often feels as she is preparing to speak in public or to travel abroad. Such moments of insecurity are described in terms of a fragmentation of self, as part of her anxiously watches the "poor thing" perform, and is amazed at her success. These are also the moments at which, mirroring the original act of self-(mis)recognition, Edib shifts back from the first to the third person, disrupting the linear, progressive plot of the autobiographical narrative.

But Edib's autobiography makes the other woman, or woman in hiding, visible in other ways. My reading of her memoirs has highlighted the precarious ways in which the narrative of the rebirth of the nation renders woman both present and absent, significant and insignificant. The section entitled "The First Glimpse," in which she imagines the military nurse as the heroine of an epic struggle, the focus and symbol of the heroes' emotional yearnings, is followed by the story of her own entry into the army as Corporal Halidé, which in turn is followed by "The Respite" and "The Epilogue," in which she hints at her gradual exclusion from national history. At the same time she constructs her story so that at its edges we become aware of other women whose stories were excluded or rendered insignificant in the new era of the establishment of the Republic.

In an ominous farewell scene after the ultimate victory, Mustafa Kemal hands over to Halidé Edib the cape he has worn throughout the nationalist struggle. The scene anticipates the moment only a short time later when Mustafa Kemal will dispense with many of the leading figures of the inner circle of the nationalist movement, including, of course, Halidé herself. At the end of the section, we catch sight of Ghul Hanum, a woman soldier who during the campaign has worn a fantastic mask of white bandages covering her face. Almost entirely hidden behind a tree, she watches the handing-over of the cape from a distance because Mustafa Kemal has refused to receive her:

> "I know she is there. I am not going to receive her," he said harshly. He went on to speak about Ghul Hanum in a way that hurt and disappointed me. In her way she had played a part in the scheme which had worked out the national destiny. In her limited, fantastic sphere she had given her very best. But he waved away the subject. (Volume II, 389–90)

If Halidé Edib is the heroine of the memoirs I take Ghul Hanum to be the anti-heroine. In a sense she represents the other, the daemonic in Halidé Edib as well as the unseemly element in the nationalist movement—which was, after all, basically a cadre movement in need of popular support. If Halidé Edib represents herself positively as a kind of Joan of Arc, it is at the expense of Ghul Hanum, who represents the negative, other-worldly, archaic, and even witchlike aspect of the woman-warrior image. She is introduced as a woman from Erzinjan (an Eastern Anatolian town) "who had had strange dreams." Ali, the Lion of Allah, the great Arab Caliph and the nephew of the Prophet, had appeared in her dreams and ordered her to join the army. Taking her only son, a lad of fifteen, she had left her home and her husband and joined the struggle. Refusing either to remove her mask or to accept work in the hospital, she insists on being sent to the front:

> She had a mild voice, but one felt uneasy as it spoke in a muffled tone behind the thick white bandage . . . there was something infinitely childish about her—she reminded me of the days when I used to pore over the heroic tales of Ali in our various homes at Scutari as a child. I did not have the heart to tell her that warfare had altered since the good old days of Ali, and that there was a lot of ugly machinery. Yet the faith of her medieval heart in the ultimate realization of the Turkish deliverance did not seem so different from ours, although our clothes and our make-up did not frighten the horses in the market-place. (Volume II, 339–40)

Here we see that the popular literature, epics, and romance stories that were part of the childhood socialization of the Ottoman élite could function as a bridge between Halidé Edib and the culture of the lower classes, mitigating the solitude she feels because of her class position and bypassing the effects of the special Western education that had, in her early years, cut her off from Turkish children of her own age. Şerif Mardin has theorized this relationship in terms of the social and cultural dynamics of the time: it was possible for the modernist élites to operate the mechanism of the "Little" culture for their own goals because it was not totally alien to them. "In the élite, then, culture seems to have consisted of two layers: a childhood layer where the very same values that were fixed on lower class adults were given a place—this is primarily true for the themes of bravery—and an adult layer of themes clustered around the reason of state."[14] At other times, however, Edib finds the gulf is too great: she describes feelings of alienation from the Anatolian peasant women, and from what she sees as their expressive sexuality. She recounts a number of instances of extreme estrangement: running away, horrified, when the village women invite "the slut of the village" to dance especially for her (Volume II, 207);[15] being mocked and attacked for her modern dress by the children of the lower class neighborhoods she visits on educational or philanthropic expeditions.

In a variety of ways, then, class difference is shown to inform her consciousness, her feminine subjectivity, and her identity as a nationalist. On one occasion, the Istanbul pashas come to visit her in her modest study at the military headquarters in Ankara. The scene is interesting in that it testifies to her need to redefine the concept of ladyhood or genteel womanhood in the light of the new, nationalist agenda. The visit of the pashas reminds her of the secure and luxurious home she has left behind in Istanbul; yet she shrugs off their pity at her reduced circumstances, preferring instead to see herself as a participant in an epic struggle (Volume II, 235–36). Although in Ankara she feels like a refugee in an alien land, gradually the country round about affords her space to construct a new vision of life: a life of "People, Horses and Dogs," as the title of a chapter in *The Turkish Ordeal* has it. The idea of the farmhouse as a future home takes shape. She is given a mare, which she names Doru, and

> . . . it was she who carried me to the villages and the wild wastes round Angora where my real initiation was beginning.[16] The orderly Suleiman who had been given us by headquarters rode with me . . . I then took long solitary rides to explore the country,

and these gave me infinite rest amid unparalleled surroundings: all above me numberless low hills, before me long stretches of undulating land, above me a clear sky and a bright sun. Up and down I rode, sometimes straying across a small plain concealed among the hills. And there I would find, nestling against a mound, a village of yellow huts, blue smoke curling upward, surprise vineyards, green orchards and silver streams. (Volume II, 192)

The idealization of village life, a new vision of a country with Anatolia as its base, was to become a major theme in the nationalist discourse and literature in the coming years. According to this ideal, the age-old discrepancy between the "enlightened" and the "subject" population was to be wiped out, subsumed in the new identity of the Turkish nation. Yet the new femininity that can be discerned in the chivalric image of ladyhood Halidé Edib assumes—and which was to become a characteristic ideal for Kemalist, nationalist women, differentiating them from traditional Ottoman ladies—can already be seen to equip the new women with a "baton" with which to orchestrate the lives of lower class men and women:

Toward the end of December the headquarters moved from Azizié to Akshehir. The ride of five hundred horsemen (a cavalry battalion accompanied the headquarters) to Tjay, where we took the train to Akshehir, stays in my memory as one of the exciting episodes of my military life. I rode at the head with Colonel Assim, the chief of staff, and he gallantly asked me to set the pace. Both Doru and I enjoyed leading the five hundred horses. Up went my hand after half an hour of trotting and we fell into an easier pace; up it went again and we tore ahead amid the formidable echo of hoofs from the hills. Especially in the valleys the echo was fantastic. (Volume II, 329)

There remains much to be uncovered about the grassroots of Kemalist feminism and its effects on women's life stories.[17] In a society in which self had typically been defined in terms of communal and familial orientations, Kemalist socialization cultivated in Turkish women the first germs of individuation. Individual women like Halidé Edib were forced to define an ethic for themselves as they pushed forward and challenged their ascribed status. Secure in her class position, Halidé puts her own story unapologetically at the center of her memoirs. She is unequivocally the heroine, in command of herself and others. Yet as we have seen, she marks points of intersection between her own and the stories of those other women who were more marginal to the epic struggle. In this way, however indirectly, she writes the other women into Turkish history as well. The army officers may not have been willing to accept Ghul Hanum because "she did not fit the actual things"; Halidé includes her, writing her back into history not only in her autobiographical account, but in her fiction-writing. In the end we could see Ghul Hanum as a complex symbol of liminality: as at once an instance of the precarious position of women in the nationalist movement, and a symbol of in/significance: a trope for the strategies of inclusion and exclusion that constitute Halidé Edib's own autobiographical negotiation with history.

Notes

1. The Turkish War of Independence (1919–1923) was fought mainly against the Greek, British, and French shortly after World War I. Halidé Edib was accorded the title "Corporal," and was later promoted to the rank of Sergeant Major for her services in the War.

2. See for instance Halidé Edib Adivar, *Turkey Faces West: A Turkish View of Recent Changes and their Origin* (New Haven: Yale University Press, 1930).

3. *Memoirs of Halidé Edib* (New York and London: Century, 1926); *The Turkish Ordeal, Being the Further Memoirs of Halidé Edib* (London: John Murray, 1928). Hereafter cited as Volume I or II, with page references given in the text.

4. See *Mor Salkimh Ev* (Istanbul: Atlas Kitabevi, 1963), serialized intermittently in the Turkish periodical *Yeni Istanbul*, 1951–55.

5. "Abla" means "elder sister" in Turkish.

6. The second volume of the memoirs was published as *Türkün Ateşle Imtihani* (Istanbul: Çan Yayinlari, 1962), serialized in the weekly magazine *Hayat* as *Milli Mücadele Hatiralari*, 1959–60.

7. Mustafa Kemal Atatürk (meaning father of the Turks) gave his account and interpretation of the nationalist struggle as a speech to the congress of his party in the parliament building over six days, 15–20 October 1927. It has been published several times by the Turkish Historical Institution and the Turkish Language Institution, and is a basic document for the history of the Turkish Revolution. It is interesting to note that Halidé Edib wrote her own account in exile just at the time Mustafa Kemal was delivering his historic speech.

8. Victor Turner, *The Ritual Process* (Chicago: Aldine, 1964).

9. See Claire M. Tylee, *The Great War and Woman's Consciousness* (London: Macmillan, 1990).

10. The novel *the Shirt of Flame* was first published in English (New York: Duffield, 1924). See also *Daughter of Smyrna: A Story of the Rise of Modern Turkey on the Ashes of the Ottoman Empire*, trans. Muhammed Yakub Khan (Lahore: Darul Kütup Islamia, 1932), later published in Turkish as *Ateşten Gömlek* (Istanbul: Atlas Kitabevi, 1969).

11. Compare, for example, Halidé Edib's construction of heroines in her autobiography and fiction with Reşat Nuri Güntekin's novel *Çalikuşu: The Autobiography of a Turkish Girl*, trans. Wyndham Deedes (London: George Allen Unwin, 1949). Here, the heroine, whose nickname Çalikuşu means "wren," is depicted by this male writer as an attractive, naive girl whose virginity and ignorance endow her with a particularly potent sexuality, and who requires the patronage of the male in order to avoid being led astray. Çalikuşu is a young idealistic woman teacher who, having been disappointed in a love affair, leaves her family in Istanbul to take up work in Anatolia (a common theme in Turkish Nationalist literature). As an unmarried woman, she is exposed to the sexual advances of the men around her. The novel is written in the first-person singular, in autobiographical form. The male character with whom the novelist most clearly identifies is Doctor Hayrullah Bey. He offers fatherly love, protection, and a paternalistic marriage to the tomboy Çalikuşu, to save her from rumors of sexual misconduct and to restore traditional morality. This depiction of female virginity as a state of unspecified but threatening womanhood seems to me to be a characteristic response among male writers to the flux in gender relations caused by this period of great sociocultural change in Turkey. Unlike Çalikuşu, Halidé Edib's heroines are defiant in the face of patronage, though they do not readily defy the code of female sexual propriety.

12. Halidé Edib mentions being impressed at school by lessons in the Christian scriptures, as well by the writings of Shakespeare and Zola. Although she does not allude to any specifically auto/biographical writings, it is perhaps worth noting that, seventy years later, I remember being encouraged to read about the lives of Florence Nightingale, Thomas Jefferson, and Helen Keller at the same school.

13. Patricia M. Spacks, "Selves in Hiding" in Estelle C. Jelinek, ed., *Women's Autobiography: Essays in Criticism* (Bloomington: Indiana University Press, 1980), pp. 112–32.

14. Şerif Mardin, "Superwesternisation in Urban Life in the Ottoman Empire in the Last Quarter of the Nineteenth Century," in R. Benedict and E. Tümertekin, eds., *Turkey: Geographical and Social Perspectives* (Leiden: E. J. Brill, 1974), p. 429.

15. Halidé Edib draws on this autobiographical material in the interesting short story "The Witch of Kalaba," in Ed. Rhys and C. A. Dawson-Scott, eds., *Tales from Far and Near* (New York: Appleton, 1930).

16. Angora is Ankara, capital city of the Turkish Republic.

17. "State feminism" is the term used by Turkish feminists today to denote the Kemalist reforms in relation to women's rights effected in the 1920s and 1930s. The Republican state advocated women's rights; introduced a secular civil code in 1926, and granted full suffrage in 1934. See Ayşe Nilüfer Durakbaşa, "The Formation of Kemalist Female Identity: A Historical-Cultural Approach," M.A. Dissertation, Boğaziçi University, Istanbul, 1987.

PART III

Subjectivities

INTRODUCTION

"The difficulty of saying 'I.'" This phrase comes from Christa Wolf's novel *The Quest for Christa T.* and is explored there in the way Wolf makes her text hover elegiacally in the space around the female subject, experiencing her as fragmentary, as absent, as "other."[1] Given that subjectivity is more (and less) than the spontaneous recognition of self by self, the difficulty that Wolf refers to, and which both female novelists and autobiographers alike experience, may well be finding a story which authorizes *her* as a subject. "The subject is a concept with a history" Margaret Whitford has written and further argues that "the successive adventures and crises of the Hegelian subject"—its picaresque journey from autonomy to splitting and displacement to eventual death—"were not *her* adventures or crises."[2] The female subject, never allowed to enter into the discourses of subjecthood in the same way as the masculine subject, never allowed to constitute herself as the (universal) subject of discourse, the subject who is, at the same time both singular and representative, is then relegated to the outside as object, body, or unfathomable spatiality. Subjectivity—the interiorized subjectivity of the Cartesian ego—relies on this kind of partitioning of mind from body, of inside from outside, of self from other selves. The privileged place of self-reflection is a place asserted through the delineation of boundaries and limits; it is also, as Diana Fuss has pointed out, of necessity, stationary.[3] Paradoxically, to begin to think about place—to shift the grounds of the question from "who is speaking?" to "where am I speaking from?"—is also to recognize that the subject is unlocalizable, that any positioning of the subject is both temporary and precarious. To make the place of subjectivity into a question is thus also to destabilize it, to open up the possibility of other places, other subjects. As Irigaray suggests, female subjectivity can be imagined only as a condition of becoming, of resistance to her positioning or containment as object within the symbolic—a movement both away and towards. Women's access to subjectivity therefore requires the transformation of both limits and perspectives, the opening up of a horizon or an elsewhere, a possibility which Christa Wolf also envisages in terms of ceaseless movement: "this long and never-ending journey toward oneself."[4]

If Freudian psychoanalysis has provided one of the most potent scripts for the understanding of modern subjectivity, it has also produced an important text of feminine resistance. Woman does not exist as an autonomous, independent subjectivity in Freudian theory, it has often been noted, but must assume her place as essentialized other, his complement, "his appropriate opposite sex."[5] However, hysteria, which Freud posited as the bedrock of psychoanalytic theory, also proved to be a protean fiction, in the words of one commentator, and *Dora*, Freud's most famous case study of a hysteric, was built on shifting sand. Not only did *Dora* "reveal the terms masculine and feminine to be unmoored in the psychic life of hysterics, but the place of the analyst was opened to as much uncertainty as that of the analyst."[6] Dora, of course, walked out on Freud, leaving him to fill in the gaps in her story himself, to attain a coherence and completeness which Dora's resistance renders impossible. The fragmentation of hysteria—the hysteric's inability to tell her own story—becomes Freud's inability to complete his case history. *Dora* has been such an important text for feminists precisely because it demonstrates a fluidity which Freud's narrative attempts to repress: sexual difference cannot be contained in the conventional plot of heterosexuality, nor can the neutrality—or indifference—of the knowing subject be sustained. If Freud, in the end, can only tell his story—the same story—the question then becomes is there a different story that a woman can tell?

The essays in this section explore this problematic: whose story, whose subjectivity, is at stake; how must the story be changed if the woman is to become its subject; from where can she say I, what space must be created within discourse for her to speak. Sabine Vanacker looks at the difference between the texts of (male) high modernism and the modernist texts of women writers like Dorothy Richardson, Gertrude Stein and H. D. Like the case history that Freud could and could not construct, (male) autobiography could be seen as the textual accomplishment of coherence, a way of completing, through the closure of the written word, a story which inevitably escapes its author. Modernism—for all its entanglement with autobiography, its (Freudian) emphasis on the structure and strangeness of the individual psyche—aims to create a "significant artistic monument," which through sublimation and distance, has refined the personality of the artist out of existence: the text stands in his place, testimony to his achieved identity as artist. For female modernists, however, according to Vanacker, the autobiographical desire, enacted in their writing, is to be present within and thus through their own writing. The text speaks where women are otherwise silent: it represents scenes where women are not heard, not given a hearing, and accords them a different recognition through its textual representation of their (silent) thoughts and feelings. In H. D.'s case one of these scenes is also the analytic scene. In her *Tribute to Freud*, H. D. achieves her own subjective vision, the mysterious, magical nature of which resists Freud's attempts at "scientific" interpretation. H. D.'s vision is also vitally present and requires her to be physically there as its witness. These writers want to do anything but disappear into textual anonymity: their aim is less to achieve completeness than endlessly to create situations which re-present them, in which they can go on performing their own presence to themselves and others.

Judith Woolf, on the other hand, draws attention in her essay to the omissions and silences within women's testimony as necessary, not as a sign of oppression. She quotes Natalia Ginzburg as saying that her memory is unreliable. In *Family Sayings*, however, that unreliability is also a form of truth-telling, a reluctance to move outside her own, necessarily limited perceptions, to share in family and national mythologies. Silence may not, as Woolf suggests, be silencing, but eloquent testimony to a trauma which cannot be put into words, which refuses the consolations of meaning and narrative. Shoshana Felman has recently suggested that "unlike men, who write autobiographies from memory, women's autobiography is what their memory cannot contain—or hold together as a whole—although their writing inadvertently inscribes it."[7] How to narrate a story which has never been experienced as having the shape or meaning of a story; how to find a form for what has no form—or memory—within discourse? For the story to be told, as Felman suggests, it may have to first enact its own event (or advent) as a story";[8] it may have to situate itself as witness to the story she (I) will become.

Notes

1. (London: Virago, 1982), p. 174.

2. *Luce Irigaray: Philosophy in the Feminine* (London: Routledge, 1991), p. 43.

3. *Essentially Speaking: Feminism, Nature and Difference* (New York: Routledge, 1989), p. 29.

4. *The Quest for Christa T.*, p. 174.

5. Jane Gallop, *Feminism and Psychoanalysis: The Daughter's Seduction* (London: Macmillan, 1982), p. 59.

6. Claire Kahane "Introduction," in Charles Bernheimer and Claire Kahane, eds., *In Dora's Case* (London: Virago, 1985), pp. 22–23.

7. *What Does A Woman Want? Reading and Sexual Difference* (Baltimore: John Hopkins University Press, 1983), p. 15.

8. Ibid., p. 17.

Further Reading

Anderson, Linda. *Women and Autobiography in the Twentieth Century: Remembered Futures* (Hemel Hempstead, Harvester Wheatsheaf, 1996).

Felski, Rita. *Against Feminist Aesthetics: Feminist Literature and Social Change* (London: Hutchison Radius, 1989), especially ch. 2.

Felman, Shoshana. *What Does A Woman Want? Reading and Sexual Difference* (Baltimore and London: John Hopkins University Press, 1993).

Gagnier, Regenia. *Subjectivities: A History of Self-Representation in Britain 1832–1920* (New York and Oxford: Oxford University Press, 1991).

Henriques, J., Hollway, W., Urwin, C., and Walkerdine, V., eds. *Changing the Subject; Psychology, Social Regulation and Subjectivity* (London and New York: Methuen, 1984).

Julia Kristeva. "A Question of Subjectivity—An Interview," in P. Rice and P. Waugh, eds., *Modern Literary Theory: A Reader* (London: Edward Arnold, 1989), pp. 128–34.

Miller, Nancy. *Subject to Change* (New York: Columbia University Press, 1988).

———. "Representing Others: Gender and the Subjects of Autobiography," *differences* 6 (1994), pp. 1–27.

Simons, Judy. *Diaries and Journals of Literary Women from Fanny Burney to Virginia Woolf* (Basingstoke and London: Macmillan, 1990).

Smith, Sidonie. *Subjectivity, Identity and the Body: Women's Autobiographical Practices in the Twentieth Century* (Bloomington and Indianapolis: Indiana University Press, 1993).

Stanton Domna. "Autogynography: Is the Subject Different?," in Domna Stanton, ed., *The Female Autograph: Theory and Practice of Autobiography from the Tenth to the Twentieth Century* (Chicago and London: University of Chicago Press, 1987), pp. 5–22.

9

Autobiography and Orality: The Work of Modernist Women Writers

Sabine Vanacker

The text preserves the past by recording it. . . . [A] written or a printed work . . . has a special kind of involvement with the past, namely, its textuality as such. Not just what a text says, but the physical text itself possesses a certain pastness. All texts are preterite. Unlike an utterance, a text is assimilated by the person who receives it not when it is being composed but after its utterance (its "outering") is over with. . . . A text as such is so much a thing of the past that it carries with it necessarily an aura of accomplished death.[1]

This quotation, from a section entitled "Text as Monument" in Walter J. Ong's *Interfaces of the Word* (1977), forms part of a prolonged investigation into the impact of literacy on the human psychological make-up, particularly in Western culture. Ong's research has analyzed how, over long centuries, oral societies have slowly transformed themselves into fundamentally altered, literate societies. From communities in which all knowledge had to be contained and preserved by means of oral telling and re-telling, we have evolved to a state of "highly interiorized literacy" in many contemporary societies. In this essay, an Ongian perspective will be used to differentiate the modernist texts of women writers like Dorothy Richardson, Gertrude Stein, and H. D. from (male) high modernism. By highlighting their attitudes to the written and printed word, we can distinguish a common autobiographical pursuit at the heart of their avant-gardism: rather than writing about their life histories for an audience of absent readers, they in fact seek to "perform" themselves as a strong female presence in front of an audience of reader-listeners.

For any culture, the arrival of writing and literacy forms an epis-temological point of no return, which is only boosted by printing tech-nology. Typically, oral societies are characterized by communal story-telling. Formal oral address and verbal prowess form part of a clan member's status and success. The knowledge and communal history of the clan has to be contained and preserved by means of continuous oral telling and re-telling in the presence of an audience. The typically literate society, on the other hand, has the option for individuals to record their own personal existence and history in utter privacy. Ordinary, unremarkable individuals in this century leave an inevitable paper trail of documents and computer data, from the shortest shop-ping list to diary extracts and official certificates of marriage and death.

In different ways, twentieth-century philosophers and critics, like Jacques Derrida, Harold Bloom, Sandra M. Gilbert, and Susan Gubar, and Walter J. Ong, have taken part in the unravelling of the powerful mythologies created around the written word; around textuality, author-ship, writerly influences, and anxieties. It is a timely discussion. Indeed, the computer technology developing in the latter half of this century is causing yet another drastic revision in our mental make-up and our perception of textuality. Rather than offering a strictly philosophical interpretation of literacy and orality, Walter J. Ong stresses the more prosaic, everyday effects of the writing technology on subjects, such as its consequences for memory span, the growth of new storytelling habits, or the painful development of printing conventions. Writers and speakers have come to associate an emotional complex of characteristics around these two states of being, orality, here regarded as the favoring of spoken language as the main means of communication, and literacy, the altered place in the world of the visile, textually-focused literate. Typically associated with speech are feelings of warmth, presence, and immediacy: the speaker and hearer(s) are considered mutually inter-active, their communication is immediate, rectifiable and their speech resounds all around them. Oral poets compose in the presence of the full force of the audience. The reality they are talking about is part of communal memory. Vital for oral narration and recitation is the per-formance level, the interaction between the teller and audience, a rela-tionship which can alter between different tellings of the same tale or even within the same tale. For the writer/reader relationship, on the other hand, there is absence and exclusion. What is written about is mostly absent either from the reader, or the author, or both; even with the author of a text present, the reader is excluding him/her. However, writing has proven to be such a stimulating and liberating invention because of ideals such as clarity, precision, and permanence which have developed around it. The evolution towards interiorized literacy is irreversible: literates can never return to any imagined, prelapsarian state of direct orality and presence. Nevertheless, societies do not partake evenly of this evolution. There are what Ong calls "pockets of orality" in predominantly literate societies, such as the American rap culture, while traces of orality persist in the insistence on oral proclamations in such ceremonies as marriage.

The written word, then, is "a thing not an event." Written words are "alone in a text," lacking the support of pronunciation, emphasis, audience-participation: lacking, in other words, the performance level.[2] They are a faculty of space and vision, not of time and aurality. For writers, the psychological effect of the absence of the audience is that the text as well as the topic under discussion become their property. The arrival of literacy means a move from one sense, the aural, to another, the visual, as the predominant mode of knowledge, and this causes different affective attitudes towards the surrounding world. As Ong summarizes it: "Sight isolates, sound incorporates":

> By contrast with vision, the dissecting sense, sound is thus a unifying sense. A typical visual ideal is clarity and distinctness, a taking apart. The auditory ideal, by contrast, is harmony, a putting together.[3]

Because it constitutes a technique which has to be actively learned, writing introduces division and alienation, but of a creative kind. As Ong points out, the technologies of writing and printing have fostered the capacity for analysis, and eventually self-analysis. As a visualist experience, writing has a distancing effect, making the writer distinguish between the writing subject and the absent object written about. Thus, the historical evolution towards the concepts of self and the individual is regarded as a result of increased literacy. Ong shows that oral societies are less experienced with self-analysis, or analysis of character. A Soviet anthropologist of the early thirties, A. R. Luria interviewed illiterate and "somewhat literate" persons and discovered that they answered questions about their characters and personalities situationally, explaining their position in their family and society rather than attempting an analysis of what they were like.[4] These illiterates, in other words, were not yet individualists, but stressed their inclusion in a community. To put it in an Ongian epigram, writing is consciousness raising.[5]

In the opening quotation, the permanence, stability, and eternity of the written work is at issue. The printed text combines the attractive potential of the eternal monument poised towards a never-ending future, with a more sinister, generally-accepted suggestion that this stability freezes the living word, and kills in order to preserve. The "aura of accomplished death" surrounding textuality becomes more poignant still when considered in the light of one of the "master narratives" of Western textuality, the genre of autobiography. The literary genre of autobiography in this sense can be considered as the final outcome of interiorized literacy, when textual analysis of reality becomes self-analysis. Karl Weintraub thus defines the essence of the genre.

> [A]utobiography adheres more closely to the true potential of the genre the more its real subject matter is character, personality, self-conception—all those difficult-to-define matters which ultimately determine the inner coherence and the meaning of a life.[6]

The importance of the genre lies not solely in the description of the life of an individual. In its traditional form, the autobiography presents an individual who has established, via his writing, a scripted coherence to his life and self which is not there in day-to-day experience, but belongs strictly to textuality. Significantly, the genre first appeared in 1809 in a text by Robert Southey, cropping up in the Romantic period with its triumphant assertion of the importance of the individual. The Romantic significance attached to the intellectual and emotional development of the single individual is in itself the result of an interiorization of literacy. The same goes for the Romantic ideal of originality. Only a long tradition of literacy could result in the perception of a writer's words as the sole possession of this writer. The narrators of tales in the presence of an oral audience could not regard their words as such, since the spoken word is fleeting, the tale can never be repeated in exactly the same way and needs to belong to the community if it is to survive at all. As a genre, autobiography has typically been assigned the function of narrating the life of a public and important individual. By the very nature of textuality, this public life presents the life as more coherent, significant, more ordered than experienced by its subject. The typical autobiography is intended to achieve closure, a solution, an order and meaning which allow the life story to be used as exemplary and didactic for the reading public. In its origins, the autobiography has served as monument to its writing subject, containing the aura of a finished, accomplished life.

Modernism and The Crisis in Literacy

In many ways, the high period of literary and artistic modernism in the first decades of this century can be defined as the pinnacle of literacy.

Indeed, considering the length of its principal works, it would seem foolhardy to regard literary modernism from the perspective of orality. *Pilgrimage, Ulysses, Finnegans Wake, The Making of Americans*—all are too long to be within mnemonic range of the oral person. They are only possible in a print culture. In fact, these texts specifically need an advanced print culture with a body of highly-sophisticated readers, supported by a highly-efficient editing and publishing network. Moreover, the secondary orality which typifies the twentieth century, according to Walter J. Ong or Marshall McLuhan, was not yet in place. Although the telephone was invented in the late nineteenth century, the great days of the radio were only to come in the thirties, and until the late 1920s the early cinema was a silent, purely visual, and consequently international medium. Thus, literary modernism coincided with a period when the interiorization of literacy was at its strongest. Simultaneously, however, writers were growing increasingly frustrated with the commercialization of the printing and distribution industries on which they were dependent. This growing unease with the evolving status of authorship and the changing make-up of the reading audience during the period resulted in the first cracks in this situation of radical literacy.[7]

As a result of these major changes in the book trade and journalism, a commercial, dominant popular literature had emerged virtually simultaneously with the avantgarde. Detective novels, Westerns, Romances were avidly borrowed and read by a new, less-educated public, many of whom were women. By the turn of the century an awareness had grown among many intellectuals of an overabundance of print and textuality. The enormous growth in periodicals and newspapers, and the boom in popular literature had a destabilizing effect on the certainties of men of letters. They felt swamped by reams of worthless print and pushed out of the cultural center. The popular genres formed an important context for the production of the modernists, who always had to confront their own unpopularity. Most readers preferred Ethel M. Dell, Elinor Glyn, or Georgette Heyer to Ezra Pound. Ironically, and significantly, modernist literature, with its attack on closed narrative, the plot, and the traditional character co-existed with the detective novel, the closed narrative par excellence. Attacked in modernist prose, the characteristics of the written medium were here over-developed: analysis, rationality, the love of stable definition. In different ways both detective fiction and modernist literature questioned language, rationality, and common-held views on reality. In fact, they responded to the same complex relationship between orality and literacy. Holquist remarks on the "radical rationality" of the detective story. Authors like Agatha Christie and Dorothy L. Sayers portray a rational detective in an over-signified world constantly in danger of stumbling into the absurd because of an overabundance of meaningful or meaningless clues. The genre calls up the specter of absurdity, only to defeat it in the last chapter where the public (and usually oral) narration of the detective defeats the written confusion, returning it to a single narrative. Detective fiction, thus, papered over these anxieties by a reassuring ending: always, in the end, the culprit is recognized and tried. Modernist literature, on the other hand, faced these questions head on.

The modernists were at one with traditionalist intellectuals in perceiving dangers emanating from this block of popular writing. Q. D. Leavis, for one, noted that the nineteenth century had not known such a great split between popular, best-selling literature and high literature.[8] Stein too remarked on this phenomenon when she discussed English literature as influenced by God and Mammon.[9] In *Everybody's Autobiography* she concluded with an example of modernist anxiety: "Of course in the nineteenth century best sellers were things that go on being, but the difference between one that is and one that is not writing that goes on being read, . . . it is not possible to describe the difference."[10] In her own meandering style, Stein is here discussing the coexistence of popular and high-brow writing. Whereas in the nineteenth century a bestseller could be equated with quality, Stein here addresses modernist worries about a possible confusion between high quality writing "that goes on being read" and the low quality, commercial bestsellers. These developments within the literary field have been characterized in a number of different ways. According to Tuchman and Fortin, the period 1840–1890 saw the development of an ideology about novel writing, to distinguish the masculine high art (realist, naturalist) novel as a genre from the feminine popular romances.[11] A hard-hitting Leavis suggests the "drug habit" of popular fiction resulted in the "herd prejudice" dominating popular writing.[12] A comment by Nancy Cunard testifies to the horror felt by artists at the way the popular press was producing ephemeral text for consumption. Spewing forth text merely to fill a daily paper is felt to be a perversion of textuality:

> An illuminating comment by Americans themselves on their newspapers is that journalists have got to write *something*—the papers have got to be filled every day, you know. . . .[13]

In her cryptic way, Stein also diagnoses the same problem. Because it is acutely tied to context and time, journalism is radically ephemeral and thus perverts the basic function of literacy and textuality, which is to rise above temporality:

Hemingway, on account of his newspaper training, has a false sense of time. One will sooner or later get this falsity of time, and that is why newspapers cannot be read later out of their published time.[14]

Newspaper text is transient, and even threatens the writing talent of an aspiring high-brow writer like Hemingway because of its lack of significance when read out of context. In an essay called "The Novel Demeuble" (1936), Willa Cather draws a very sharp distinction indeed:

In any discussion of the novel, one must make it clear whether one is talking about the novel as a form of amusement, or as a form of art; . . . One does not wish the egg one eats for breakfast, or the morning paper, to be made of the stuff of immortality. The novel manufactured to entertain great multitudes of people must be considered exactly like a cheap soap or a cheap perfume, or cheap furniture. Fine quality is a distinct disadvantage in articles made for great numbers of people who do not want quality but quantity, who do not want a thing that "wears," but who want change,—a succession of new things that are quickly thread-bare and can be lightly thrown away.[15]

Cather's harsh distinction between high culture and mass consumption suggests her horror at popular literature and art, as well as an acute feeling of loss. Popular art and writing have stolen literature and its tradition from literary women and especially literary men. In his autobiography, Richard Aldington reveals his horror at the thought that he might actually have "slipped" into low quality reading.

Now that was really a stroke of good luck. From the obsolete sensationalism of Ainsworth I might have passed to more recent brands, and have ended up as one of those unhappy people who take their intellectual pleasures so sadly with newspapers, horror stories, jig-saw puzzles, and detective novels.[16]

These reactions are indicative of the response by many intellectuals and modernists to the onslaught of popular, ephemeral, insignificant textuality. As a result of the perceived threat by popular fiction, the modernist avantgarde took care to distance itself by becoming more difficult, more hermetic, and by limiting its accessibility to the general public.[17]

Modernism then can be interpreted as a position taken vis a vis a perceived crisis in literacy. A highly self-conscious literary movement, modernism is a stock-taking by the literary and artistic world. Literary modernists confront their now unloved literary tradition and react against the affronts to significant textuality by popular novels and journalism. Edged out themselves from the living interests of society, these modernists retrace their steps, trying to reconnect with the significant texts of the literary tradition. In the programmatic or critical articles by Eliot and Pound we can find a variation on the reflex phenomenon described by Harold Bloom as "anxiety of influence." It is not a fear of the previous tradition, but rather of the popular tradition threatening to unseat "men of letters" from the center of culture.[18]

For male modernists the presence of too much print, and too many different readers to read all this text, proved a determining factor in their avantgardism. As Walter J. Ong indicates, the initial written document in a largely-oral society is an almost magical document, a basis for order which a mainly-conservative society refers to again and again. In the modernist era of ephemeral popular journalism and novels, that kind of mystique was mourned by many (male) modernists. Many of the literary ideals proposed by Eliot, Pound, and others are indicative of this loss. Their theoretical essays aim to reinstate the significant, eternal text, linked to the name of a possessive Author. It is interesting that both Pound and Eliot focus on the metaphor of the trained, accurate scientist for the new poetry they are suggesting. Their anti-romantic, or rather anti-sentimentalist attitude combines with a sublimation of their art as hard, objective, precise, experimental, and scientific. Hence, Eliot talks with contempt of the spilt pot of treacle of Romanticism.[19] Pound's imagism also stresses toughness, direct treatment of the thing, "whether subjective or objective," no more words than strictly needed, and the musical phrase to replace a robotic rhythm of previous poetry.[20] The image of imagism is "that which presents an intellectual and emotional complex in an instant of time," ultimate complexity condensed into a highly significant, small piece of text. Moreover, Pound is attracted by the idea of limiting access to literature, advocating a clear distinction between the scientist and the pupil-scientist. He suggests this categorization in literature, where the "[f]reshmen" "are unfortunately not confined to a definite and recognizable class room."[21] His advice to young poets stresses the craft, the training, the professionalism of poetry. He calls the young poet a candidate like one aspiring to a medieval guild (or about to take an exam), or a neophyte asking to be admitted to a brotherhood.[22] In reaction to the sentimental nineteenth-century poetry of women and clergymen, poetry is business again, a matter for the career poet who undergoes a long training in a tradition. No longer is everybody eligible to write. There is a duty towards the scientific community: "if a man's experiments try out one new rime, or dispense conclusively with one iota of currently accepted nonsense, he is merely playing fair with his colleagues when he chalks up his result."[23] But the real motive behind this astringency is expressed later: "Poetry is *an art and not a pastime*; such a knowledge of technique; of technique of surface and technique of content, that the amateurs will *cease to try to drown out* the masters."[24]

Equally important is a renewed link-up with the literary tradition. Aldington's autobiography, *Life for Life's Sake*, describes a visit to Watts-Dunton, a friend of the late Swinburne, by now an old man himself. His reason for intruding on Watts-Dunton, he says, was

> a sentimental one. Swinburne had known Landor; Landor, Southey; and at one time Southey was very friendly with Shelley. The chain was a short one, and I was never likely to get humanly so near to Shelley again. He was only five hand-clasps away. In my enthusiasm I didn't even stop there, but somehow made the link back to Pope, and through Wycherley and Davenant to Shakespeare. An absurd fancy, but my own.[25]

Even though the visit does not really prove very satisfactory, making Aldington feel like a respectful tourist, the literary line is important for him, so that he can inscribe his authorship into his autobiography. With his usual forcefulness, Pound discusses his interest in the literary tradition as a finding out "once and for all" what remains to be done in poetry. He is thus presenting poetry as a finite closed system, a matter of discovery and experiment, rather than endless creativity.[26]

Significantly, Eliot also combines the scientific metaphor with the concept of impersonality, the depersonalization of a sacrificing poet:

> The progress of an artist is a continual self-sacrifice, a continual extinction of personality.
>
> There remains to define this process of depersonalization and its relation to the sense of tradition. It is in this depersonalization that art may be said to approach the condition of science. I therefore invite you to consider, as a suggestive analogy, the action which takes place when a bit of finely filiated platinum is introduced into a chamber containing oxygen and sulphur dioxide.[27]

The poet is the catalyst for his art, never the expresser of his autobiography, only someone who might use events from his life as the object of his writing.[28] Eliot rejects Wordsworth's autobiographical vision of literature: "'emotion recollected in tranquillity' is an inexact formula."[29] This is replaced by *"significant* emotion," i.e. "emotion which has its life in the poem and not in the history of the poet."[30] Joyce's version of impersonality, the artist paring his fingernails, expresses the same ideal: "The personality of the artist, at first a cry or a cadence or a mood and then a fluid and lambent narrative, finally refines itself out of existence, impersonalizes itself, so to speak."[31]

To the excess of popular, ephemeral, insignificant text, then, many modernist men reacted by grasping control of the professionality of literature, by distancing themselves from the amateurs, elevating the text to the precision instrument of a scientist, by insisting on the unemotionality which was anathema to the sentimental novel, by realigning themselves with the great literary tradition, and by paring down the text to the absolutely meaningful.[32] In various ways, they were searching for the text as significant artistic monument, for the eternal word.

The Position of Women Modernists

As far as modernist women are concerned, no such a perception of modernism as a response to a perceived crisis of literacy can be assumed. In line with Ong's theories, we can suggest that their relationship both to orality and literacy was different. Profound literacy has produced radically visualist societies. As a means of acquiring knowledge, we now favor sight over sound, unlike oral societies. Feminist epistemologists and anthropologists, like Emily Martin and Evelyn Fox Keller, have recently investigated the consequences for women of the visualism of Western epistemologies, suggesting how an ideology has developed that views the female pole as Other, nature, the dark continent where the light of science will eventually penetrate. The viewpoint of the male visile was recorded in the permanence of texts, with women as only the seen object, made up of a visible surface and an unknown interior.[33] Thus society's pervading visualism fostered a perception of men as the writers, the scientists, whereas the seen reality and women became objects of writing. Even though Stein and H. D. had several years of university education, modernist women writers like Richardson, Stein, and H. D. were profoundly aware of how they were circumscribed by male textuality and male narrative plots. For them, ironically, the modernist enterprise was to be different, centered on a basic autobiographical intention, the need strongly and effectively to perform a female presence via textuality. All three authors testify to this profound if ultimately impossible desire to push female presence through the medium of textuality.

In *Bid Me to Live*, for instance, H. D. seems to be aware of the fact that she may be used as material in the autobiography of her male fellow artists. She has her autobiographical character Julia warn off Rico (read: D. H. Lawrence) from employing her as a character.

> But I am aware of your spider-feelers, I am not walking into your net. I am not answering your questions, "What room have you? What room has Vanio?" Not quite so obvious as "Do you sleep together?" I am not telling you of my reactions, or if there were or were not reactions on his part. A nice novel, eh Rico? So Rico, your puppets do not always dance to your pipe.[34]

Concomitantly, women's relationship to the speaking situation also varied drastically from that experienced by male speakers. Richardson, Stein, and H. D. recognized the ideology which dictated that women's talk supported male talk, and did not have an end to itself. In her story of a young, late-Victorian woman making her way through the world, Richardson obsessively returns to the topics of speech and silence, as her autobiographical alter ego Miriam chafes at her ideologically-assigned speaking role. She recognizes how, as a woman, her chat is meant to be merely sociable, smoothing over ruffled conversational feathers, filling silences, keeping the conversation light and unthreatening. Walking with an unusually reticent male interlocutor, Miriam shows herself acutely aware of the usually subservient function of her conversation.

> She tasted a new sense of ease, walking slowly along with this strange man without "making conversation." He was taking her silence for granted. All her experience so far had been of companions whose uneasiness pressed unendurably for speech, and her talking had been done with an irritated sense of the injustice of aspersions on "women's tongues," while no man could endure a woman's silence.[35]

Similarly, noticing angry silences around the dentist's office tea table in *The Tunnel*, the secretary Miriam feels disastrously compelled to fill in these conversational voids.

> There was nothing left now in the room but the echoes. . . . If now she could endure for a moment. But her mind flung hither and thither, seeking with a loathed servility some alien neutral topic. She knew anything she might say with the consciousness of his thoughts in her mind would be resented and slain.[36]

In this attempt to pretend normality, a frustrated Miriam "hit out with all her force, coming against the buttress of silent angry forehead with random speech." The expected happens: she discovers that she has inadvertently been tactless. Her well-intended effort at feminine conversation to deflect a stormy situation degenerates into an angry, impotent Miriam appearing to show off her knowledge of languages.

> "Time flies," responded Mr Hancock grimly. She recoiled exhausted by her effort and quailed under the pang in the midday gas-lit room of realization of the meaning of her words. . . . "'Tempus fugit,' I suppose one ought to say," he said with a little laugh, getting up. "Oui," said Miriam angrily, "le temps s'envole; die Zeit vergeht, in other words."[37]

Miriam's servility, her pandering to male emotions through conversation, betrays her speech, as it leaves the man in full control to retort. Hancock's put-down shows her her verbal impotence. Again, Miriam recognizes that the much propounded feminine ideal of silence serves an ideological function vis a vis an oppressive male presence:

> Opening a volume of Mendelssohn she played, from his point of view, one of the *Songs without Words* quietly into the conversation. The room grew still. She felt herself and Mr. Tremayne as duplicates of Harriett and Gerald, only that she was a very religious, very womanly woman, the ideal wife and mother and he was a bad fast man who wanted to be saved. It was such an easy part to play. She could go on playing it to the end of her life, if he went on in business and made enough money, being a "gracious silence" . . .[38]

The late nineteenth-, early twentieth-century female speaker in a normal household situation could not hold her own against the more competent, authoritative, and confident male speaker. These women modernists' specific relationship to speech and consequently to writing means that the topics of orality and literacy become very definite themes in their texts. In *The Making of Americans* Stein describes the "being" of her alter ego Martha Hersland. She equally presents a young girl straining to project effective speech but failing, as she is a speaker to whom nobody listens:

> This one, and the one I am now beginning describing is Martha Hersland and this is a little story of the acting in her of her being in

her very young living, this one was a very little one then and she
was running and she was in the street and it was a muddy one
and she had an umbrella that she was dragging and she was crying. I will throw the umbrella in the mud, she was saying, she
was very little then, she was just beginning her schooling, I will
throw the umbrella in the mud, she said and no one was near her
and she was dragging the umbrella and bitterness possessed her, I
will throw the umbrella in the mud, she was saying and nobody
heard her, the others had run ahead to get home and they had left
her, I will throw the umbrella in the mud, and there was desperate
anger in her, I have throwed the umbrella in the mud, burst from
her, she had thrown the umbrella in the mud and that was the
end of it all in her. She had thrown the umbrella in the mud and
no one heard her as it burst from her, I have throwed the umbrella
in the mud, it was the end of all that to her.[39]

Equally, in *Her*, H. D. presents one of her many autobiographical personae caught in a psychological crisis which is to a large extent a linguistic one. In this novel, a grammatical complication fronts the linguistic difficulty for women in becoming self-sufficient, competent
speakers in a language which offers no significant place for them in its
grammar. Her Gart's predicament is most evident when she attempts
to "speech" herself, to say in conversation who she is. Grammar
denies her as a speaker: "I am Her" is a logical quandary.[40] Grammar is
biased against women: to try to speak as a woman, to say I, results in
contradiction. H. D. formulates a proto-Lacanian awareness of alienation and absence in speech with reference to the practical experiences of the woman speaker. By saying who she is, Her is merely saying she is not: I am Her, meaning I am someone else. Self-identification
is here utterly impossible, a dilemma the more poignant in the speaking situation, in the absence of capital letters. Hermione's final name,
Gart, is equally ludicrous and, since it is used for a version of the past
Hilda Doolittle, this indicates the extent to which H. D. saw herself as
a stranger, an outsider: "She said, 'I am Hermione Gart,' but Her Gart
was not that."[41] Not unexpectedly given this naming problem,
Hermione suffers from a lack of definition. Her identity crisis is also
described in images of fluidity, as "drowned." Her self-definition is
too "slippery" and her fingers "slipped" off her sense of identity.[42]
Her's slippery self is almost over-determined in the text, since her
first name is constantly in danger of slippage, of disappearing into
the grammar of a sentence. She is a speaking subject constantly threatened by a take-over by her own speech; a female speaker who is

absent as she attempts to speak her presence. Because she cannot
define herself grammatically, cannot define a separate space with a
clear-cut edge for herself, Her has no clear access to language, and
hence to reality. She cannot distinguish clear boundaries; the difference
between herself and what surrounds her. Almost a Kristevan "bab-
bler," H. D.'s autobiographical persona flows into reality, and can no
longer make distinctions. Defending George during a quarrel with
her mother, "Hermione heard Hermione speaking, saying something
out of a play, words had been written for her, she was repeating words
that had been written."[43] Even though she rejects being a "foul parrot"
to her mother's accusations, Her is not present while speaking, not
in charge of her own words. In fact, women's social function prevents
them from speaking their own words, as they have to feed a polite,
sociable conversation. In *Her*, social small talk is bewildering to
Hermione's reeling mind. Part of Chapter IV and the greater part of
Chapter V are devoted to the tactful conversation at Nellie Thorpe's
and the meeting with Fayne. The formal conversation is experienced
as limiting by Hermione, and by the silent Fayne Rabb.[44] Having to
explain why she failed her exams to this company, Her finds it hard to
"be there" in conversation. She does not perform knowingly as a
speaker, and a few pages later nearly falters under their questions
which are like a "Tibetan prayer wheel":

> She did not actually hear the words she uttered. . . . She went on
> talking, not knowing what she said, she seemed to explain herself
> not knowing why she did it. . . . (I didn't know I had said any-
> thing) . . . Words went round, had odd ways of tacking off, bil-
> lowing out, full sail.[45]

Under intense pressure, the autobiographical persona of *Bid Me To Live*
Julia, like Her, is not even sure whether she is speaking herself, or
whether she is enunciating dialogue written by a playwright: "and
speaking, as if from outside, like someone in a play, Julia heard Julia
speaking." This feeling of being controlled by outside events returns
again and again.[46] Bella even acts badly, "as if she were bent on speaking
her lines, this particular set of words, she flung out, tonelessly," "as if
she were speaking lines, not very well stressed, lines she had learned,
knew perfectly." She is compared to a "foreign exotic, bright parrot"
uttering toneless words put into its head, once again the epitome of the
absent woman speaker, not voicing her own lines.[47]

   Dorothy Richardson reacts to the absence of the competent
woman speaker in charge of her own words. In her essay "the Reality of

Feminism" she tries to recover speech for women. Women are located at the origins of civilization: they "invented" social life, their speech a powerful tool to keep their family together:

> Woman was a differentiated social human being earlier than man. The "savage" woman who first succeeded in retaining her grown son at her side, invented social life. Up to the era of machinery, *i.e.*, during the agricultural and civic centuries, the home was the centre of productive service.[48]

Richardson is turning the tables, proving that women have only recently been alienated from what before was their authentic invention, the ability to knit social life together through everyday speech. They have been reduced to servile talk, only to flatter, support, and sustain male conversation and the masculine self-image: "Henceforth her sole asset was her sex, her sole means of expression her personal relationship to some specific male—father, brother, husband or son. She lived on her power to 'charm.'" Richardson's primal woman seems Iocasta in reverse, a mother who manages to tie her son into society productively via speech, rather than lose him from society through her silent suicide as in the Greek original. Richardson argues that retaining the grown son in the female atmosphere is the single action which originated civilization. Her presentation of the oral sphere of productively and truly talking women was a reversal of the many Freudian myths doing the rounds among her contemporaries. Consequently, Richardson advises women to advance into the world, "doing the world's housekeeping," in order to socialize and feminize the public world.[49] For these three authors, literary modernism is not primarily a defense of an age-old literary history against omnipresent literate diarrhoea. As relative newcomers to the profession of authors, they could view the literary text in a positive way, as a certain liberation from their non-presence in the oral situation, where, like children, women were meant to be seen not heard.

Modernist Autobiography by Women Writers

For women modernists, then, the literary text was not in danger, but offered instead a double attraction. The isolation typical of the written situation allowed for escape from a position of weakness as woman speakers. Thus, their modernism centered on what was in fact an autobiographical pursuit, an attempt to push the experience of living as a woman through into text. But since they did not want to disappear behind their own textuality, Richardson, Stein, and H. D. in fact offered perverse readings of the genre of autobiography. They developed textual life stories which paradoxically refuse closure. Richardson's autobiographical *Pilgrimage* radically rejects closure, its two-thousand pages never bringing her persona Miriam to a moment of rest from which the previous life can be defined and characterized. Instead, the text proceeds slowly, focusing not on definition and story line but on the minute evocation of the conversations and situations in which Miriam takes part. In a review of Richardson's novels for *The Little Review*, May Sinclair stressed the lack of plot or drama in the first three novels and referred to complaints of formlessness.

> Nothing happens. It is just life going on and on. It is Miriam Henderson's stream of consciousness going on and on. And in neither is there any grossly discernible beginning or middle or end.[50]

Both Stein and Richardson offer a metaphor for autobiography which underlines the unending, continuous ideal; the impossible rejection of closure. Stein's two explicitly autobiographical texts make great play of her habit of copying and recopying her own text, of the fact she never threw any text away. They also offer a prolonged discussion of repetition and repeating, the retelling and reperformance of past events, which make them present to herself again. Her typically Steinian, prosaic metaphor for this type of modernist autobiography was "nutting."

> It is like nutting. You go over the same ground ten or a dozen times and each time you see nuts that you had not taken. The pleasure is in the eye seeing them but if you did not take them there would be no pleasure in the eye seeing them . . .[51]

Stein's very oral style is used to underline the presence of the autobiographical subject, engaged in a conversation with the reader, performing the past for the fantasy of the audience. According to her daughter, H. D. offers a similar image of autobiography as open-ended, never finished yet strongly present:

> "Like working on a sampler," she confided, years later. "So many stitches and just so many rows, day after day. If I miss even one day, I drop a stitch and lose the pattern and I feel I'm never going to find it again."[52]

Richardson too shows her awareness of orality and aurality and her delighted perception of the writing situation as a boost for the female individual. She presents us with the life story of a consciousness in being, a communicative autobiography evoking the interrelating of a young woman and her surroundings. Richardson's metaphor for writing is that of a creative environment.

> Here, amidst the dust-filmed ivy leaves and the odour of damp, decaying wood, was *the centre of her life.* The rickety little table was one now with its predecessors, the ink-stained table under the attic roof at Tansley Street, first made sacred by the experience of setting marginal commentaries upon Lahitte's bombastic outpourings; and the little proud new bureau at Flaxman's, joy for her eyes . . . and, later, depth, *an enveloping presence in whose company alone,* with an article for George Taylor being written on the extended flap, *she could escape both the unanswerable challenge of the strident court* and the pervading presence of Selina, and *becoming,* . . . the permanent reminder amongst easy and fluctuating felicities, of *one that remained,* so long as its prices were faithfully paid, both secure and unfathomable.[53]

This is not writing which offers clarity, insight, understanding. Instead, Miriam recognizes other ideals as essential to her writing: the feeling at the center of her own life, of writing as a comforting presence, as company, as a protective environment for the writer, allowing her to escape a wearying sociability. Again, Dorothy Richardson's essay, "On Punctuation," expresses unusual ideals for her writing. She follows the male modernist rejection of commercialized, mechanized print and the alienated reading that goes along with it. But this modernist attitude is combined with a specific goal, a renewed access to an early textuality which is presented as almost oral:

> Only to patient reading will come forth the charm concealed in ancient manuscripts. Deep interest there must be, or sheer necessity, to keep eye and brain at their task of scanning a text that moves along unbroken, save by an occasional full-stop. But the reader who persists finds presently that his task is growing easier. He is winning familiarity with the writer's style, and is able to punctuate unconsciously as he goes . . . It is at this point that he beings to be aware of the charm that has been sacrificed by the systematic separation of phrases. He finds himself *listening.* Reading through the ear as well as through the eye. And while in any way of reading the ear plays its part, unless it is most cunningly attacked it co-operates, in our modern way, scarcely at all. It is

left behind. For as light is swifter than sound so is the eye swifter
than the ear. But in the slow, attentive reading demanded by
unpunctuated texts, the faculty of hearing has its chance, is
enhanced until the text *speaks* itself.[54]

This is different and paradoxical ideal for textuality, not the closed,
clear, analytic, and permanent text, but a text which speaks to a hearing
reader, and consequently acquires a presence. In a different, stylistic
way, Stein's autobiographical texts, *The Autobiography of Alice B. Toklas*,
Everybody's Autobiography, and *The Making of Americans* evoke the same
ideal. Her metaphor for her writing, the "nutting" which allows her to
go over the same ground again and again and delightedly to discover
new nuts, belongs to a Steinian preference for presenting her life in
Paris and her return to America in its now-moments rather than as the
narration of past events. Combining this theme with a highly oral-
sounding style, this is the talking Stein, addressing an audience as if it
were hearing her in the present rather than reading at a later moment.
Nowhere is this more obvious than in *The Making of Americans*, where
the autobiographical facts move to the background to feature Stein in
the process of speaking her autobiography. Unlike the traditional ideal
author, she does not present us with a finished, edited, authoritative
text, but instead performs the process of composing, "writing everything as I am learning anything."

> Every one is not a whole one, now I am waiting a little for an
> inspiration about this thing to explain completely my feeling. I
> will now soon be telling my feeling about men and women, . . . I
> am writing everything as I am learning anything. I am writing
> everything as I am learning anything, as I am feeling anything in
> any one as being, as I am having a realization of any one, I am
> saying everything then as I am full up then with a thing, with
> anything of any one.[55]

Presenting herself in the process of "nutting" her own life story, Stein
the modernist is in fact Stein the speaker attempting to perform in a
written medium, to crash a now-moment into a medium that is by definition preterite.

In a different, but comparable, way, H. D. breaches convention to
achieve a similarly perverse textuality, stretched in the direction of
speech. The most pregnant moment in this regard is the ultimate
Writing which her seer-persona witnesses in *Tribute to Freud*, the vision
of hieroglyphic writing on the wall of her hotel room, "dim light on

shadow, not shadow on light. It was a silhouette cut of light, not shadow." First there are static pictures of a bust, goblet, or cup, a "spirit-lamp," followed by a dynamic writing "drawn or written by the same hand." The narrator is unsure whether the writing is projected by her-self or comes from outside herself. While she turns to Bryher, the mov-ing picture acquires an aural-aspect, a sort of pictorial "buzzing," like ants or small people.[56] Not only a highly significant, magical text, the visionary writing in this scene is, paradoxically, also writing-in-action, writing in performance with the audience actually present. For H. D. the writing sought in her visionary project is not a static, defined text, but a dynamic text, stretched towards orality and radically present. Typically, when she expresses her fears of punishment for her visionary writing, this is associated with the spoken situation, and not expressed as a sup-pression of the written word. Struggling through a visionary crisis by means of autobiographical remembering, the narrator of *The Gift* has recurring nightmares combining her terror in the Blitz with the fear of annihilation as a female speaker:

> The snake has sprung at me and . . . I shout through the snake-face, that is fastened at the side of my mouth, . . . The snake falls off. . . . He has bitten the side of my mouth. I will never get well, I will die soon of the poison of this horrible snake. . . . How ugly my mouth is with a scar, and the side of my face seems stung to death. But no, "You are not stung to death," says dark Mary, who is enor-mous and very kind . . .[57]

Gertrude Stein, Dorothy Richardson, and H. D., then, show a marked interest in the autobiographical position or, more broadly, in self-writ-ing: an interest which is not generally regarded as part of modernist aesthetics. In fact, they redefined the genre of autobiography, develop-ing modernist styles and themes which centered around the wish for a permanent and strong presence almost physically facing the reader. In a different relationship with both orality and literacy, their need to express self-performance by way of autobiography resulted in an alternative female accent on the modernist revolution in language. All three indi-cated a strong awareness of the psycho-social alienation experienced by women in the speaking situation. Absent women speakers like Miriam Henderson, Martha Hersland, and "Hilda" from The Gift are poignantly aware of, even obsessed with, their inability to hold their own and to feel truly present in the oral sphere. In this context, writing is felt to benefit women. If the speaking situation results in a woman's absence, then the absence of a male interlocutor allows for a woman's presence. Surprisingly, but consistently, what Richardson, Stein, and H. D. appreciate in the medium is the feeling of self-presence it offers. As such, the writing these autobiographers aspire to is a perverse textuality, located on the boundary between the written and the spoken medium. As she paradoxically attempts to incorporate characteristics like presence, immediacy, and performance into the text, the woman speaker/writer is attempting to come forward in her text, to turn her readers into an audience and make them listen. Their modernist goals are to develop writing as a strong presence, so much so that you can almost hear it. Their textual transgression in favor of women's presence, then, allies them with the genre of autobiography. As autobiographies *Pilgrimage, Bid Me to Live, Her, The Gift, Everybody's Autobiography,* and that quirky text *The Making of Americans* reject closure, and are specifically shaped to keep the autobiographical narrator alive and in front of her audience. Their metaphors for writing highlight a modernist redefinition of autobiography which is in fact a rejection of the "aura of accomplished death" of the typical male autobiography. By reinterpreting the genre from this perspective, Stein, H. D., and Richardson, managed to make autobiography into the never-finishing performance of the female self, and not the definitive, significant male life-history.

Notes

1. Walter J. Ong, S. J., *Interfaces of the Word: Studies in the Evolution of Consciousness and Culture* (Ithaca and London: Cornell University Press, 1977), pp. 232–33.

2. Walter J. Ong, S. J., *Orality and Literacy: The Technologizing of the Word,* New Accents, gen. ed. Terence Hawkes (1982; London and New York: Methuen, 1991), pp. 32, 101.

3. Ong, *Orality and Literacy,* p. 72.

4. In an informal conversation, subjects were asked to isolate from a series of words the word that does not belong, a game demanding abstract thinking and analysis. Luria showed that this type of thinking was not used by oral subjects—they thought situationally: if items, like log, hammer, hatchet, and saw belonged to the same work situation they were all "alike," as a 25-year-old illiterate peasant said (Luria 1976, p. 56 quoted by Ong 1991, p. 51— *Cognitive Development: Its Cultural and Social Foundations* was only published in Russian in 1974 and in English in 1976).

5. Ong, *Orality and Literacy,* p. 179.

6. Karl J. Weintraub, "Autobiography and Historical Consciousness," *Critical Inquiry* 1, no. 4 (June 1975), p. 824.

7. From the 1830s, and especially after 1850, changes in the Victorian publishing system and late Victorian journalism had important effects on the practicalities of writing. From the middle of the nineteenth century, periodicals and journals were boosted by the disappearance of three forms of taxation, the Advertisement Tax (1853), the Newspaper Stamp Duty (1855), and the Paper Duty (1861). Bonham-Carter refers to a real explosion in the last quarter of the nineteenth century: "between 1870 and 1900 the number of newspapers rose from 1390 to 2448, while magazines increased from 626 to 2446" (Victor Bonham-Carter, *From the Introduction of Printing Until the Copyright Act 1911* (London: The Society of Authors, 1978), pp. 175–76. The real boom occurred in popular journalism, with the invention of modern, popular entertainment papers like *Tit-Bits*, started by George Newnes in 1880–1881, *Answers to Correspondents* by Alfred Harmsworth (1888), or *Pearson's Weekly* by Sir Cyril Arthur Pearson (1890). With their text organized in bite-size "tit-bits," these were reading matter for the newly literate. A similar rationalization of publishing houses during the 1830s meant that they started to specialize in certain areas like fiction or travel. Inventions like ink-blocking on cloth during the 1840s had allowed the publication of cheap six-shilling one-volume novels, another factor boosting the importance of the poor, less educated market (Q. D. Leavis, *Fiction and the Reading Public* (London: Chatto and Windus, 1932; reprint, London: Bellew Publishing Company, 1990), p. 152.

8. Leavis, pp. 169–70.

9. Gertrude Stein, "What is English Literature?," in *Lectures in America*, with a new introduction by Wendy Steiner, p. 11–59 (New York: Random House, 1935; reprinted by Beacon Press, 1985; London: Virago, 1988, offset from Beacon Press with introduction), p. 12.

10. Gertrude Stein, *Everybody's Autobiography* with an introduction by Janet Hobhouse (New York: Random House, 1937; London: William Heinemann, 1938; reprint London: Virago, 1985, offset from William Heinemann, ed.), pp. 224–25.

11. Tuchman and Fortin, p. 3.

12. Leavis, pp. 7, 67.

13. Nancy Cunard, "The American Moron and the American of Sense— Letters on the Negro," in *The Gender of Modernism: A Critical Anthology*, ed. Bonnie Kime Scott (Bloomington and Indianapolis: Indiana University Press, 1990), p. 79.

14. Gertrude Stein, "A Transatlantic Interview 1946," chap. in *A Primer for the Gradual Understanding of Gertrude Stein*, ed. by Robert Bartlett Haas (Los Angeles: Black Sparrow Press, 1971).

15. Willa Cather, "The Novel Demeuble," in *Not Under Forty* (London, Toronto, Melbourne and Sydney: Cassell, 1936), pp. 47–48.

16. Richard Aldington, *Life for Life's Sake: A Book of Reminiscences* (New York: Viking, 1941; reprint, London: Cassell, 1968), p. 38.

17. Michael Holquist, "Whodunit and Other Questions: Metaphysical Detective Stories in Post-war Fiction," *New Literary History*, vol. 3, no. 1 (Autumn 1971), p. 137.

18. However, in their belated efforts to live off their pen, serious writers like H. G. Wells, called a "mass-manufacturer of words" (Bonham-Carter 1978, p. 180) or modernists like Djuna Barnes and Dorothy Richardson, found themselves producing a similarly large number of essays and reviews, actually increasing the sea of ephemeral text.

19. See for instance, Thomas Stearns Eliot, "Tradition and the Individual Talent," in *Selected Essays*, 2nd revised and enlarged edition (London: Faber and Faber, 1951, first published in 1919), p. 18.

20. Ezra Pound, "A Retrospect," in *Literary Essays of Ezra Pound*, ed. with an Introduction by T. S. Eliot (London: Faber and Faber, 1954), pp. 3–4.

21. Pound, p. 6.

22. Pound, pp. 5, 6.

23. Pound, p. 10.

24. Pound, p. 10, italics mine.

25. Aldington, p. 44.

26. Pound, p. 11.

27. Eliot, p. 17.

28. Eliot, p. 18.

29. Eliot, p. 21.

30. Eliot, p. 22.

31. James Joyce, *A Portrait of the Artist as a Young Man*, Triad Panther Book (1916; London, etc.: Granada, 1981), pp. 194–95.

32. Not all male modernists reacted in this way, however. One alternative solution to the excess of print awash around the writer and reader of the period was Bob Brown's invention of a telex-like machine which would, amazingly, speed up print in front of the reader's eyes and which required a pared-down, dynamic style of writing, calling his new poems "readies" in parallel with "talkies" (Ford, 1975, p. 309).

33. Evelyn Fox Keller, "From Secrets of Life to Secrets of Death," in *Body/Politics and the Discourses of Science*, eds. Mary Jacobus, Evelyn Fox Keller, Sally Shuttleworth (New York and London: Routledge, 1990), pp. 177–92. Emily Martin, "Science and Women's Bodies: Forms of Anthropological Knowledge," in *Body/Politics and the Discourses of Science*, pp. 69–83.

34. H. D., *Bid Me To Live* with a new introduction by Helen McNeil and an afterword by Perdita Schaffner (New York: Grove Press, 1960; reprint, New York: Black Swan Books, 1983; reprint, London: Virago Press, 1984), p. 164.

35. Dorothy Richardson, *Backwater* in *Pilgrimage 1*, including *Pointed Roofs*, *Backwater*, *Honeycomb* with an Introduction by Gill Hanscombe and a Foreword by Dorothy Richardson (1979; reprint, Virago Modern Classics, no. 18, London: Virago, 1989), p. 219.

36. Dorothy Richardson, *The Tunnel* in *Pilgrimage 2* including *The Tunnel*, *Interim* with an Introduction by Gill Hanscombe, Virago Modern Classics, no. 18 (London: Virago, 1979a), p. 171.

37. Richardson, *The Tunnel*, p. 171.

38. Richardson, *The Tunnel*, p. 27.

39. Gertrude Stein, *The Making of Americans: Being a History of a Family's Progress* (Paris: Contact Edition, 1925; reprint, London: Peter Owen, 1968, written 1906–1908), p. 388.

40. H. D., *Her*, with a new introduction by Helen McNeil and an afterword by Perdita Schaffner (New York: New Direction Books, as HERmione, 1981; reprint, London: Virago Press, 1984), p. 3.

41. H. D., *Her*, p. 3.

42. H. D., *Her*, p. 4.

43. H. D., *Her*, pp. 94–95.

44. H. D., *Her*, pp. 50–51.

45. H. D., *Her*, p. 54.

46. H. D., *Bid Me to Live*, pp. 48, 50, 63. In her psychological breakdown, Hermione has the same theatrical awareness: "Words said over and over, over and over. They were a stock company playing in a road show, words over and over. All very well cast for the parts, can't get out of this show, it's too fu-uunny" (H. D., *Her*, p. 40).

47. H. D., *Bid Me To Live*, pp. 98, 101.

48. Dorothy Richardson, "The Reality of Feminism." Review of *Towards a Sane Feminism* by Wilma Meikle, *Woman and the Church*, by Rev. B. H. Streeter,

Woman in the Apostolic Church, by T. B. Allworthy, *Woman's Effort*, by A. E. Metcalf in *The Gender of Modernism*, p. 402, originally published in *Ploughshare*, n.s. 2, no. 8 (September 1917), pp. 241–46.

49. Richardson, "The Reality of Feminism," p. 402.

50. May Sinclair, "The Novels of Dorothy Richardson," *The Little Review* 5, no. 12 (April 1918), p. 6.

51. Stein, *Everybody's Autobiography*, p. 111.

52. Perdita Schaffner, "Sketch of H. D.: The Egyptian Cat," in *Hedylus* by H. D. (Manchester: Carcanet New Press; Redding Ridge, CT: Black Swan Books, 1980), p. 145.

53. Dorothy Richardson, Dimple Hill, in *Pilgrimage* 4 including *Oberland*, *Dawn's Left Hand*, *Clear Horizon*, *Dimple Hill*, *March Moonlight*, with an Introduction by Gill Hanscombe, Virago Modern Classics, no. 18 (London: Virago, 1979), pp. 523–24.

54. Dorothy Richardson, "About Punctuation," in *The Gender of Modernism*, p. 414.

55. Stein, *The Making of Americans*, p. 540.

56. H. D., *Tribute to Freud*, with an Introduction by Peter Jones (New York: Pantheon Books 1956; reprint Carcanet Press, 1971), pp. 50–53.

57. H. D., *The Gift*, ed. Griselda Ohanessian, with a new introduction to the American edition by Perdita Schaffner (New York: New Directions, 1982; London: Virago Press, 1984), p. 57.

10

Silent Witness: Memory and Omission in Natalia Ginzburg's Family Sayings

Judith Woolf

I have written only what I remember, so if this book is read as a chronicle it could be objected that it is full of gaps. Even though I am dealing with real life, I think it ought to be read as a novel; in other words, without asking either more or less of it than a novel can give.[1]

—Natalia Ginzburg

In her study, *Fascism in Popular Memory: The Cultural Experience of the Turin Working Class*, Luisa Passerini alerts the reader to the symbolic structuring frequently given to recollected events in the oral testimonies which form a major part of her evidence and comments that:

The order in which memories are recalled undermines the notion that the chronological order is inherently "natural" and automatic. It underlines the fact that all stories are based on conventions. In written autobiography, in fact, reflection, a form of active engagement with one's own past, predominates.[2]

Natalia Ginzburg's preface to *Family Sayings*, her account of her family's experiences during the Fascist period and its aftermath, makes it plain that this engagement with the past may be expressed not only through what is related but also, and just as significantly, through what is left unsaid. Ginzburg's book, one of the most intriguing texts by

Italy's greatest post-war woman writer, radically questions the conventions of written autobiography and with them the underlying assumption that every life has, or indeed even is, a story. Instead of attempting to guarantee the truth or reality of the narrative by asserting, whether explicitly or implicitly, that what we are being told is the story of her life, Ginzburg prefaces her book, in which she is both character and narrator, with the disclaimer: "This is not in fact my story but rather, in spite of gaps and omissions, the story of my family." While she claims to have invented nothing, she warns us that "the memory is unreliable" and that in any case, "There are . . . many things which I remember but have omitted to write about, including many which concern me directly."[3] Far from writing the self, Ginzburg almost appears to be trying to write herself out of the record. A text so full of voluntary and involuntary omissions , she suggests, can only be read as a work of fiction.

This essay considers the importance of silence and omission in Ginzburg's *Family Sayings* as well as some of the questions these issues raise for our reading of autobiography, especially female autobiography. In the course of the argument I call as witnesses the historians Luisa Passerini and Susan Zuccotti, the scientist and autobiographer Rita Levi-Montalcini, and also the novelist Virginia Woolf, who grew up subject to pressures that in many ways resembled those in Ginzburg's own family but who found a very different solution to the problem of transforming the raw stuff of memory into fiction. All these kinds of narrative, as Passerini reminds us, are forms of active engagement with the past in which storytelling conventions are used, consciously or unconsciously, to impose a symbolic pattern on events. This is just as true of the seemingly factual genres of history and autobiography as it is of fiction or oral reminiscence.

Like Passerini's informants, Ginzburg begins her book not with her birth or her earliest memory but with an apparently insignificant little scene which encapsulates what are for her the dominant features of family life. This scene, imprinted through countless repetitions in which her father angrily scolds his children for their clumsiness at table, establishes not only the father's intolerant and dominating character and the highly ritualized nature of family interaction, but also the voice and the viewpoint through which Ginzburg will control her text, a child's remembered viewpoint, powerless and partly incomprehending but sharply and coldly observant, communicated by a detached adult voice. Unlike Woolf's *To the Lighthouse*, which is concerned with exploring the inner life of the characters, what is thought and felt but left unsaid, Ginzburg's book gives us an alarmingly clear vision of what lies on the surface, implicitly claiming that it is only by studying the surface, the irrational but stylized ticks and quirks of speech and behavior, that we can understand how the family really functions.

The book's title, *Lessico Famigliare*, literally means family lexicon, and Ginzburg uses this lexicon, a shared private language which codifies a comic private mythology, to set up the protective and threatening figures of her father and mother, who tower over the world of her childhood like Easter Island statues, grotesque and larger than life. These parental figures derive much of their confidence and power from interpreting their own lives in terms of a collection of stories and sayings which changes only by accretion and from which nothing is ever lost. The Easter Islanders ceased to make statues when the trees ran out; having deforested their island, they could no longer transport their vast totems from the quarries where they were carved. In her 1951 essay "Silence," Ginzburg suggests that for her own generation the words have run out:

> Those ponderous words that served our parents are a currency that has been withdrawn and which no one accepts. And we realize that the new words have no value, that we can buy nothing with them . . . They are no use for writing books, for linking us with someone we love, for saving a friend.[4]

Those "meagre, barren words" are the vocabulary of the neo-realist novel, in which young Italian writers, among them Ginzburg herself, expressed their disillusionment with all rhetoric, the tyrannical bombast of the Fascist regime under which they had grown up, the utopian propaganda of the divided left for whose resistance movement many of them had fought, and the obsolete personal language of drama and emotion, the "words from old opera libretti," which seemed to have no place in the grey post-war world. The friend that this new impoverished language failed to save was her fellow writer Cesare Pavese, whose greatest novels express a vision of life at once lyrical and almost totally bleak and whose suicide in 1950 is described in *Family Sayings*. Ginzburg was to retain from the doctrinaire austerity of neo-realism both a prose style of stripped-down simplicity and a life-long preoccupation with the subject of non-communication between wives and husbands, parents and children, would-be lovers who find that their love is too anemic to survive. In *Family Sayings*, though, she returns to the rich and comic private language of her childhood, ironically adopting a version of her mother's storytelling role as transmitter of the family lexicon.

The task of the autobiographer is often to make public a version of what has hitherto been private, known only to an intimate circle. Ginzburg, on the contrary, gives us a private and deheroized version of events that have become part of twentieth-century European history. Ginzburg's family sheltered the socialist leader Filippo Turati during his escape from Italy. Her brother Mario was involved in what has become known as the Ponte Tresa affair; caught with his friend Sion Segre attempting to smuggle anti-fascist literature over the Swiss border, he escaped by throwing himself fully clothed into an icy river and swimming back across the border to safety and exile. The mass arrests and anti-semitic newspaper articles that followed were the first indication that Mussolini's shift towards a closer alliance with Hitler would lead a few years later to the Racial Laws which stripped Italian Jews of their civil rights. Ginzburg's husband Leone, a leader of the armed resistance, was tortured to death in Regina Coeli prison in Rome during the German occupation. If we turn to the index of Susan Zuccotti's *The Italians and the Holocaust*, these names are all there: Turati, Filippo; Segre Amar, Sion; Ginzburg, Leone; and with them, in what amounts to a roll call of the opponents of Fascism, disproportionately many of them Jewish or half Jewish, are Ginzburg's father Giuseppe Levi , her brothers Alberto, Gino, and Mario, her sister Paola with her husband Adriano Olivetti, and Natalia Ginzburg herself.

It is illuminating to compare Zuccotti's version of the rescue of Turati with Ginzburg's account in *Family Sayings*. For Zuccotti, this is a stirring tale of courage and daring, and she sets the scene accordingly.

> Late in 1926, young Carlo Rosselli was involved in an adventure worthy of a Hollywood film. Filippo Turati, former member of Parliament and highly esteemed elder statesman in the moderate wing of the Socialist Party, was clearly in danger. When his life-long companion Anna Kuliscioff died the previous year, Fascist thugs threatened violence at her funeral. Since then, they had continued to harass Turati. The old man was too weak and ill to survive a beating. Because he was unable to obtain a passport, his friends persuaded him to emigrate secretly[5]

The name Carlo Rosselli is one which still has a powerful resonance for Italian readers. The founder of the anti-fascist organization Justice and Liberty, he became not only a hero of the resistance movement but also one of its chief martyrs when, in 1937, he was assassinated in France along with his younger brother Nello, by French fascist killers hired by the Mussolini regime.

As news of their murders flashed around the world, more than 200,000 people accompanied their hearse to Père Lachaise cemetery in Paris.[6]

Zuccotti draws with straightforwardly unquestioning admiration on the legend of the Rosselli brothers, all the more so because a book about the Holocaust, even one concerned with Italy where more than eighty-five percent of the small Jewish population survived, needs all the heroes it can find. This is an important factor in her account of the rescue of Turati. After describing how the fugitive was hidden in a number of safe houses, including the home of Ginzburg's family in Turin, Zuccotti gives the story the appropriate dramatic ending for "an adventure worthy of a Hollywood film":

> One icy night in December 1926, Adriano Olivetti . . . met Turati in Turin and drove him down twisting mountain roads, avoiding a number of road blocks, to Savona on the Ligurian coast. There he waited five days for a motor launch, in the company of Carlo Rosselli, Ferruccio Parri (first prime minister of Italy after the war), and Sandro Pertini . . . Finally, in a winter storm, with waves breaking over the boat, no stars in the sky, and a faulty compass, they struggled toward freedom. After twelve harrowing hours, they found themselves in Corsica.[7]

By contrast, Ginzburg adheres strictly to her promise to write "only what I remember," giving us a private and comic view of events through the eyes of a ten-year-old child, frustrated in her longing to give away the exciting secret that the guest she has been told to call Paolo Ferrari is really Filippo Turati.

> Lucio said to me, without much interest, "There's a man with a beard in your house who slips away from the living-room as soon as I get here."
>
> "Yes," I told him, "Paolo Ferrari!"
>
> I was longing for him to ask me some more questions, but Lucio didn't ask anything else. He was banging on the wall with a hammer to hang up a picture he had done and brought me as a present. It was a picture of a train . . .
>
> I told him, "Don't bang the hammer like that! He's old, he's not well, he's in hiding!"

"Who?"

"Paolo Ferrari!"

"Look at the tender," said Lucio. "Look, do you see, I've even painted the tender."[8]

Her family, far from being presented as selfless and intrepid, are shown as absurdly inefficient conspirators , blithely unconscious of the scale of the risks they are running. Indeed, Ginzburg's mother rapidly comes to remember Turati's stay simply as an agreeable social event.

> Paolo Ferrari was safe in Paris; but by now everyone in our house had got bored with calling him Ferrari so they called him by his real name. My mother used to say, "He was such a nice man! I really enjoyed having him here."[9]

Ginzburg excises from the story everything that she was unaware of at the time, including something she discovered shortly afterwards, that one of the "two or three men in raincoats" who arrived with Adriano Olivetti to drive Turati to the coast was Carlo Rosselli himself. His named presence would have brought an incongruous note of heroism into the story. If we cut from *Family Sayings* to Rosselli's defense of his actions at his subsequent trial, we can see just how careful Ginzburg is not to sound this heroic note.

> "A Rosselli secretly hosted at Pisa the dying Mazzini, an exile in his own land. It was logical that another Rosselli, later, would make an effort to save from the Fascist fury one of the most noble and unselfish spirits of his country."[10]

This is rhetoric of the most impressive kind, an attempt to testify to a truth that is being warped beyond recognition by the distorting glass of Fascist ideology, but it is rhetoric none the less, a political speech in the context of a political trial. Ginzburg, by contrast, tells us a quite different truth: that historic events are not necessarily experienced as historic by those who live through them. As we have seen from Zuccotti's account, this is a kind of truth that historians, by the very nature of their trade, are seldom able to show us, and it justifies Ginzburg's scrupulousness in recording "only what I remember." To the eyes of the watching child, her parents show no signs that they are rising to the challenge of what Zuccotti describes as a Hollywood drama; even the confusingly transparent lies they tell her about Turati's identity correspond to earlier parental lies. It is only when Adriano Olivetti arrives with the "men in raincoats" that for a moment she sees the commonplace transformed.

> Adriano was starting to lose his hair and now had a square, almost bald head ringed with frizzy blond curls. That evening, his face and his thinning hair seemed to be swept by a gust of wind. His eyes were frightened, resolute and happy. I was to see those eyes two or three times in my life. They were the eyes he had when he was helping someone to escape , when there was danger and someone to be taken to safety.[11]

This wordless glimpse, all the more vivid because it also contains the child's ordinary perception of Adriano, will later prove to be a key moment in the structure of the book.

In Ginzburg's account of the Ponte Tresa affair and its aftermath, there is an even more striking omission. Again, we are shown a view of events from inside the family group. Having already set up her brother Mario as a far from heroic figure, violently and irrationally quarrelsome and with a tendency to sulk, Ginzburg now demonstrates the protective power of the family lexicon by foregrounding her mother's idiosyncratic reactions to his famous exploit and its consequences. With one son in exile and her husband and another son in jail as suspected conspirators, Lidia Levi shields herself from the potentially intolerable pressure of threatening circumstances by making a comforting catchphrase out of some comic and peripheral aspect of them. Thinking of Mario's dangerous swim across the turbulent River Tresa, in which he was nearly shot by an Italian border guard and barely escaped drowning:

> My mother, sounding happy, astonished and scared, kept clasping her hands and saying,
>
> "Right into the water with his coat on!"[12]

While it is important to remember that Ginzburg is here giving us a deliberately-stylized version of the memories of a daughter still in her teens, there is evidence that she was not the only one to be struck by her mother's capacity for self-protective humour at this time. Anna Foa, whose own father and brothers were among those imprisoned during the Ponte Tresa affair (her brother Vittorio, who was not released until the fall of Mussolini in 1943, was later to marry Ginzburg's friend Lisetta Giua), remembers Lidia Levi joking in the police station waiting-room about what they could expect from the Fascist authorities.

She complained that one day the government would open all the safe-deposit boxes belonging to the Jews. "Do you know what I am going to do?" she said. "I'll put a chamber pot in my safe-deposit box."[13]

In the course of this episode there is a scene in which Ginzburg describes her mother inviting the novelist Pitigrilli, who had himself been in jail, to visit the house and advise her about arrangements for supplying the prisoners with food parcels and clean clothing. The young Natalia already knows of this notorious writer, whose books are considered by her father to be highly unsuitable for a schoolgirl like herself. What the adult Ginzburg has long known by the time she comes to write *Family Sayings*, but neglects to tell the reader, is that this visit was heavy with dramatic irony. Pitigrilli was in fact an agent of OVRA, the Fascist secret police, and many of those arrested during the Ponte Tresa affair were rounded up on account of his spying.

Alexander Stille tells the story in *Benevolence and Betrayal: Five Italian Jewish Families Under Fascism*. Pitigrilli, whose real name was Dino Segre, was an illegitimate cousin of Sion Segre Amar, Mario Levi's friend and fellow-conspirator.

His father was from a well-to-do Jewish family, while his mother was a poor Catholic girl. As the bastard child of an undistinguished mixed match, young Dino's arrival was a Segre family scandal. His parents did not marry until he was eight. His descriptions of childhood are universally bitter, reflecting the ostracism he suffered.

He was later to take his revenge by becoming an Edmund to his cousin's Edgar. "What in the world could be more beautiful than to be a bastard," he once wrote, "so that one can despise everything, without making an exception for one's own father and mother?!"[15] He infiltrated the Turin circle of Justice and Liberty, of which his cousin was a member, and informed on them with such success that eventually the whole group was behind bars or in internal exile and Pitigrilli's lucrative secret profession was gone. He was unmasked at the end of the war, when his copious reports to his spy-masters were discovered and made public, among them his own account of the visit to the Levi household that Ginzburg describes. We can see from his claims to have the key to far more information than he actually conveys that spy reports too are "stories based on conventions."

Before [his arrest] Giuseppe Levi . . . was able to warn his family. They burned many letters in a fireplace. Since not all were burned entirely an attentive examination would probably reveal some letters from [Carlo] Rosselli . . .

Mario Levi, who managed to escape to Switzerland . . . is now probably in Paris and with the Rossellis. With the excuse of going to take him clothing and money from his family, I think I can learn much from him. Now that he is free he should talk very openly.[16]

By confining the narrative to what she was aware of at the time, Ginzburg puts this sinister and dramatic material beyond the boundaries of her book. In doing so, she is not necessarily concealing it. When *Family Sayings* was published in 1963, most of her Italian readers would have been likely to have heard of Pitigrilli's role as an OVRA agent and to know about the rescue of Turati and the significance of the Ponte Tresa affair. The book operates, to some extent, by exploiting the ironic distance between events as an historian might relate them, with hindsight and from the outside, and the private, inner narrative of memory, which foregrounds the apparently comic and trivial in order to tell its own symbolic and personal story. For the informed reader, the omissions are part of the text, a code through which these distinctions can be made and understood. However there are also more complex ironies at work. While Ginzburg's book is far from being an artless collection of reminiscences, it is crucially concerned with oral storytelling, which she presents as enabling a family embattled within and beleaguered without to form a mutually-protective bond, controlling the present through a shared and stylized version of the past. This storytelling is necessarily subject to, indeed dependent on, omission. Luisa Passerini found that the recollections of her oral sources also contained omissions when they were asked about their experiences during the Fascist era (omissions which imply a reading of the past that has already become problematic for the Italy of Forza Italia and its neo-Fascist allies).

The identification of Fascism with evil and a source of national shame, and the consequent desire to keep quiet about it, even among those not actually responsible . . . signifies that power makes those who are subjected to it complicit in its exercise. This involvement explains the frequent recurrence in the memoirs . . . of a sense of shame , guilt, silence and injury . . .

Oral recollection, oscillating as it does between silence and censorship on the one hand, and the recall of the minutest, almost "insignificant" episodes on the other hand, brings us back to these issues.[17]

Silence can simply be omission, but it can also be a powerful unspoken presence in the text. Superficially, by writing the book Ginzburg is simply transmitting and adding to the family lexicon, but if we look more closely it becomes apparent that her storytelling is radically different from her mother's. This will become clear if we compare the mother's silence about the death of her brother Silvio with Ginzburg's silence about the death of her husband Leone.

Silvio was that brother of my mother's who had killed himself. In our house his death was always swathed in mystery; and though I know now that he killed himself, I don't really know why. I think it was mainly my father who was responsible for spreading that air of mystery round the figure of Silvio, because he didn't want us to know there had been a suicide in the family, and perhaps for other reasons too which I don't know about. As for my mother, she always used to talk about Silvio very cheerfully, having such a sunny nature that it embraced and coloured everything, making her recall only the bright side of people and events and draw a veil over grief and misfortune, to which at most she would sometimes spare the passing tribute of a sigh.[18]

The mother's references to Silvio recur throughout the book, memories so happy and unshadowed that they make his death seem "unintelligible." While Silvio's suicide is a minor mystery, Leone Ginzburg's death is central not only to the book but to its author's life, and Ginzburg's silence about the brutal circumstances of that death and her own overwhelming grief becomes a narrative black hole which draws the entire text towards it.

They arrested him . . . and I never saw him again.

I found myself back with my mother in Florence. Misfortune always made her feel the cold, and she would muffle herself up in a shawl. We didn't talk to each other much about Leone's death. She had been very fond of him, but she didn't like to talk about the dead and besides she was far too busy washing and combing the children and making sure they were warmly dressed.[19]

The distance between the silence that Ginzburg describes here, her mother's silence as she busily recreates her past maternal role by caring for their daughter's children, and the silence that Ginzburg herself enacts by shifting the focus of the narrative away from her own bereavement to her mother's sudden aging, her mother's pallor, her mother's need to wrap herself in "a purple angora shawl," is one that can be measured by turning to an essay that Ginzburg wrote in 1946, "The Son of Man."

> Once the experience of evil has been endured it is never forgotten. Someone who has seen a house collapse knows only too clearly what frail things little vases of flowers and pictures and white walls are . . . A house is not particularly solid. It can collapse from one moment to the next . Behind the peaceful vases of flowers, behind the teapots and carpets and waxed floors there is the other true face of a house—the hideous face of a house that has been reduced to rubble.[20]

Because of this terrible and ineradicable knowledge, "there is an unbridgeable abyss between us and the previous generation." Ginzburg's mother, though profoundly shaken by "terrors and misfortunes," still has a house to put in order.

> The broken windows were patched up with plywood, and my father had stoves put in the rooms because the central heating didn't work. My mother immediately sent for Tersilla, and when she had Tersilla in the ironing room in front of the sewing machine, she gave a sigh of relief and felt that life might return to its old rhythm. She got floral fabrics to cover the armchairs, which had been in the cellar and were stained here and there with mould.[21]

Silence, in narratives by women, is too often seen as disempowerment, evidence of a legacy of oppression and suppression. It is important to stress that Ginzburg has not been silenced, nor is she merely reticent or stoical; rather by her silence she places Leone's death at the center of the text, creating a space from which the reader is forced to retreat with narrative greed unsatisfied. The closing paragraph of *Winter in the Abruzzi*, an essay written in 1944 describing the period that she spent in internal exile with her husband and children, helps to explain why, for Ginzburg, Leone's death lies beyond narrative.

My husband died in Rome, in the prison of Regina Coeli, a few months after we left the Abruzzi. Faced with the horror of his solitary death, and faced with the anguish which preceded his death, I ask myself if this happened to us—to us, who bought oranges at Giro's and went for walks in the snow.[22]

The key word here is not horror but solitary. The fact and the circumstances of Leone's death can be recorded, but any attempt imaginatively to recreate the experience of his dying can only be a fiction. All stories, even the most terrible, console us by creating the illusion that words can shape and control the past. In *Family Sayings*, that work of fiction in which nothing has been invented, Ginzburg attests to the unassimilable reality of her husband's death by refusing to fictionalize it in this way. The horror and the solitude are conveyed by silence.

For an historian such as Zuccotti, the death of Leone Ginzburg, like the rescue of Turati, is one of many significant details that can be selected and pieced together to form a coherent public narrative. For the child Natalia, the rescue of Turati was experienced as part of the continuity of daily life, while for the adult Natalia her violent bereavement was a trauma which severed her connection both with the past and with her own past self. In the 1949 essay, *My Vocation*, she describes it as

a real, irremediable and incurable grief that shattered my life, and when I tried to put it together again I realized that I and my life had become something irreconcilable with what had gone before.[23]

In *Family Sayings*, both of these episodes show us the impact of history in Zuccotti's sense (a large-scale pattern of events, meaningful not only to those who witness or suffer them) on an individual life and they are linked, too, by the figure of Adriano Olivetti. It is he who comes to tell Ginzburg that her husband has been arrested and to take her and her children into hiding. The omission here is one that no attentive reader could fail to register, Ginzburg does not need to put into words the danger that Adriano helps to save them from, the danger that also menaces Adriano himself and every other Italian Jew. Instead, and very movingly, she describes how that time of nightmare severance from the certainties of a known world is made endurable by his presence.

I shall always remember, as long as I live, the great comfort it was to me that morning to see his familiar figure which I had known since my childhood, after so many hours of solitude and fear . . . and I shall always remember his bent back as he stooped to collect our scattered clothing and pick up the children's shoes in a humble, kindly attitude of patient compassion. And when we escaped from that house, he had the same face as when he came to us to fetch Turati, the breathless, frightened, happy face he wore when he was taking someone to safety.[24]

In her childhood, that look on Adriano's face had for a moment transformed everyday life into history. Now it is history at its most terrible which is transformed for a moment by the healing ordinariness of a human gesture. This is why, in a book which so consistently deheroizes its characters, Ginzburg makes an exception for Adriano Olivetti.

> I met him in the street one day in Rome, during the German occupation. He was on foot, walking by himself with his wandering gait, his eyes lost in the perpetual dreams which veiled them in a blue haze. He was dressed no differently from anyone else, yet he looked like a beggar in that crowded street and at the same time he looked like a king. Like a king in exile.[25]

Where her parents' stories are protective and consoling precisely because they are continually retold yet always remain the same, Ginzburg uses the recurring motifs of her mother's dislike of talking about death and Adriano's "breathless, frightened, happy face . . . when he was taking someone to safety" in order to emphasize the shift from comedy to tragedy, which is also a shift from childish ignorance to adult knowledge for the narrator/persona. The final section of the book returns us to the family lexicon, still unchanged for Ginzburg's now elderly parents but completely redefined for the reader, and here too omission has a significant part to play in the shaping of the text. *Family Sayings* begins and ends with the voice of Ginzburg's father, an irascible tyrant whose alarming but ultimately unsuccessful attempts at total domestic control paradoxically serve to inoculate his family against the fear of the more sinister tyranny that threatens them from without. When police agents arrive at six in the morning to search the house and arrest her son Alberto, Lidia Levi smuggles the envelope containing her bills into her daughter's schoolbag . . .

> because she was afraid that my father might catch sight of them during the search and scold her for spending too much.[26]

His peremptory and eccentric personality dominates not only *Family Sayings* but also the autobiography of his most distinguished student, the Nobel prize-winning scientist Rita Levi-Montalcini.

Born in 1909, seven years earlier than Ginzburg, Levi-Montalcini grew up in Turin in a free-thinking, middle-class Jewish family similar in many ways to Ginzburg's own, especially in the autocratic control that the father exerted over his children's lives and the daughter's consequent sense of distance and constraint. Unlike *Family Sayings*, Levi-Montalcini's *In Praise of Imperfection* adheres closely to the conventions of classic autobiography, conventions which enable its author to resolve her feelings of guilt and regret, inside the narrative at least, with an anguished but formal deathbed scene in which she loses her father but at last begins to love him. However, while implicitly claiming that she is simply relating the story of her life, Levi-Montalcini too makes use of recurring elements to structure her text, in this case "a Master-disciple relationship"[27] with her old professor which over the years becomes a quasi-filial one and culminates in a second, very different deathbed scene.

A significant figure in both books is Giuseppe Levi's friend and fellow scientist Tullio Terni, a passionate lover of the arts who infects first Mario and Paola, united in their affected cultivation of melancholy, and then Ginzburg's mother, that inveterate recaller of past time, with his enthusiasm for Proust.

> "*La petite phrase!*" my mother used to say. "It's so lovely when he talks about *la petite phrase*! Silvio would have liked it so much!"[28]

In spite of having built him up into a major comic character, Ginzburg records his death only in passing; a paragraph listing the friends of her parents who have failed to survive into the post-war era ends with the information that "Terni had died too, in Florence."[29] It is Levi-Montalcini who tells us the story that this phrase conceals. After the war, the National Academy of the Lincei, a learned body which had been suppressed by Mussolini, reconstituted itself and expelled forty of its members for their involvement with Fascism. Though Terni had been no more than a passive sympathizer with the regime, Giuseppe Levi, as acting secretary for the commission conducting the purge, felt morally obliged not to make an exception for his old friend. Terni, already suffering from depression, committed suicide.

> He used a vial of cyanide . . . like the ones he had given to his family at the time of the Nazi invasion, in the reasoned belief that if they were ever captured by the SS it would be the wisest and quickest solution.[30]

The tragic irony here is that though Italian Jews were among the most determined opponents of Fascism, there were also many who, proud of their new assimilated status in a united Italy, became ardent early supporters of a regime which eventually deprived them of their civil rights and, after the German invasion and reinstatement of Mussolini as nominal head of the puppet Republic of Saló, collaborated in sending them to their deaths.

We need to look at Ginzburg's silence about Terni's suicide in the light of the much more significant omissions that she makes in choosing to end her narrative with her mother and father, elderly now but essentially unchanged despite all they have endured, still telling each other with undiminished zest the old stories that each has heard so many times before. Giuseppe Levi was to die, aged ninety-two, of cancer of the stomach two years after Ginzburg published *Family Sayings*. Levi-Montalcini's moving account of her final meeting with the old man unaffectedly elevates him from a comic character to an heroic one, "consumed neither by old age, nor suffering, nor by the knowledge he had of his approaching end" which he accepts "with a stoic serenity."[31] This capacity for obstinate and rational courage had been thoroughly tested in the final years of his life. The death of his wife—Levi-Montalcini calls her "his adored life-companion Lidia"[32]—eight years previously had been followed a year later by the amputation of his left leg above the knee, an impairment he had accepted with a proud and testy refusal of pity or assistance.

In ending her narrative where she does, before her mother's death, Ginzburg has made a novelist's decision. Unlike the parents of Alberto's wife Miranda, transported by the Germans to an "unknown destination" because they believed that "no one is going to harm peaceful people like us,"[33] the end of the book presents Ginzburg's parents, both of them socialists and Giuseppe Levi a Jew, not merely as foolhardy but fortunate survivors but as almost mythological figures. Passerini tells us that "'fixed identity' . . . can be considered a specific feature of self-representation in oral narration" whereas "it is, on the contrary, typical (historically) of written autobiography as a genre that it is 'the history of the development of the personality.'"[34] Ginzburg's refusal to present herself as the central character of her own written narrative enables her to return us at the end of the book to the fixed identities which her mother and father have created for themselves by the incessant process of oral storytelling, identities as powerful and unchanging as those of parents seen through the eyes of a child. To have come through so much and still to preserve those identities intact seems, in its absurd way, a triumph of the human spirit, and yet their affirmation of the past is, in a very real sense, also a denial. It is in order to achieve this celebratory yet ambiguous ending that Ginzburg chooses not to leave us with the image of the maimed but indomitable old widower that Levi-Montalcini describes. It is for this reason too that she suppresses the story of Terni's suicide. Those fixed and fictive selves enable the parents to weather death and loss while remaining fundamentally untouched in their own comic and private narrative universe. Only the silence at the heart of the book, surrounding the death by torture of Leone Ginzburg, reminds us that this is a fiction. Ginzburg's parents are unvulnerable, in other words, only because they are comic characters in a narrative controlled by their novelist daughter who has learned, as they have not, how fragile and delusive is the protection afforded by irrational optimism.

If *Family Sayings* is thus doubly fictive, in what sense can we claim that Ginzburg, or indeed any autobiographer, is telling us the "truth"? A comparison with Virginia Woolf's *To the Lighthouse* may help to clarify this. Woolf's novel makes no public parade of being anything but a work of fiction, yet in her diary she describes the experience of writing it as a kind of self-psychoanalysis or exorcism, freeing her at last from the haunting presences of her mother and father, and refers to a letter in which her sister Vanessa claims that on reading it she "found the rising of the dead almost painful."[35] That Woolf's novel too contains significant omissions is not in itself surprising; we would expect a novelist using autobiographical material to adapt or disguise it to some extent, both for literary and for personal reasons. However in *To the Lighthouse* the changes are often very transparent. Though nominally set on the Isle of Skye, the place descriptions unmistakably point to St. Ives, where the Stephen family had a holiday house, while the three deaths which punctuate the central section of the novel are those of Woolf's mother, half-sister, and brother. Indeed, the very material that Ginzburg omits from the end of *Family Sayings* forms the pivot of *To the Lighthouse*, the terrible moment of loss on which the poetic action of the novel is poised.

> [Mr. Ramsay stumbling along a passage stretched his arms out one dark morning, but, Mrs. Ramsay having died rather suddenly the night before, he stretched his arms out. They remained empty.][36]

It is all the more interesting to look at what is omitted from a text in which such painful material is included.

Woolf grew up in a family that was dysfunctional in more than just that shattering series of bereavements. "That house of all the deaths," as Henry James called it, was one in which the names of the dead, though endlessly brooded on, were never mentioned. In her auto-biographical fragment, "A Sketch of the Past," Woolf describes finally breaking this taboo when she was in her mid-twenties.

> I remember when Thoby died, that Adrian and I agreed to talk about him. "There are so many people that are dead now," we said.[37]

While Woolf's mother was alive, the tensions in a disparate family group to which both parents had brought offspring from previous marriages remained decently concealed, only to show up shockingly after her death (helping to confirm for Woolf the myth of a lost golden age). Of those four step-siblings, Laura, Leslie Stephen's eldest daughter, was mentally handicapped, while Julia Duckworth's children by her first husband, the pampered George, and Gerald, and the put-upon Stella, were all to be sources of division and pain. Stella's courtship and marriage, Stella's illness and death, each in turn became the pretext for hysterical displays of family emotion, while Woolf famously accused both Gerald and George of sexually molesting her.

It is difficult to know quite how to judge these accusations (a difficulty compounded by the over-literal and sensationalist readings of certain recent critics).[38] Woolf's description[39] of Gerald's gropings sounds like a reliable childhood recollection of a form of interference that one imagines a good many middle-class small girls must have suffered at a period when their adolescent brothers had few other sources of information about female anatomy, but what are we to make of her dream-like memory of "a long thick fish wriggling on a hook in the larder, and Gerald beating it to death with a broom handle?"[40] In the case of George, the main evidence is "22 Hyde Park Gate,"[41] a piece written to be read aloud to Bloomsbury's Memoir Club. This describes an evening so baroque in its accumulation of bizarre social embarrassments that long before we reach the bedroom scene it is clear that Woolf is speaking as raconteur rather than witness. Any description of sexual abuse presented to an audience as an entertaining tale is likely to be unreliable, and there is no way of judging whether Woolf is exaggerating this part of her story too or, on the contrary, concealing the extent either of George's assault or of her own complicity in it. It is even possible that sexual abuse is being used, wholly or in part, as a metaphor for other kinds of violation. In a memoir written at the end of her life, Woolf describes, with still lively anger, coming down to dinner in a new green dress and George (a quite different George—only her hatred for him is the same) telling her to "Go and tear it up."[42] It was George too who acted as master of ceremonies at her mother's deathbed, officiously wrapping his half-siblings in towels and giving them hot milk and brandy before leading them in to kiss the corpse.[43]

All this dark and tangled stuff, which Woolf herself seems to have been unable to get into focus, vanishes behind the water-color shimmer of *To the Lighthouse*. There is no literary reason why the Ramsays should have eight children, but the logic of wish-fulfillment demands that they should be there round the dinner table, all of them full brothers and sisters, not one of them "an idiot." Of the girls, Woolf herself is Cam, while Prue is plainly Stella, no longer a jealously exploited stepdaughter but Mr. Ramsay's true child. Laura is eliminated by allowing Vanessa to double as the artistic Rose and the harassed Nancy, housekeeper to her widowed father. The hated George is replaced by Woolf's favorite brother Thoby who becomes not only Andrew, the eldest son, but also James, the youngest, who steers the boat on the trip to the lighthouse as Thoby used to do at St. Ives.[44] In this novel written to celebrate the memory and to lay the ghost of the mother that she remembers as never having individual time for her, Woolf has also blotted out her younger brother Adrian, the child her mother "cherished separately" calling him "My Joy."[45] Roger and Jasper are simply ciphers, added to make up the numbers. It is in the context of this dream family that Woolf sets out to resolve her feelings about her parents, resurrecting her mother in Lily Briscoe's painting, which is also the novel, and freezing her father into the permanence of art as Lily draws that final stroke on her canvas which is both the lighthouse itself and Mr. Ramsay, liberated for ever from egotism and self-pity, leaping "lightly like a young man, holding his parcel, on to the rock."[46]

If we compare Woolf's novel with *Family Sayings*, the similarity in structure is evident. In each book, a family ruled by idiosyncratic but strongly traditional parental figures, having survived a devastating period of destruction and loss, both literally and symbolically rebuilds a house in which a former pattern of life can be re-established. This similarity is all the stronger because of the ways in which Woolf has reshaped family history into fiction. By bringing forward the date of the narrative by a decade or so, the private agony of Thoby's death is subsumed into the public cataclysm of the First World War, while as we have seen the final restoration of a lost order owes more to wish than to memory. The crucial difference between the two texts is that for Woolf bereavement and trauma are located at the heart of the family experience while for Ginzburg they are sharply separated from it. Turning back to Ginzburg's book from the impressionistic constructs of *To the Lighthouse*, its focused and unsparing clarity of vision makes it appear to be mapped precisely on reality and yet, as Woolf reminds us, the felt experience of living does not have this coherent and unitary quality. Through the clarity of the telling, Ginzburg is deliberately mythologizing the past, showing us not how events were experienced but how they are recalled. Memory, her source material, is also her real subject matter.

Woolf, by contrast, can be seen as writing not to recollect but to undo the past. Indeed, it is possible to read the closing sequence of the novel in terms of a symbolic pattern in which James represents justice and Cam forgiveness, while Lily Briscoe stands for art. Refracted through the prism of art, justice and mercy converge and become one and Woolf is at last able to look with detachment and acceptance at the father whose excessive demands and devouring self-pity had poisoned her youth. The year after the publication of *To the Lighthouse*, she notes her father's birthday in her diary and calculates that had he lived he would have been ninety-six . . .

> & could have been 96, like other people one has known; but mercifully was not. His life would have entirely ended mine. What would have happened? No writing, no books;—inconceivable. I used to think of him & mother daily; but writing *The Lighthouse*, laid them in my mind.[47]

Woolf's ability to feel and record this sober and objective gratitude for her father's death shows that *To the Lighthouse* is not merely an exercise in aesthetic wish-fulfilment but a means of resolving long-standing feelings of anger and guilt. Where Levi-Montalcini reconciles her conflicting feelings about her relationship with her father by means of a formal deathbed scene, accepting, through the use of this nineteenth-century narrative device, the finality of loss and the inevitability of regret, it is perhaps only by writing the end of *To the Lighthouse*, in which as Cam she forgives her father and as Lily she abstracts and crystallizes the moment of forgiveness into art, that Woolf can dissociate her rational relief at her father's death from the irrational guilt of having wished and thus symbolically caused that death.

Ginzburg, too, at the end of *Family Sayings*, leaves her parents suspended in an unchanging present moment, but it is the collective present moment of memory. Recollections of countless similar episodes have been collated into one reflexive scene in which her parents' repetition of the stories in the family lexicon has itself become part of the lexicon. Ginzburg's essays make it plain that during her formative years she feared and disliked her father and often resented her mother, but

Family Sayings neither foregrounds nor attempts to resolve these emotions, and neither does it concern itself with love, that unmentionable subject between parents and children. Lidia Levi may indeed have been her husband's "adored life-companion," but the only proof their daughter offers us either of shared parental affection or of her own adult feelings for those twin pillars of her childhood world is this archetypal final scene, from which Ginzburg herself is absent or present only as a silent witness.

Notes

All quotations from Natalia Ginzburg, *Lessico Famigliare* (*Family Sayings*) are in my own translation and page references are given for the Italian text. *Family Sayings* has been translated by D. M. Low (London: Hogarth Press, 1967; revised and reprinted, Manchester: Carcanet, 1984).

1. Natalia Ginzburg, *Lessico Famigliare* (Turin: Einaudi, 1963), p. 5.

2. Luisa Passerini, *Fascism in Popular Memory: The Cultural Experience of the Turin Working Class*, trans. Robert Lumley and Jude Bloomfield (Cambridge: Cambridge University Press, 1987), p. 27.

3. Ginzburg, *Lessico Famigliare*, pp. 5–6.

4. Natalia Ginzburg, *The Little Virtues*, trans. Dick Davis (Manchester: Carcanet, 1985), p. 70.

5. Susan Zuccotti, *The Italians and the Holocaust: Persecution, Rescue and Survival* (London: Peter Halbab, 1987), p. 243.

6. Zuccotti, p. 254.

7. Zuccotti, pp. 243–44.

8. Ginzburg, *Lessico Famigliare*, p. 83.

9. Ginzburg, *Lessico Famigliare*, p. 85.

10. Zuccotti, p. 244.

11. Ginzburg, *Lessico Famigliare*, p. 84.

12. Ginzburg, *Lessico Famigliare*, p. 102.

13. Alexander Stille, *Benevolence and Betrayal: Five Italian Jewish Families under Fascism* (London: Jonathan Cape, 1992), p. 119.

14. Stille, pp. 106–7.

15. Stille, p. 109.

16. Stille, pp. 110–11.

17. Passerini, p. 67.

18. Ginzburg, *Lessico Famigliare*, pp. 44–45.

19. Ginzburg, *Lessico Famigliare*, pp. 167–68.

20. Ginzburg, *The Little Virtues*, pp. 49–50.

21. Ginzburg, *Lessico Famigliare*, pp. 168–69.

22. Ginzburg, *The Little Virtues*, p. 8.

23. Ginzburg, *The Little Virtues*, p. 67.

24. Ginzburg, *Lessico Famigliare*, p. 174.

25. Ginzburg, *Lessico Famigliare*, p. 174.

26. Ginzburg, *Lessico Famigliare*, p. 100.

27. Levi-Montalcini, p. 59.

28. Ginzburg, *Lessico Famigliare*, p. 66.

29. Ginzburg, *Lessico Famigliare*, p. 178.

30. Levi-Montalcini, pp. 56–57.

31. Levi-Montalcini, p. 205.

32. Levi-Montalcini, p. 203.

33. Ginzburg, *Lessico Famigliare*, p. 183.

34. Passerini, p. 61.

35. *The Diary of Virginia Woolf*, vol. III, ed. Anne Olivier Bell (London: Hogarth Press, 1980), p. 135. Vanessa Bell's letter is quoted in Quentin Bell, *Virginia Woolf: A Biography*, vol. II (London: Hogarth Press, 1972), p. 128.

36. Virginia Woolf, *To the Lighthouse*, 3rd ed. (London: Hogarth Press, 1977), pp. 199–200.

37. Virginia Woolf, *Moments of Being: Unpublished Autobiographical Writings*, ed. Jeanne Schulkind (London: Chatto and Windus for Sussex University Press, 1976), p. 107.

38. See particularly Louise DeSalvo, *Virginia Woolf: The Impact of Childhood Sexual Abuse on Her Life and Work* (London: Women's Press, 1989).

39. Woolf, *Moments of Being*, p. 69.

40. Woolf, *Moments of Being*, p. 114.

41. Woolf, *Moments of Being*, pp. 142–55.

42. Woolf, *Moments of Being*, p. 130.

43. Woolf, *Moments of Being*, p. 91.

44. Woolf, *Moments of Being*, p. 115.

45. Woolf, *Moments of Being*, p. 83.

46. Woolf, *To the Lighthouse*, p. 318.

47. Woolf, *Diary*, p. 208.

PART IV

Lives in Practice

INTRODUCTION

In *A Room of One's Own* Virginia Woolf could famously only find a way of encompassing the female subject—making room for her[1]—by refusing to be bounded by the usual proprieties of genre. Theoretical discourse in her essay quickly becomes autobiography or rather a mode of personal rambling which refuses the authoritative stance of theory. Yet autobiography is itself no less problematic since for Woolf the female I is as yet a figure of possibility, moving between women's historical exclusion and their inscription in the future. I, for Woolf, names "someone who has no real being"; however by re-routing autobiography through fiction Woolf is also able to set into motion a questioning of the "truth" of historical fact: "Fiction here is likely to contain more truth than fact."[2] Woolf installs fiction in the gaps left by history—she creates a life, for example, for her cultural predecessor, Shakespeare's sister—and thus offers another—but equally plausible—reading of history. She begins where history leaves off, claiming authority for a different form of representation. At the same time, her fictional history reflects back on the notion of "historical truth" suggesting that it is more arbitrary and partial than it seems, dependent ultimately on the guise of truth and the power that goes with repetition.[3]

The essays in this section of the book are all concerned—as Woolf herself preeminently was—with foregrounding the idea and moment of enunciation in writing, removing the mask of critical objectivity as a way of opening up different and multiple approaches to meaning and truth. As Nicole Ward Jouve argues in the Introduction to her book, *White Woman Speaks With Forked Tongue: Criticism as Autobiography*, it is all too easy for critics—even for critics of autobiography—to forget how they are themselves implicated in the texts that they write. "Are there ways of writing that are not autobiographical in the most complex sense?" Jouve asks. Her response to contemporary debates about the subject is, instead of giving in to a sense of terminal difficulty, to perceive these as a reason for renewed engagement." "Any writing constructs and betrays a subject. It is not a question of choice. One might as well make something of the process."[4] Making something of the process is both to accept that all meanings are provisional—that we are always "subjects in process"—and, at the same time, to see the possibility thus opened up for new forms of writing and creativity.

Her own essay in this collection explores her attempt to reconstruct her family history during the period of the First World War. In her foreword to the essay Jouve adds another layer to the complicated overlapping of discourses and temporalities that she sees must constitute any attempt to come to terms with history. The original text, she reveals, was written at a time when, faced by the imminence of bereavement, she turned to other, more distant family deaths for consolation and the perspective that war and the colossal scale of war-time death could bring. Inevitably this autobiographical note complicates rather than explains the writing, interposing a hesitant, equivocal motivation between the writing and the person. Indeed, we could perhaps interpret this authorial voice as struggling against a metaphorical as well as a literal death, for if, within the text, the author brings the dead to life again through their letters and their writings, she also attempts in the foreword to add another living layer to a writing which could be seen— in contemporary critical terms—as containing her own authorial death, freezing the time of writing into the past monument of a text.[5]

Jouve is concerned, in various ways throughout her essay, with interrogating the binary opposition of public and private history. Her fictional intervention into the more public record of war precisely questions the separation of histories and discourses, redirecting the details of history through the language of fiction, insisting on analogies and repetitions within her own writing. As in the letters she refers to and quotes from, she perceives a flow of information and emotion between battlefront and homefront, male and female, external and internal worlds, which History as public discourse has elided or ignored. Fiction thus, in much the same way as it did for Woolf, becomes a way of questioning the authority invested in historical truth, a way of foregrounding another intimate, obscure and, almost inevitably as well, feminine, history. Ultimately this mixing of discourses has an ethical as well as an aesthetic purpose for war is also lived as private, internal event; the reverse, as Jouve suggests, that private wars and personal catastrophes have a connection with national events may also be true, if we were able to attribute a proper importance to the subjective and perceive its power. As Hélène Cixous writes—and Jouve's text reveals—"I and the world are never separate."[6]

Marion Shaw is also concerned with the writing of lives, this time her own role as the biographer of Winifred Holtby. Biography, as Woolf again recognized through the numerous experimental forms she developed, is difficult to separate from fiction: it is also traditionally intimately allied with death, and with the authority bestowed on writing by endings. The biographer both participates in and transcends the death of his subject: as Woolf noted—converting into fiction a feature of her own family history—"when one of them dies the chances are that another of them writes his biography."[7] How far does biography attempt to displace the uncertainties of the autobiographer into the completeness of the biography, containing one life within another? How far does the biographer, in Shaw's words, both "invent and enclose" its subject? Does the biographer inevitably become—whatever her knowledge of her subject—a presence within the biography? A feminist biography—so Shaw suggests—should perhaps foreground its selectivity and partiality—by refusing completeness, the authority of one (deadly) conclusion. She quotes Liz Stanley's belief that a feminist biography should accept multiplicity: "'she was like that and like that' should be its motto."

For Vicki Bertram, it is the subjectivity of the reading process itself which turns every critic into an autobiographer. Before critical opinions solidify there is another process, one which engages and implicates the subjectivity of the critic. Later the critic may disavow, even to herself, the personal origins of her reading. What Bertram suggests is that it is not a case of the critic engulfing text in her own self, but being sceptical—just as the feminist autobiographer has to be—of an objectivity which masks the personal investment of the critic. Personal criticism could be a name for a certain relation to the text, where detachment and empathy coexist. The relationship between text and reader inevitably involves struggle, doubt, and uncertainty, and converts any act of reading and criticism into a process rather than a single event. Why do we pretend that we can suddenly handle this relationship effortlessly? Why are we not more frank about the provisionality of our criticism, as well as our ownership of it? Is the authority of the critic after all a fiction? And is the best and most honest approach for historican, biographer, and critic alike, as Jouve advocates, simply—and perhaps not so simply—"to make something of the process?"

Notes

1. This phrase is from Shoshana Felman, *What Does A Woman Want* (Baltimore and London: John Hopkins University Press, 1993), p. 128.

2. *A Room of One's Own* (London: Granada), p. 6.

3. See Tania Modleski, *Feminism Without Women* (New York and London: Routledge, 1991), pp. 55–56.

4. (London: Routledge, 1991), pp. 2, 10.

5. Paul de Man famously linked autobiography to epitaph and analyzed it in terms of a "chiasmic" crossing of death and life, speech and silence in his essay "Autobiography as De-facement," *Modern Language Notes* 94 (1979), pp. 919–30.

6. "Preface" to *The Hélène Cixous Reader*, ed. Susan Sellers (London: Routledge, 1994), p. xv.

7. *Night and Day* (Harmondsworth: Penguin, 1992), p. 27. Quoted in Julia Briggs, "Virginia Woolf and 'The Proper Writing of Lives,'" in John Batchelor, ed., *The Art of Literary Biography* (Oxford: Oxford University Press, 1995), p. 245.

Further Reading

Ascher, Carol, De Salvo, Louise, and Ruddick, Sara, eds. *Between Women* (Boston: Beacon Press, 1984).

Farran, Denise, Scott, Sue, and Stanley, Liz. Writing Feminist Biography, *Studies in Sexual Politics*, vols. 13–14.

Hanscombe, Gillian, and Myers, Virginia. *Writing for Their Lives: The Modernist Women 1910–1940* (London: Women's Press, 1987).

Jouve, Nicole Ward. *White Woman Speaks With Forked Tongue* (London: Routledge, 1991).

Kaplan, Cora. "Autobiography, Gender and History," in *Sea Changes: Essays on Culture and Feminism* (London: Verso, 1986).

Marcus, Laura. "Personal Criticism and the Autobiographical Turn," in Sally Ledger, Josephine McDonagh, and Jane Spencer, eds., *Political Gender: Texts and Contexts* (London: Harvester Wheatsheaf, 1994).

Miller, Nancy. *Getting Personal* (London and New York: Routledge, 1991).

Sellers, Susan, ed. *Delighting the Heart: A Notebook by Women Writers* (London: Women's Press, 1989).

Stanley, Liz. *The Auto/biographical "I": The Theory and Practice of Feminist Auto/biography* (Manchester: Manchester University Press, 1992).

Wilson, Elizabeth. "Telling It Like It Is: Women and Confessional Writing," in Susannah Radstone, ed., *Sweet Dreams: Sexuality, Gender and Popular Fiction* (London: Lawrence and Wishart, 1988), pp. 21–46.

11

Their Wars

Nicole Ward Jouve

I have kept a diary since I was ten, but I never thought of writing an autobiography. I marvelled at people who did: they felt they mattered, they had self-importance. They were able to see themselves; they knew where they were in relation to their lives.

But from an early age I was always interested in family history. One branch of my family had lived in or around Marseilles since the early part of the seventeenth century. My mother, who fifteen years ago had a fad for family trees, got as far back as Justine and a Baptistin Jouve who were servants in a fine house in the hills outside Marseilles and, being illiterate, signed the register on their wedding day with a cross. By the beginning of this century, small or not so small tradesmen and women and shopkeepers had produced an only son, Xavier Jouve, who'd made it to the liberal professions. He was a doctor and went to the First World War and served over five years, only being wounded once, and not grievously. He was one of the lucky ones.

There were a lot of aunts, great-aunts, second cousins, and family friends in my childhood, all with tales to tell about the family past. There were good storytellers among them, one in particular whom we called Mimi Marraine and who kept us spellbound. Nothing out of the ordinary had happened to anybody. But there was affection, remembrance, and a sense of wit that made the ordinary tales riveting. Marcel Pagnol had spent the country bits of his childhood on the other side of the hill where my father and aunt, during and after the First World War, and my cousins, brother, and myself during and after the Second World War, spent ours.

About twenty years ago I got interested in writing down some of the tales, or simply the information that was still around. I had noticed that one generation was disappearing, and with it its knowledge of the previous ones. Suddenly no one is left to give you that vital piece of information you were too foolish to bother about when those who knew were alive. I remember going to pay a visit to my grandmother's grave with Mimi Marraine who had been her young cousin. And Mimi Marraine taking me on a tour of the various graves and vaults in the Marseilles Saint-Pierre cemetery and telling me about André Alliès who'd been twenty and had his head blown off by a shell on his first day at the front as, sitting astride a canon, he bit into a sandwich. And about that mysterious sister of my grandmother's whom everyone had agreed never to mention again after she . . . And then, of course, Mimi Marraine died, and her memories with her.

The piece that follows is the fruit of death. I was living in the USA at the time and flew home to Marseilles several times in the course of the winter in which my brother died. As, to busy myself, I sorted through old suitcases, several bunches of papers and photographs of my grandfather's surfaced. I was intrigued. I'd been told that my aunt had burned all my grandfather's papers, especially his World War I diary, after my grandmother's death—she had survived him over ten years. When questioned about why she'd done it my aunt had said there was nothing of interest—her father had been anti-war—and her parents' letters were for their eyes only. Yet I found several packets of letters, an early war diary, lots of notebooks, lots of photographs, and maps which somehow had survived.

I had time in those days. I began a minute reconstitution of my grandfather's activities during the first two months of the war, by using his bit of diary, historians' accounts of the period—August 1914 and the battle of the Marne in September—French writers' diaries and descriptions of the war, and the French War Office's vast collections of documents, and sometimes hour by hour maps of the Alsace-Lorraine battles. I traced the movements of my grandfather's regiment. But from the start—perhaps because I'd almost always had the oral tales from the women in the family—I also began, using the letters from his mother and father that my grandfather had kept, to write about the family at home, especially my grandmother and great-grandmother. They'd written to him every single day and my grandfather had replied every single day (barring those in which battles were raging or they were too much on the move). The two lots, home and front, lived for the other's letters. My grandfather's letters were read and commented on by family and friends. He numbered them. By December he was going towards two hundred.

Reconstituting my grandparents' lives during World War I, and imagining the childhood of my father and aunt who'd only been little in 1914, I was making myself temporarily forget grief at my brother's death. The old deaths consoled me as it were for the fresh one. Or, living immersed in the scale of death World War I had produced, and which scandalized my grandfather from the first day of slaughter, I was reducing to size—or dramatizing?—the death of a brother much younger than myself, who ought not to have died before me.

Then I stopped midway—four hundred pages written, two months of the war barely covered, acres of material to go through: if I did want to write this history, I had to find another way. I am still looking for it.

The piece that follows was written as both exemplar of, and reflection on, the work I had been doing: I hadn't got as far as 1916. But I had become particularly concerned with the relations between home and front, between the sexes. I am very interested still, and am reflecting about what psychoanalysis has to say about the relations between inner and outer violence—in famous people as well as among those groups of people who by participating, enthusiastically or reluctantly, make wars possible. It is a reflection that recent conflicts—the Gulf War at the time the piece was written—the war in Bosnia today—continue to keep alive.

And autobiography? I am now beginning to see with much more clarity than when I wrote how the trials and sins of one generation lead to those of the next. "Mortiferous zones" some analysts call them: those areas of wreckage one generation passes on to the next. I see my grandparents' story as the wreck of a couple, leading to other later wrecks. But also, there was great love between them, there is great love in the later generations: and yet, repeatedly it went astray. How terrible that love should so often be the worst casualty of war. Worst because the failure of love leads to more failures, which lead to more wars . . . There would be no wars outside if there were no wars in the human heart.

Their Wars*

President Bush says, "Read my lips." It is difficult to read the lips of American presidents. To know whether their own words make them move. American words make lips move little. American voices are a crucible in which the sharp angles of many voices have melted into one. American voices make noises which could be of peace, since the diversities of human voices have fused in them.

President Bush speaks. The world listens. He speaks of war. Thousands die. The repercussions are endless.

---

*Previously published in *Women: A Cultural Review*, vol. 3, no. 3 (Oxford University Press, 1992). Reprinted by permission of Oxford University Press. Translated extracts from *Leurs Guerres*, work in progress by Nicole Ward Jouve.

My lips move. I speak. The audience, the friends, are interested, or bored. Something I say moves someone. They think about it. Then they forget. Or they don't.

A Kurdish woman is running in the night. The sky is lit by exploding shells. She carries a bundle on her head, with a plastic can, containing water perhaps, and a kettle tied to it. She holds a little girl by the hand, and on the other side half-carries, half drags, a little boy. The Iraqi army is bombing her village. There are already three hundred villages in Iraqi Kurdistan which are in ruins. Nowhere to go but the desert. Nothing in the desert. Nothing for it but to return in a few days, prop together some of the larger pieces of concrete, or corrugated iron, and make a home of it. If the little boy by her side grows up to be good with a rifle, and brave and bold, and becomes a Peshmerga and can speak at rallies, he may become a leader. Not the woman though. She moves her lips. She does not speak. She screams. Nobody hears. As the nationalisms everywhere flare up, as human voices make a separatist, a self-aggrandizing or a defensive virtue of their quiddity, there is no fused language: speech aborts. In the Babel din of age-old grievances, ambitions and bloodshed, only screams are left.

What is it about politics, about power, that can so multiply some individuals' impact upon others that they will have an effect a thousand, a millionfold greater than that of other individuals who may in real human terms be their equals or their betters? Is it culture, the need for human societies to be hierarchically structured and governed? Is it that power, in a formula that remains striking, has gone to the sex that kills, not to the sex that gives birth? Can ambition, character, geopolitics, inborn advantage, call it development or socio-sexual expectations, make such a crucial difference? Does Bush live a million times more than me, and me a million times more than the Kurdish woman? Yet all three of us can only eat our dinner once, if we're lucky enough to have one.

President Bush belongs to History. My family and myself belong to the privileged category of those happy people who, a French saying has it, have no history, but if they wish have a right to fiction and, possibly, to biography. We touch History when there is a revolution, a civil war, when we meet someone famous, or when our men go to war. We touch History through those of our men who go to war, not through the women who send them parcels and wait. Our obscure men touch the public domain when they make war. Women remain inside the private kingdom: at best the statistics or briefly individualized material of social history, of feminist searches for those who are "hidden from History." In their private homes or hovels, women breed boys who will become

Peshmergas or First World War cannon-fodder, and girls who like them will wait, or flee the bombs. Yes, some women at the time of the First World War became nurses, made munitions, worked on the land, in factories, in offices. Some today do gain access to power, some even fight. But on the whole, at any rate at the time of the First World War, the majority of women remained in the private domain. History, or so at least it seems to me, in that period remained a public realm to which the individual gained access only in so far as he, and rarely she, was part of some collective grouping whose violence, visibility, or command of a scientific discourse made significant in terms of power, or the lack of it. My family, from Marseilles in the south of France, touches History, thanks to my grandfather who was a doctor during the First World War.

We are in the little town of Apt, in Provence. September 1916. Lise is seven. She's been able to read since she was four. She is happy to be at Aunt Adèle's. Maman smiles here, sometimes she even laughs. The only thing is, there is that horrid room to cross to go to the loo. There is no light. It's big. It smells of straw and dust and dried pooh. You have to cross a corridor between cages where the hens are. It is because Aunt Adèle keeps hens that there are such good omelettes with truffles, they've told her; it's one of the local specialties. That's all right with Lise: but in the meantime, the hens move in the dark. You hear rustling feathers, throaty cries, things swell. Sometimes cacklings make her jump, she rushes into Alex's arms. He's as scared as she is but he pretends not to be. They take each other by the hand to go to the loo; she sits while he does it, then he sits to wait for her. If it's a big one and it takes time, they make appreciative or patient faces at each other. At home, when they were little, Alex showed her a trick. He held his little tap and pulled the skin and a red tip came out. He thought that was clever. Lise guffawed to please him; she was relieved not to have such a cumbersome toy. A little tap and a water-tank, really, when it's so simple to pee through a hole. Tonight the children stare into each other's eyes, straining to hear the noises beyond the partition, their stomachs knotted at the thought of the semi-darkness to cross again. What if one of the cages opened?

Aunt Adèle is nice. She calls them "my little rabbits." She makes very good rabbit stews. She is very good at baking. With her floury arms she weighs down on the pastry roll that goes and comes while the succulent puddle of dough spreads. Lise likes the roundness of the arms, the vigorous fingers that knead. She is surprised that Aunt Adèle can manage to bend over: her dress is as stiff as cardboard. That's because she decorates her own dresses herself, with brushes and real paint out of tubes. Maman says, "Adèle is very artistic." Afterwards, the paint hardens, the painted piece with the violets or the petunias stands up all by itself. Adèle is so artistic that she can't go out very much. "An hour at the most," she says, "either by carriage or on foot." That's because her hats are so heavy, with those pine cones she paints in all colors, blue-red or gold to match her dresses. "I have hats that weigh more than a kilo," she says proudly. With their being so heavy, you can't wear them too long, or else it's the migraine or a stiff neck. When Lise is grown up, she will be an artist also. But she will make things that don't stop you from moving about.

The scent of chicken casserole rises up from the kitchen. Lise is flat on her bed. Bliss! Maman has just brought her *Suzette's Weekly*. There are beautiful poems in it that make you cry. Lise enjoys crying. If it's not too long, she will learn "A soldier confides in his little parcel" by heart; she'll recite it after dinner. And everyone will say, "Good Lord, what a clever child!"

> My dear little parcel, I have you, I hold you,
> And my heart can no longer contain its emotion.
> To the desire of opening you up like a child I yield . . .

Lise feels her tears well up. The parcel smells of the verbena that grandmother puts inside her white linen. There is tobacco, a pipe, socks, chocolate . . . chocolate . . . has Aunt Adèle got any left in her cupboard? . . . yes, she must have. And then the little soldier finds a letter from his Maman!

> My beloved son, with this letter,
> You will recognise the gifts from our hearts.
> Think of what we made you promise;
> Frenchmen must return victorious! . . .
>
> . . . Pursue one aim, one only: victory!
> And if one day farewells must be told,
> May our tears exalt your glory
> Be blessed, my son . . . Go! Believe in your God.

Lise wonders whether Maman writes these kinds of letters to Papa. Something makes her suspect not. Maman keeps moaning, "But when will this war be over!" Perhaps that's not a good thing. We must be brave, Aunt Adèle says, and she's an artist. You only have to see how heartened the little soldier is by his Maman's letter!

My good little parcel, this sublime message
Has firmed up my valour, my faith.
Yes, to the end, Maman, worthy of your courage
I will defend Right.

In wet clay and wind, under rain or snow,
I will get him, the Accursed One that came to attack us . . .
And we shall crush the sacrilegious horde . . .

A shudder of hatred for the invader runs over Lise's back. Her foot on the counterpane crushes an imaginary horde. "Let an impure blood quench the thirst of our furrows."

This same Wednesday, 29 September, Xavier, Lise's and Alex's father, "médecin aide-major" in an ambulance in Tartigny, near Amiens, writes in his notebook:

General Verreaux in *L'Oeuvre*: "Strongest advance: 12 kilometres over three months means an advance of 4 kilometres per month (at one point). The depth that needs to be covered to get back to the border is 70 kilometres. But 70 divided by 4 = 18. It would therefore take 18 months to reach the border (at one point), for let us not expect to find the terrain free. Everytime we advance, at the fourth as at the twelfth kilometre, we find masterpieces of defensive organisation."

One month later Xavier notes:

Brayon, my "infirmier major," returning from leave has seen at Saint Just military station a soldier raging at being sent back to the front. He had been freed and returned from Germany for being grievously wounded. He was protesting against being sent back to the front, showing to the entire station that he no longer had either penis or balls. The captain who'd come to shut him up, on seeing him went away without daring to say anything, seeming to think that he was right.

The Germans were constructing 135 submarines per year.

In *L'Oeuvre*, 7 Nov., in the serialized *Le Feu* by Barbusse, a novel. Inside the trench:

A gust of wind, more violent than the others, forced our eyes closed and made us choke. When it had passed and we could see the tornado fleeing through the plain, in places gripping and shaking its muddy rags, digging holes in the water of the trenches that were gaping open as long as a whole army's grave—we continued: "Peoples struggle today so as to be rid of the masters that lead them. This war here, it's like the French Revolution continuing."

"Yes," Xavier comments between brackets, "only the masters will change; just like the Revolution, the leaders alone changed names."
     The links between the first and second text are many. They are united by their dates. Xavier was Lise's and Alex's father. He thought about them all the time, as can be seen from his letters home. He daily received letters, sometimes parcels, from his wife. Like his children he liked good food and, like them as a city-dweller he was afraid of hens. He often told how, one night on guard-duty with his friend Léo Guesde at the Fort de la Colle Noire near Toulon they had trembled because noises kept coming from a bush nearby, and had thought a spy was hiding to murder them. At dawn they had discovered a hen trapped in the branches.
     But the first text belongs to the register of fiction, the second to that of History. The first is written in the feminine mode, centered on inner-ness, a little girl's stream of consciousness. A canny critic would detect traces of an autobiographical female voice, in its interest in the process of "becoming a woman." For instance, the little girl's desire to become an artist like Aunt Adèle is bound by the prescribed though unconscious limits of what being an artist can mean for a woman from the provincial bourgeoisie. The little girl has independence and common sense: she is dimly aware of those limits and has decided that she will look for a less constraining activity when she is grown up. In real life, the partial model for Lise will become a sculptor, love handling clay. But she'll decorously stop when she gets married. The second text is in the masculine mode, focused on journalistic data, on military science. It is produced by a think-ing male subject. The poem in the first text is typical of what little french girls were made to read in the period, both at school and in books and magazines. It idealizes and sentimentalizes the war, it inculcates notions of patriotism and religion. The man, the father, reads the papers, reads a good and realistic war novelist, Barbusse, collects accurate pieces of news. He is sceptical about propaganda and cynical about all idealizations, patriotic or socialist. On the one hand peace, on the other, war. Interior, the front. Women and children in the one, fighting men in the other. Calm and health, death and wounds. The polarizations are many. It is not sur-prising that on 30 June 1918, having gone back to the front after a few days' leave, Xavier should write to his wife:

My darling child,

Back here. Our existence is like a bad dream. One keeps wondering if it's reality we are living. In Marseilles I had trouble believing that the life I was living with you was only for a few days and was not true life. Here I hear things that straightaway put me back inside the war. Darling Isette, you found me stupefied, stunned. Yes I am when I see people from the interior going on with their hardly-changed lives, and when I think of what our life here is like.

And yet there are connections between the two texts. To Alex's game with his "little tap" there answers the abominable amputation of the soldier who was being sent back to the front. The soldier has suffered the ultimate punishment, felt at least to be so by the other men, for having been born of the sex whose gender sentences to war. You could argue that the father was at war, like the rest of the French army, to protect his family, so that it should not be subjected to the fate of the people from Noméiny, shot or burnt alive during the German advance into Lorraine in August 1914. Or so that the banal but precious life that his near and dear were leading should be allowed to continue. Or, like Barbusse, you could say the reverse. You could maintain that it is because ordinary people count for so little in the calculations of governments and military leaders that wars can take place, and that trench warfare revealed men's solidarity with each other, filling them with horror at what was being inflicted upon them, and that this would lead to the end of all wars. That was the view of Léo, Xavier's socialist friend, the son of Jules Guesde who was, with Jaurès, one of the main socialist leaders and thinkers in the pre-war years. A few months after Xavier's entry in his notebook, the Russian Revolution will erupt. Lastly, like recent historians, you could suggest that the First World War was won by the countries which not only possessed the strongest industrial resources but above all by those which had the best-fed populations. The contents of the little soldier's parcel, along with the sense of plenty in Aunt Adèle's house, show that there was no food supply crisis in France at the time, whereas in Germany people were already suffering food shortages, even hunger.

You could therefore produce a historical reading of the passage about the little girl. You could let each element become imbued with a general dimension, become symptomatic as it were. But it's the reverse process that I'm engaged in. I want the "interior" to weigh as much as the front, to occupy as much space. My hypothesis is that individuality

counts as much as collectivity. That significance need not be built upon
the larger meaning. That each individual, whether important or not,
intelligent or not, famous or not, counts just as much as any other. That
the Kurdish woman, President Bush, and myself, are equal. I can only
hook into History centrifugally, not centripetally. My grandfather's
notebook for August 1914, because it had survived, could make sense
for me of the historical accounts and analyses of the beginning of the
war. All notes for the period of the battle of the Marne had disappeared
(perhaps everyone was much too busy to make notes . . .), and no
amount of detailed reading of War Ministry Annals, even hour after
hour, enabled me to imagine or re-live a thing about my grandfather, his
regiment . . . Only Maurice Genevoix's *L'Eté 1914* helped.

This is not just because the imagination cannot reach beyond the
self or its blood-bonds. I do think that if one could understand a collection of different and passionate individuals in a given period, even if
they were not a typical social grouping, one might have some insight
into why wars smolder and burst out. All my life I have given myself
mental slaps whenever I caught myself thinking that the crises in my life
strangely echoed, or paralleled, various world crises. It occurs to me
today that the Greeks were after all not so wrong in showing, through
their kings and queens, that when plague has taken possession of one
family it can go on to devastate an entire city. We, the ordinary, the
obscure, think that we do not have power. What if we were all kings
and queens? What if, as some argue, the wing-beat of a butterfly affected
all space? What if effects were horizontal, not just vertical, and political
power only one of those effects? What if the power of words, as Poe
and Baudelaire stated, never ceases to have eddying repercussions? If not
only every shell that's shot and blows up a house, a monastery, ancient
ramparts, but every action that pollutes water, every gas that rises, could
contribute to destroy the planet? If true life, the true source of power,
were to be found in the banal, the little? If the pain of the "interior," in all
senses of the word, were equal to the pain of the front, and related to it?

Xavier writes to his wife on 23 July 1918. The German advance is
devastating, France on the brink of defeat:

Very darling Isette,

This nightwatch, we haven't been disturbed. Our morning has
been spent bandaging . . .

I am writing to you from my room, near the window.

I hear the noise of the diners' forks down below.

We're on the second round of the meal tonight. The tin mugs clatter, but the conversation is nil. Wherever he goes the chief surgeon casts a tragic coldness. What a strange man! Very miserly with leave. His secretary, a male nurse, keen to visit his sick wife, volunteered to give blood (for a blood transfer). It's worth ten days' leave. He's the fifteenth male nurse Fricker has bled. I'd readily volunteer if I could get leave. Fricker continues in a deep black mood in the midst of all his pitiful wounded. What a spectacle! He goes round the sheds to flee from these sad groans. What sadness!

Two days later, upon receipt of a letter from his wife:

Isette. What shall I write? I do not know. My head is broken. I received your letter of Monday 22 at noon. I read it through at table, then straight-away I went 200 metres down into the park, in a meadow to conceal my grief. I just lay there, with your letter in my hand, stupefied . . . What are my vicissitudes and little troubles compared to your sorrow? I am bowed down by it . . . Truly, I had rather be ill than in such pain. I re-read your letter. Tears come to my eyes. If at least my grief could be some use—I see you alone with our two little darlings near you. I see you alone, always alone—I see you alone, climbing the road to the Aygalades. I see you alone at home.

I am overwhelmed by the fatality that weighs upon us. No, my Isette, never would I have believed I could suffer as much as I have in this war.

12

"Invisible Presences": Life-Writing and Vera Brittain's Testament of Friendship

Marion Shaw

Let any woman imagine for a moment a biography of herself based upon those records she has left, those memories fresh in the minds of surviving friends, those letters that chanced to be kept, those impressions made . . . What secrets, what virtues, what passions, what discipline, what quarrels would, on the subject's death, be lost forever? How much would have vanished or been distorted or changed, even in our memories? We tell ourselves stories of our past, make fictions or stories of it, and these narratives *become* the past, the only part of our lives that is not submerged.[1]

During the late 1930s, two women labored at auto/biographies: Virginia Woolf was engaged on the appalling grind of her life of Roger Fry, published in 1940, and was writing her autobiographical "A Sketch of the Past"; Vera Brittain was slowly writing *Testament of Friendship*, her biography of Winifred Holtby which is also an account of herself as one half of a relationship "which continued unbroken and unspoilt for sixteen incomparable years." This also was published in 1940.

More than fifty years later I am writing a biography of Winfred Holtby. This essay relates to one of my major concerns, which is to recognize both Brittain and her biography as powerful presences in Holtby's life and legend, yet not to take them on trust, but to see what else there was to Holtby, to tell another story of her life. Part of this essay scrutinizes Brittain's narrative for what was left out, what there is new to say about Holtby.

But in showing that Brittain's account is not the whole truth, the danger is that of proposing an alternative, truer story. As far as the finished biography is concerned, this may be what will have to happen. To be readable, and therefore marketable, biographies must make a mapping of their subject, and decide that she or he not only did this and that, but was this and not that as a character. My map of Holtby, though different from Brittain's, will invent and enclose Holtby as surely as Brittain's has done. Virginia Woolf, who so persistently, subtly, and self-consciously worked over the auto/biographical terrain, knew this when she wrote in *Orlando* that of the many selves out of which a person is built up, "one on top of another, as plates are piled on a waiter's hand," biographers such as herself must choose for their subjects "only those selves we have found room for."[2] It is her probing of the compelling yet unsatisfactory mystery of life-writing which sets the terms of the other, meditative aspect of this essay. A biography itself cannot take time out, so to speak, to ponder its own rationale; but an essay like this, in a book like this, asks those questions which are the submerged agenda of the act of life-writing: why has this been chosen and not that, what are the autobiographical pressures that shape it, what has been created and not merely discovered?

Woolf and Brittain had a point of contact in Holtby who in 1932 had published the first study in English of Woolf and had visited her during the writing of it. Brittain sent Woolf her biography of Holtby and this arrived just as *Roger Fry* was being finished. Woolf was unenthusiastic about *Testament of Friendship*: ". . . tho' I wrote Vera a polite letter, I somehow didn't enjoy or wholly like her Life: too petty and that horrid little reviewer's gossip; she had a good deal more to her than V. B. saw . . . it was a scrambling gasping affectionate book: and W. H. deserved a better."[3] Her own biography, *Roger Fry*, she thought of as differently analytic and dispassionate. It was "an experiment in self suppression" and "there was such a mass of detail that the only way I could hold it together was by abstracting it into themes."[4]

Both women were exercised by the question of truthfulness in biography. Woolf ponders this in "A Sketch of the Past" where she meditates upon her childhood and the influence of her mother and her half-sister, Stella, and their untimely deaths. Although Woolf believes she should strive to capture the facts of what happened—to "fit a plug into the wall; and listen to the past"—at the same time she is sceptical about the value of this: ". . . people write what they call 'lives' of other people; that is, they collect a number of events, and leave the person to whom it happened unknown."[5] What is missing from such "lives" is the important "invisible presences" which Woolf explains as:

. . . the consciousness of other groups impinging on ourselves; public opinion; what other people say and think; all those magnets which attract us this way to be like that, or repel us the other and make us different from that; . . . well, if we cannot analyse these invisible presences, we know very little of the subject of the memoir; and again how futile life-writing becomes.[6]

In a glide from the lives of other people to herself, Woolf concludes by saying: "I see myself as a fish in a stream; deflected; held in place; but cannot describe the stream." This is an image she uses of the difference between the public world of work and the private self in *Between the Acts* when Giles, the stockbroker who earns the money to keep Pointz Hall functioning but would rather have been a farmer, thinks to himself, "So one thing led to another; and the conglomeration of things pressed you flat; held you fast, like a fish in water. So he came for the week-end, and changed."[7]

Vera Brittain begins *Testament of Friendship* with the image of a stream, but this time it is the subject of the biography who is the stream and who names herself as such. Brittain recalls that Holtby, on being asked to write her autobiography, replied:

I don't see how I can write an autobiography . . . I never feel I've really had a life of my own. My existence seems to me like a clear stream which has simply reflected other people's stories and problems.[8]

If Woolf is troubled by the difficulty of surmounting the boundaries of self to connect with "the consciousness of other groups" which "tug this way and that" every day and keep "the subject of the memoir . . . in position," the apparent problem with Holtby is to identify the auto/biographical subject at all. She is, it seems, not the fish but the watery medium which reflects the self-fish lives of others.

In their musings more than fifty years ago, Woolf and Brittain articulated a debate on biography which has renewed currency nowadays. The problems they confronted are to do with the relationship between the "subject of the memoir" (as Woolf puts it) and the "invisible presences" of other people, public opinion, and the world of work: how to capture that web of connectedness which radiates out from the subject and without which the subject is life-less. There is also the relationship of the subject with the biographer. Both Woolf and Brittain knew their subjects intimately and so were presences while they were alive, but additionally they are posthumous presences, tugging the subject this way and that, holding the fish in place in the stream of their own interpretation and in the context they select for the subject of their life-writing. Both knew that what they wrote had to do with themselves as much as or more than with their subjects: not only the thematic abstracting they did but their life-writing as personal exploration, as autobiographical therapy. In recalling the writing of *To the Lighthouse*, Woolf says: "I suppose I did for myself what psychoanalysts do for their patients. I expressed some very long felt and deeply felt emotion [about her parents]. And in expressing it I explained it and then laid it to rest." But of course she has not laid it to rest entirely because "A Sketch of the Past" is her mother and father and Stella remembered yet again. For Brittain, the perspective and detachment developed during the years of writing have clarified memory and modified the bitterness of loss; although far less self-consciously than Woolf, she too has revisited her own past and written her own story through that of her friend. In the process, both women extracted a truth for their own purposes, a relative truth.

Woolf admits to the reductive nature of what she is doing in "abstracting . . . into themes" the massy, fragmentary, and disturbing details of Fry's life in order to show a life lived according to principles rather than accident. Brittain's purpose was no less exemplary. This was not only to write a personal elegy on "the best friend whom life has given me" (p. 4) but more generally to celebrate female friendship as potentially equal to the great male friendships of history and literature. Her theme is "loyalty and affection" between women as "a noble relationship," but it is a theme fraught with problems during a time when female friendships are "mocked, belittled and falsely interpreted" (p. 2). The false interpretation she fears is that of a lesbian relationship between herself and Holtby which gossip had certainly proposed and which they had apparently talked and joked about together. So anxious is Brittain to disclaim a lesbian connection that she begins her biography defensively, as in the following passage where she describes female friendship as a preparation for marriage and motherhood, where, in fact, she imposes a heterosexual limitation on the friendship she is about to describe:

> . . . loyalty and affection between women is a noble relationship, which, far from impoverishing actually enhances the love of a girl for her lover, of a wife for her husband, of a mother for her children. (p. 2)

In telling Holtby's story, Brittain looked for her model to one of the few biographies of a woman by a woman: "I turned, as often, to Mrs.

Gaskell's *Life of Charlotte Bronte*." In particular, she aligned herself with Gaskell's outspokenness over Bronte's relationship with her family, and she approvingly quotes Gaskell's statement that "I came to the conclusion of writing truly if I wrote at all: of withholding nothing." This gave Brittain permission to be less than charitable to Holtby's sister and perhaps also her mother, both of whom she disliked and, in the case of Holtby's mother, was jealous of. Otherwise the resemblance between Gaskell's and Brittain's biographies is not obvious. Gaskell's biographical method is both self-effacing and inclusive of others (which is not to say it does not have its own agenda) whereas Brittain's is one of self-reference. *Testament of Friendship*, as its title proclaims, is about the relationship between two people as it is remembered and mourned by one of them. Like "the great male friendships of history," this friendship takes on an idealized quality which is nourished by the notion of Holtby's transparent personality and her selflessness. This is a theme continued by Brittain into her writings subsequent to *Testament of Friendship* and it tends to diminish Holtby into a pitiful saint, a foil, so it seems, to Brittain's more successful and (heterosexually) fulfilled life:

> How sadly conscious I felt that I had always accepted from her so much more than I gave, and now could give no more. None of her books published in her lifetime had sold remarkably, so she helped mine to sell magnificently. The only man whom she really loved failed her, so she identified herself with my married happiness. Her burdens were great and intolerable, so she shouldered mine which were often trivial. When she learned that she must never have children, she shared in the care of ours.[9]

Brittain's appropriation of Holtby extends also to her use of Holtby's own words. Brittain's intention in including this autobiographical evidence is "to let her make her own contribution." Yet as it turns out, Holtby's "own contribution" is highly selective because it largely comprises her correspondence with Brittain. Even within this constraint there are selective processes operating which illustrate how subjective and singular is this truth about Holtby. To explain what I mean here I wish to take one month in Holtby's life and examine ways in which the narratives of this time rub against each other to unsettle the biographical finality *Testament of Friendship* appears to offer.

The month in question is from late June to late July 1926. Holtby had gone to South Africa in January of that year to lecture for the League of Nations Union and also to see her friend Jean McWilliam with whom she had served in France during the war. As various accounts make clear, Brittain was jealous of Holtby's other friends, and Jean McWilliam must have seemed a threat to Brittain's pre-eminent position in Holtby's affections, not least because Brittain herself had uncoupled their own relationship the year before by marrying the political scientist George Gordon Catlin and going to America with him. By mid-1926, however, after being cold-shouldered by American publishers, and perhaps finding marriage less engrossing than she had believed, Brittain had decided to return to England for six months in order to rescue her career as a writer. She was also eager to resume her relationship with Holtby on the old grounds, that is, by sharing the flat in Maida Vale they had shared before her marriage. This was the first move in a negotiation which finally resulted in a household in which Brittain and her two children, Holtby, and Gordon Catlin on his six-monthly visits to England, made their home, with the addition of a couple, the Burnetts, who housekept for them. What was eventually to be a very satisfactory arrangement for Brittain, and to some extent for Holtby too, began its crucial shaping during this month when both Brittain and Holtby were returning home from America and South Africa respectively. Brittain's nervousness about this reunion is recalled in *Testament of Friendship*:

> At Tilbury my mother met her, and she spent a night in Kensington [the Brittain family home] before going on to Yorkshire [Holtby's family home]. Amongst other accumulated documents, she found there a sheaf of letters from me. I was due back from the United States in mid-August . . . to recover the lost contacts at home. Thanks to one of those idiotic misgivings which long separation provokes, I had found—Heaven knows how or where—some imaginary lack of response in Winifred's vivid, delightful letters, and had written suggesting a little sadly that perhaps she might not want to share the flat again during my six months in England. (p. 261)

Brittain had voiced her misgivings in a letter of late June 1926: "Sometimes I feel anxious, because you said 'I will meet you at Southampton if possible,' but 18 months ago you would have said 'I *will* meet you at Southampton.' Is something very wrong at home, Sweetieheart, or is it that time and distance are making me apprehensive about you as I used to be about Gordon?" Letters seem to be missing from this period but there must have been more of this kind in the "sheaf of letters" awaiting Holtby, sufficient to make her write back a troubled, self-accusing, and emotional letter. Brittain reproduced some

of this letter in *Testament of Friendship*; in the following extract from the
letter itself, those parts of Holtby's letter which were not included in
Testament of Friendship are given in italics:

> I do not find demonstrative intimacy an easy thing. *I had never
> thought to show such natural demonstrative affection as I find rises
> quite naturally now from my love for you. But expression of this love is
> only the outward and visible form. It is called forth from me when you
> are near, or when, as today, a long silence is broken by a series of letters
> that bring me poignantly near to you. Your presence breaks down a
> sort of inhibition that makes me otherwise unconsciously reluctant to
> show my feelings.* This is probably a mean and ungenerous spirit
> which hesitates to surrender an iota of its selfish integrity. I do
> not excuse it. I am only trying to explain. *It is not that I love you
> less. I love you quite absurdly.* But this inarticulateness, this inhibi-
> tion against the expression of love, is always ready to rise up in
> me. *The coldness is the insincerity, not the warmth. But I do not even
> recognise it myself for coldness, and, though I know I have no right to
> ask it, I must ask you to trust my love.* I wish that it were other-
> wise. I wish that I had not this subconscious desire to possess
> myself completely. *"Away with love,"* it says. *"No surrender. No
> surrender." But the love is there, and myself, my conscious, deliberate,
> reasoning self, desires it to be there, knows that it is a matter of enrich-
> ment, not impoverishment. My love for you is all gain to me.* I think
> that all love is gain. Only at times, *especially when tired or very
> full of business*, an instinct beyond thought comes between me
> and the expression of love. *This is badly expressed. There is a thun-
> derstorm somewhere in the distance, and I was only in bed three hours
> last night, and today has been passed in a whirl of talk and letters. I
> can't think properly.*[10]

The letter continues vehemently: "Oakwood Court [Brittain's parents'
home] is full of you. I feel you. I need you every hour. Listen, my
heart . . . you must believe these things—for they are true. I love you. I
need you. I want to be with you." In *Testament of Friendship* Brittain
suppresses most of these avowals, weaving into those she does retain
small extracts from another letter, in particular two sentences in which
Holtby says, "Nothing could change me except your changing. Not
your attitude towards me, I mean, but towards life."

The effect of Brittain's selection for publication of lines from her
friend's letter, and her inclusion of lines from other letters, is to
enhance the idea that has been strongly present during the whole of

her editing of these accounts of this episode, namely, that theirs was a friendship based on qualities of rationality and mutual regard for certain moral and social values. It certainly was a "noble relationship" of this kind, but it was also intense, hungry, and anxious in ways that Brittain did not want, or could not bring herself, to acknowledge. In her editing of the correspondence of this time, if she does not directly belie the main import of Holtby's response, she does smooth away the stress of Holtby's writing, the strains of what she is saying, along with the self-abasement of Holtby's assurance of her love for Brittain and her willingness to respond within the terms set by Brittain. This is particularly acute in her conclusion to the manuscript letter in which she picks up Brittain's comment that she is apprehensive about her "as I used to be about Gordon." Holtby refers her feeling, indeed defers her "pleasure," to Brittain's husband: "My little love, if you doubt—ask Gordon if it could be possible, having loved you, to cease. His answer will be adequate, perhaps, as my intention . . . We will make this winter a time of profitable work for you if we can. For me, it will be pleasure. I wish Gordon were to be here too." Her final sentence summarizes her capitulation to Brittain's needs and complaints: "Thank you for all your letters—and forgive me, my small sweet love."

What was there to forgive? As far as the existing letters are concerned, it seems no more than the apparent inclusion in one of Holtby's letters (which no longer exists) of the phrase "if possible" and the fact that she did not underline *will* in saying that she would meet Brittain at Southampton. But it is by such trifles that intense friendships, like love affairs, are conducted and establish their power relations: who gives and who takes, who is strong and who weak.

It is tempting to see Vera Brittain as the villain of this episode, a powerful manipulator of the evidence. As editor and biographer she deprives Holtby of emotional substance and complexity, and as friend she is tyrannously exacting; a double action rendering Holtby invisible, no more than a stream reflecting Brittain's own desires. Several people who knew them both, like Storm Jameson, St. John Irvine, and Ernest Rhys, believed this to be true and came to dislike Brittain for it, as well as for other reasons. Self-centered, suspicious, and tactless, she was not popular, particularly not with women. She knew this herself, as is obvious from another letter she wrote to Holtby in the summer of 1926:

No wonder Lady Rhondda loves you, and Percy [Harris] and Mr. Hutchinson, and all the nice, nice people that I wished loved me, and who never do. The wonder always is that you do love me, that you see more in me than what most people see—which is a combination of egotistical bitterness plus a kind of insincere prettiness plus an intermittent (and, as they think, designing) attraction for men.[11]

The ambiguous compliment of this comment once again negates Holtby in heterosexual terms (the implication being that, Percy and Mr. Hutchinson notwithstanding, Holtby isn't attractive to men, which is why people love her) and at the same time is highly seductive towards her, attributing to her powers of love and perception beyond the common. It was an appeal that Holtby could not resist because, as the letters of this time indicate, if Brittain needed to be demonstrably loved beyond the norm, Holtby needed to demonstrate her capacity to love beyond what might be thought reasonable, even to the extent of a denial of self-interest amounting to self-annihilation.

The picture I start to create from the unpublished and suppressed accounts of this month in 1926, what one might call Holtby's hidden autobiographical contribution, is that, having compensated for Brittain's departure by visiting South Africa and begun to protect herself by distancing her feelings, she now finds herself called upon to give an intimacy of friendship similar to that of their time together before Brittain's marriage. Although she is willing to do so, she must have reservations: she must remind Vera, and herself, that Vera is now married, that Gordon has to be included, and the heterosexuality of that relationship brought into alignment with their friendship. When Holtby writes: ". . . ask Gordon if it would be possible, having loved you, to cease. His answer will be adequate, perhaps, as my intention," there is a capitulation on her part not only to Gordon's preeminent position as Brittain's "lover" but also to the superiority of his means of response. As husband, he can respond physically in ways that Holtby cannot, and because of his position he can speak of love, can assume an accepted (because heterosexual) discourse of love, that Holtby is excluded from. It is in this light that Holtby's protested inarticulacy earlier in the manuscript letter may be read: "I want so much to make you see, and I can only flounder stupidly in words," she says, but her "stupidity" is that of a negotiator for whom there are no accepted means of communication, to whom the future is uncertain and in which she is only ever likely to be supernumerary, the surplus single woman in attendance on a married couple.

Britain's account of these changes and development in their relationship in *Testament of Friendship* occupies no more than a page, including the extract from the letter quoted above. When she does record the final move into a triangular household, she does so with even greater brevity and briskness. "When G. decided to change his American professorship to a half-time post so that our family could be born and reared in England, she [Holtby] suggested joining the household from which he would so often be absent. The Maida Vale flat, we agreed, would be too small [and in] September [1927] we moved into an upper maisonette . . . off the Earl's Court Road." What Holtby thought about this move into a matrimonial home (indeed, what Gordon thought about it too), why she chose a mode of living in which, Persephone-like, she would be displaced for six months of the year, is not recorded in *Testament of Friendship*.

Perhaps traces of the stress of this time are to be found in the fictional work that Holtby wrote after she returned from South Africa, her novel *The Land of Green Ginger*. Its large, fair, enthusiastic, and slap-dash heroine, Joanna, is to some extent a self-portrait, and there is a brief appearance of a Brittain-like character in Joanna's "small ardent" friend Rachel. However more significant is Joanna's weariness from dealing with other people's troubles, most obviously those of her husband, Teddy. In his religiosity and self-pity, he bears some resemblance to Holtby's unsatisfactory male friend, Harry, but his easy jealousy, his histrionic behavior and his demands on Joanna are reminiscent of Brittain's relationship with Holtby: "[Joanna's] distraction lay always in her loving heart, which warmed too easily to pity . . . Teddy stood in the doorway, making a sensation. Joanna knew that he had got over his mood. [Her] fatigue fell off her like the weight of Christian's sins."[12] Joanna's escape after Teddy's death, like Holtby's after Brittain's marriage, was to South Africa. Holtby never went to South Africa again although she brought back from her visit there in 1926 a powerful commitment to Black trade unionism which was quite independent of Brittain's concerns.

Apart from this oblique working over in *The Land of Green Ginger* of the sensitive territory of difficult and demanding relationships, there seems to be little else remaining in published form of Holtby's own testament of friendship. There is no more than a cursory mention of the unsettled nature of this period in what survives of her correspondence with the other close friend she habitually wrote to, Jean McWilliam. Here, all that Holtby says is in a letter dated 27 July 1926, written from her Yorkshire family home ten days after her letter of re-commitment to Brittain: "My own affairs are uncertain at the moment. After six months' complete independence, I shall let them be guided by other people's convenience for the next six." The letter was published in *Letters to a Friend* (1937),[13] edited by Alice Holtby (Holtby's mother) and Jean

McWilliam, and its cool summary of her situation also plays a role in a public view of Holtby as unselfish, cheerful, calm, and even dispassionate in her response to change. *Letters to a Friend* pre-dated *Testament of Friendship* as a published document and made, therefore, a prior and perhaps preemptive biographical strike, stressing a cheerful, energetic, and combative Holtby who belonged to a time and a friendship before she met Brittain. Brittain makes a veiled allusion in the introduction to *Testament of Friendship* to this undoubtedly rivalrous publishing act, when she comments on the superficiality of the "hasty portrait": "I could no more have produced a truthful study . . . in the months following her death than I could have written *Testament of Youth* immediately after 1918" (p. 4).

A late rejoinder to *Letters to a Friend* and a final account of this period comes from a volume published in 1960, *The Selected Letters of Winifred Holtby and Vera Brittain*, edited by Vera Brittain and Geoffrey Handley-Taylor. Privately printed, in a limited edition of 500 copies, the volume served to mark the quarter centenary of Holtby's death and was prompted, so Brittain says in the Introduction, by "the wish of many readers and admirers . . . to have some hitherto still unpublished work of hers issued." Otherwise, it had been Brittain's intention to "leave this correspondence unpublished during my lifetime." In *Selected Letters* radical editing of the letters of this period has taken place so that even less of the stress and indecision remain. All that is left of the impassioned parts of Holtby's letter of 17 July 1926 is this:

> I have so much to say. Oakwood Court is full of you. I feel you, I need you every hour.

> We will make this winter a time of profitable work for you if we can. For me, it will be pleasure. I wish that G. were to be here too.

The heavily edited selection Brittain and her assistant make from the correspondence is focused on work, writing, and marriage, particularly marriage which emerges on the part of both Holtby and Brittain as a topic to be discussed with the slightly sceptical good humour befitting two emancipated, feminist, and rational women of the modern age. The storms of Brittain's insecurity and Holtby's self-abasement have left even less trace than in *Testament of Friendship*, the only evidence of them being a letter from Brittain of 30 July 1926 which, typically for *Selected Letters*, sensibly resolves its emotional disclosures into general discussion and analysis:

I don't think in my heart of hearts I ever doubted you *weren't* different; I really understood all the time that you were engrossed and overfull of work and travel . . . What really started me wondering, I think, was little postcards from your mother forwarded by mine—and assumptions by mine that you wouldn't . . . prefer the arrangement that I was basing all my plans on. In normal conditions one would take no notice of such things, but . . . after a year of facing assumptions on the part of everybody that because one is married one won't want to lead the same sort of life as one did before, it is different. [W]hen people meet you and think you unmarried, their first question always is "What's your job?" But when they know you are married, they ask: "What is your husband?"[14]

Brittain was understandably determined not to dwindle into a wife and her modern views on the benefits of a "semi-detached" marriage and her drive to advance her career as well as to marry and have children made her reliant, perhaps to the point of ruthless exploitation, on her friend's selflessness. Writing of her future plans to Holtby in an unpublished letter written on the eve of her return home from America in 1926, she said: "Here they are, my red-hot irons, and the drawing them out with the best possible effect depends entirely on you." One of the best possible effects was the family which became established in the maisonette off the Earl's Court Road in 1927. It was unusual: a *menage a trois* of Holtby, Brittain, and Catlin, with the later addition of Brittain's two children; there was also a stream of visitors, particularly Holtby's African associates. This household transcended the norms of bourgeois heterosexuality, and in its inclusivity it broke down the barriers between private and public service; it also allowed for the endurance and strengthening of the female friendship at its center. This way of living was an exceptional feminist achievement and this is what *Testament of Friendship* celebrates. But the costs of this achievement both in terms of Holtby's contribution and of the image Brittain so strenuously aimed to convey of the nobility of that friendship should also be recognized and, in a different way, celebrated.

This celebration is where I, as Holtby's latter-day biographer, come in. I am concerned with giving Holtby a self she seems to lack in Brittain's account and to do this I have to break down, or at least relativize, the "truth" of *Testament of Friendship*. Brittain's biography is like a dragon at the gates of Holtby's life; or, to continue Woolf's trope, it is a powerful stream flowing with guilt and high principle which obscures the fish of Holtby's self to such an extent that she seems to be the object and not the subject of her own life. It would be easy to write altogether of the stream of history which held her in position, notably of the progressive movements of the interwar years to which she seems to have been an index, and of the exhausting program of work she put herself through. She was an exemplary feminist/socialist of her period and to write of her as such would be a worthwhile act of bio-historical reclamation. But in doing so would I be repeating Brittain's act of testamentary depersonalization, writing of the invisible presences and not the fish of Holtby's self? For although Woolf is right in that one cannot know the "subject of the memoir" without analyzing the invisible presences, surely a subject must be a presence also?

All that remains of Holtby now is a number of texts, her own and those of others, and if Holtby-as-subject is to be discovered it is through these that I must do it. Yet, as surely as Vera Brittain, I too shall select, arrange, and authorize those texts according to the "truth" of my biographical interpretation, for I too am becoming an invisible presence in the life of Winifred Holtby. On the evidence of this essay, I appear to be bringing to life-writing a woman more troubled and insecure, less "noble" perhaps, but also less elegiac, than the figure in *Testament of Friendship*. That would be in line with most modern biographies in which nobility and selflessness are seen as sham, and public strength as a front behind which to hide weakness and loneliness. This leans temptingly towards a romantic reading of Holtby in which she is the misunderstood victim, a thwarted lesbian, perhaps, certainly exploited and unfulfilled, her brave struggle minimized by the egocentrism of her friend.

In her biography of Mary Kingsley, Dea Birkett says that she is aware that she has "*created* and not *revealed* Mary Kingsley":

> Depending on the audience I am writing for, which of her writings I have read most recently, or even my mood, I may set out to either defend or destroy her. I do not put this down, as some biographers might, to Mary Kingsley being an elusive, essentially unknowable person, endowing her with a certain mystery. I see these constant shifts in my assessment of her as integral to the creation of my subject.[15]

This is not to say that events should be falsified or tracts of written evidence ignored; the plug into the wall of the past should be firmly connected. But in the matter of invisible presences and of the selection, arrangement and emphasis of the evidence, then Dea Birkett is surely right in suggesting that this is creation rather than revelation, and that as created fiction it too is unstable according to the many and changing presences in the life of the biographer. I am acutely aware that the "creation" of Winifred Holtby's life is for me a challenging act of autobiography: I come from the same area—the East Riding of Yorkshire—as Holtby; she died almost at the point at which I was born, and my mother—like Holtby a first-generation educated woman, and a powerful influence on me as was her mother on Holtby—was almost the same age. My own life now has grown into a mode similar to Holtby's; my life is lived, like hers apparently was, in the public sphere of work rather than within the intimacy of a conventional family. I want to do and see things in the public world like she seems to have done. I am becoming a stream. Part of the biographical appeal of Holtby could be to prove that it is all right to be like that, that in its very transparency such a life is fulfilling. For Holtby it was, or at least for most of the time and with most people, though not always with Vera Brittain, as we have seen. Feminist biography, Liz Stanley has said, should accept the diversity and complexity of a person's life, not straighten it out into a single narrative: "'she was like that *and* like that' should be its motto."[16]

At the same time, a biographical narrative that is too dispersed and undecided will disappoint its readership. Readers desire and expect a narrative, a story of someone's life. But of course the readership itself is not homogeneous: Yorkshire people who remember the Holtby family, students taking Women's Studies courses, feminist historians, or the common reader who engaged Woolf's attention so warmly—this diverse readership will constitute invisible presences who will bring to the biography assumptions and demands which will also tug the subject of the memoir this way and that. I too am deflected by the presences of those potential readers of the text, those unseen negotiators in the act of life-writing, who will ask in yet another way: What is the relationship between the subject and her context, the life and the writing of the Life, the stream, and the fish? To quote Stanley again: ". . . lives, and the writing of lives, are all intertextually complex and . . . to every statement about them should be appended another beginning 'And also. . . .'"[17]

Notes

1. Carolyn G. Heilbrun, *Writing a Woman's Life* (London: The Women's Press, 1989), p. 51.

2. Virginia Woolf, *Orlando* (Harmondsworth: Penguin Books, 1942), pp. 217–18.

3. Nigel Nicolson, ed., *Leave the Letters Till We're Dead: The Letters of Virginia Woolf, Vol. 6, 1936–41* (London: The Hogarth Press, 1980), p. 379.

4. Ibid., p. 426.

5. Virginia Woolf, *Moments of Being* (London: Grafton Books, 1989), p. 78.

6. Ibid., pp. 89–90.

7. Virginia Woolf, *Between the Acts* (Harmondsworth: Penguin Books, 1987).

8. Vera Brittain, *Testament of Friendship* (London: Virago Press), p. 1. Page references are henceforth given in the text.

9. Vera Brittain, *Testament of Experience* (Glasgow: Fontana Books, 1980), pp. 133–34.

10. Letter from Winifred Holtby to Vera Brittain, 17 July 1926, Winifred Holtby Collection (WHC), Hull Central Library. Copyright with kind permission of the literary executor of the Holtby estate, Mr. Paul Berry.

11. Letter from Vera Brittain to Winifred Holtby, 30 July 1926, WHC.

12. Winifred Holtby, *The Land of Green Ginger* (London: Jonathan Cape, 1927), p. 41.

13. Winifred Holtby, *Letters to a Friend*, ed. Alice Holtby and Jean McWilliam (London: Collins, 1937), p. 419.

14. *Selected Letters of Winifred Holtby and Vera Brittain*, ed. Vera Brittain and Geoffrey Handley-Taylor (London and Hull: A. Brown and Sons, 1960), p. 148.

15. Dea Birkett, *Mary Kingsley: Imperial Adventuress* (London: Macmillan, 1992), p. xxiii.

16. Quoted Birkett, p. xxiii.

17. Liz Stanley, *The Auto/biographical I: The Theory and Practice of Feminist Auto/biography* (Manchester: Manchester University Press, 1992), p. 18.

13

"Tidal Edges" in Contemporary Women's Poetry: Towards a Model of Critical Empathy

Vicki Bertram

Diane Freedman uses the metaphor of tidal edges to evoke the disorienting but exhilarating experience of reading poetry.[1] The ragged shape of the poem's right-hand margin resembles an aerial view of waves creeping along the beach, in contrast to the straight line of justified prose. Her point is that poetry destabilizes the reader's firm sense of self, demanding a fuller subjective involvement in the reading process, akin to the dissolution of boundaries between reader and text. There are, she writes, "no clear edges at all"—no certainty as to where the poem ends and the reader—or reading—begins.

This blurring of the distinction between the text and the subjectivity of the reader forms the topic of this article. I am interested in the processes of reading poetry, and in particular, in the way critics maneuver themselves from the position of readers—affected by and involved in the text—to that more detached perspective required for critical assessment. Contemporary poetry criticism adopts the convention of the impersonal critic, and thus betrays no sense either of the processes involved in the reading, nor of the reader reacting to the poem's argument. I find the neutral, level voices of such criticism disappointing: they wrap up the poems too neatly, as though their meanings were obvious and uncontroversial. In this essay I suggest that poetry critique would be enriched by the recuperation of those earlier stages of response, when the critic begins to make decisions about emphasis and interpretation. It is at this stage that the critic's subjectivity is so important. Later on, the personal origins of their reading disappear, and the criticism slides back into the rhetoric of the great "universal themes" of lyric poetry. Shifting the emphasis to this earlier stage might produce more lively debate about the poets' ideas, since it would record readers' reactions instead of concentrating solely on potted descriptions of the poets' themes. It would also form a challenge to the still-healthy hegemony of objective criticism that dominates discussions of contemporary poetry.

My argument is not entirely original, of course—Adrienne Rich is probably the most famous proponent of a style of criticism in which the critic is "active participant and identifiable voice."[2] In the course of this essay I shall examine the characteristics of this approach, and point out some of what I believe to be its failings. I wish I had a better model to propose, but I can also see problems with the alternative I offer—hence the hedgy "towards" of my title! My aim is to develop a way of holding the three components—poem, poet, and reader—in delicate balance, so that a blending of subjectivities can take place, in which none of the three dominates or engulfs the others.[3]

The knotty problem of autobiography is the underlying theme of this piece. Feminist literary criticism over the last twenty years has deconstructed the supposed objectivity of traditional evaluative criteria. Critics like Jane Tompkins, Nicole Ward Jouve, and Nancy Miller have promoted a style of more personal academic writing,[4] in which the critic's personality, perspective, and politics are acknowledged as determinants in their work. But the inclusion of this autobiographical material can be simply distracting, shifting attention from text to critic and, while some critics' lives might make gripping reading, it is probably fair to say that the vast majority are pretty dull.[5] In order to keep the focus on the poem, I advocate a cagey compromise in which the autobiographical ingredients of any reading combine so subtly with other knowledges that they leave only a faint—but identifiable—trace in the written critical response. I would call this a subjective approach, as opposed to an autobiographical one, since its aim is to situate the critic's authority, keeping the emphasis on the text, rather than to use the text to relate the critic's life-story.[6] But there is a further difficulty with this model's underlying endorsement of the authority of experience, since the idea of empathy which I am promoting directly contradicts this kind of identity politics. Such empathy requires a paradoxical state of being conscious of one's own identity and at the same time, able to imagine a position beyond/outside that identity; identity politics view such transcendence with profound suspicion. Because of this unresolvable tension, I have used the endnotes to record a sort of counter-argument. While it does not provide solutions, I hope this piece will generate debate around the oddly-neglected area of poetry criticism.

Strange Bedfellows? Reconceptualizing the
Relationship Between Theory and Poetry

There is still very little critical work published on contemporary
women poets in the United Kingdom and Ireland. What there is tends
to adopt a classic liberal-humanist approach, castigating the work for
being too concerned with specifically female experiences.[7] As a feminist
my problems with this should be obvious, but attempts to outline a
feminist poetics strike me as equally problematic.[8] I am uncomfortable
with their almost exclusive preoccupation with content, since not only
does this mean neglecting formal aspects of the poem, but it also
encourages a literal-minded critique that actually works against the far
more subtle potential effects of poetic form.[9] In terms of the way these
two approaches handle the reading process, the first completely ignores
it, setting out from the premise that the poem has already been read,
and its meaning assimilated; while the latter may end up over-empha-
sizing the critic's personal experience of the poems to the exclusion of all
else.[10] Either (specious) objectivity or the tricky terrain of autobiographical criticism: both seem unsatisfactory. There has to be a way of
achieving a more satisfactory balance: a critical empathy, as I have called
it, which would preserve the sense of participation, alongside a more
detached critical perspective.

Much contemporary poetry by women addresses a quite specific
audience—an audience of other women.[11] The communications explore
and articulate aspects of female experience, and they appear to be more
open than most contemporary men's poetry. They seem to demand the
reader's involvement. They make frequent use of personal pronouns,
drawing the reader into an intimate conversation, and often their conclusions refuse the comforting resolutions offered by rhyme and conventional form.[12] In my teaching I have seen that women do respond to
these poems very intensely; they feel they are being directly addressed,
and the reading leads to lively discussion. It is also clear that male readers encounter problems with the specificity of a female addressee when
faced with this material. It is an intimate dialogue from which they feel
excluded. Even though many of the poems do not cover "essentially"
female experiences, it is hardly surprising that women tend to relate to
them more immediately. If our criticism paid more attention to the
processes and reactions of reading this poetry, we might create a more
frank atmosphere in which "difference" could symbolize less of a
boundary wall and more of a tide-mark.[13]

One of the hardest things about writing this is that it has brought
my own critical persona into direct collision with my stubbornly unre-

constructed self. I read poetry looking for meanings and truths and other unspeakables; I read it for the comforts of humanism, the reassurances of identification, the pleasures of making sense/meaning, even (insane boldness) truth! At the same time, I know all about the fictionality of the I, the endless deferral of meaning, and the impossibility of Truth. Yet I believe that poems can still offer such forbidden fruits, even while I know that I should not seek them.

So, in good autobiographical fashion, a confession to start with: In April 1994 I helped organize *Kicking Daffodils*, a conference and festival of women's poetry. There were academic papers, poetry readings, and forum discussions, with panels made up of a mix of poets and critics. Over the weekend, several delegates expressed their disappointment that, although there were lots of poets present, still two distinct groups seemed to emerge—the poets in one, the academics in the other. I had hoped to bridge that divide; it has always struck me as a particularly depressing symptom of the isolated position of intellectuals in the United Kingdom—whether self-imposed or enforced. There is something potentially quite sad about large conferences devoted to the work of contemporary writing, rooms full of critics eager to express their appreciation, and no practitioners in sight. In my bleaker moments I think of the depressing adage, "those that can, do; those that can't, teach."

But why does this division persist? After all, some individuals might wish to see themselves as both poet and academic. Perhaps it was just an accident of human psychology that produced that cluster of poets round one table: catapulted into an alien environment, people make for familiar faces rather than plunge into a group of strangers. It was not surprising that the poets knew each other from the reading circuit, and the academics from the feminist conference circuit. But some time after the event I realized that I had anticipated the divide for other reasons—I had expected the poets to be skeptical about academics and the whole conference scene. I imagined they would view us as eccentric types who read all sorts of obscure implications into their work, making bizarre connections between bodies and texts, harping on about signifiers and the Imaginary. But as I listened to the poets—at their readings, and in discussion—I was surprised how often I heard the same language of high theory that I spend time justifying to feminist students impatient with its elitism. Nuala Ni Dhomhnaill addressed over one hundred of us in the closing session, chatting as if we were in her front room, and amidst the anecdotes about large freezers and family life, she paused for a brief meditation on Kristeva's theory of abjection. Medbh McGuckian delighted in prodding a few soft feminist underbellies in her ingenuous impatience with the idea of an exclusively feminine language. Far from bewildered skepticism, these poets knew all about the problematics of representation and debates over a feminine imaginary. I had unconsciously been subscribing to a Romantic notion of poetic activity, in which the dreamy poet, visited by inspiration, simply transcribes what turn out (once the critic intervenes!) to be pearls of wisdom. The poet gives them a quick polish; her formal skill makes them gleam, but she does not trouble herself with questions of meaning. I'd imagined her as a woman inspired, plunging into the pool of her unconscious, not as a frazzled critic at the word-processor, jabbing obsessively at the cut and paste buttons. That was the role of the academics: cautious, painstaking, utterly unromantic. Finally I learned that the poet's role is far closer to the critic's than I had imagined; now I want (well I would, would I not?) to move the critic's role closer to that of the poet.

Indeed it now seems to me that many of the most important issues facing contemporary feminism are being explored in poetry. Because of its formal versatility, because in poems language is freest from the constraining expectations of realism, and because of its apparently paradoxical combination of compression and spaciousness, poetry can say difficult things differently, can hold contradictions together long enough for their complexity to be felt. Back in 1987 Jan Montefiore noted the special potential of poetry as a vehicle for theoretical speculation, but there has been little reaction from critics since.[14] Poets may well be the unacknowledged legislators of contemporary feminism—and yet there is still little public or published discussion of their work. This is not only a loss in terms of poetic developments, but also, crucially, it is a loss for feminist thought. While a few critics have explored the subversive strategies of feminist poetry, or considered the viability of a female poetic tradition, none actually seem to spend much energy on the theoretical implications of the contents.[15]

Realizing how rigidly I had compartmentalized theory and poetry in separate boxes helps me to understand the difficulties I had working on my PhD thesis on contemporary women poets. At the time I felt it was a problem of authority: having castigated the inadequacies of liberal humanist aesthetics, I was left with no evaluative criteria to put in their place. I kept feeling that I had to prove why a particular poem was worthy of study, but I didn't know what constituted proof. I was attracted by the idea of moving away from evaluation altogether, and concentrating instead upon "my pleasure as a reader," as Rebecca O'Rourke advised,[16] but it felt like a bit of a skilful evasion. At some point, before you start writing, you have made choices about which poems to focus on. To pretend I had no evaluative criteria was somewhat disingenuous, even though I did not spend my time judging the quality of the poems. The only feminist approach I could find struck me as being too reductive: the implicit criteria appeared to be that a poem's themes were well-suited to feminist analysis. This meant that the poems selected were all about recognizable issues (male violence, marriage, racial/religious or other divisions between women, sexual inequality, lesbian desire, power); those that weren't explicitly feminist were quietly excluded. Consequently, although content was, in a sense, the deciding factor, and I have just lamented the lack of critical attention given to the content of contemporary poetry, there was not a great deal of complexity to be discussed in these poems. The ones that tackled more ambivalent, murky areas of experience and emotion did not fit into this feminist agenda. I wanted to explore poems that allowed for ambivalence, contradiction, and confusions. And because I wanted the formal skills and techniques of poetry to get some attention too, I ended up trying to reclaim the conventional criteria, divested of their traditional sexism, with what I hoped was a clear sense of the other components of identity that may contribute to readers' differing perspectives.

At the viva, my examiners commented on the curious absence of theoretical models in the thesis; why, they asked, did I not make use of the work of Angela Davis when I was writing about race and gender, or of Hélène Cixous in my exploration of the relationship between body and text? They also remarked on the strangely indirect way in which I presented crucial issues about poetry, gender, and representation: they seemed to emerge almost by chance from discussion of a particular poem. They advised me to "foreground the ideas" in the thesis. Essentially what they meant, I think, was that I should theorize more— about lesbian poetics, chameleon personae, and the tensions between testimony and appropriation.

I had shied away from applying theoretical frameworks for a combination of reasons. I had felt that to do so would be to impose an alien reading structure on a text that had nothing to do with such abstruse models. I suppose I felt (as my misguided fears at the conference reveal) that the poets would disapprove, or see such a reading as a perfect example of the intellectual show-off. But there were also ethical considerations. How appropriate was it to invoke the theoretical insights of French philosophical tradition, with their highly specialized, privileged terminology, when I was writing about a Caribbean woman's poetry? Kadiatu Kanneh has expressed misgivings about the racial analogies employed by Cixous.[17] But even without such anxieties about the appropriateness of her metaphors, it felt uncomfortable to bring such high theory to bear on writing that so wittily debunks Eurocentric obsession with the cerebral.[18]

Important revelations about my understanding of the relationship between poet, poem, and reader are buried within these confusions. Just as my account of a poet's inspiration was shaped by Romanticism, so too was my account of the experience of reading poetry. As reader, I should be a loyal and attentive listener; I had a duty to remain true to the poet's intention.[19] Depending, clearly, on the kind of poem, I saw this process as an intense transport, an out-of-body experience, something very private and inevitably subjective. I felt that, if I were to approach the poems armed with my briefcase of feminist theories, I would be denying the intimacy of that reading experience, assuming a coolly-detached, analytical persona and holding the poem at arm's length to dissect it. It would feel disloyal and willfully deceptive, as though I was trying to deny its previous power to move me.

So clearly, then, theory and poetry occupied very different compartments in my mind. And yet it is not that I am "anti-theory" per se, at all. My discomfort is with the way in which theories so easily become reified, detached from the original context of their formulation. An individual's work is reproduced in summary form as "X's theory," often a feeble travesty of the depth and subtlety of the original writing. Theories are lined up like off-the-peg blouses in a high-street store. To give an example: a "Cixousian approach," quite apart from its phonetic clumsiness, seems horribly reductive. To my mind, Cixous does not proffer an extractable theory, but enacts a way of reading and writing.[20] So many of the summaries of her work reduce the blend of rich intellectual eclecticism and individual style to a series of bare propositions which wrench the ideas embedded in her texts out of context. I do not flatter myself that my writing style has anything of that richness, but it was that almost organic relationship between reader and text, that embeddedness, and that skillful, nuanced presentation of subjectivity that I was striving for. In digests of Cixous's writing, perspective gets disengaged from the subjectivity that shapes it, and is transformed into an objective framework. Nevertheless, it felt to me as though any single theoretical framework would prove inadequate to the demands of this poetry, because of its need for an involved response.

This reluctance to apply someone else's theoretical framework to the poems I was reading helps make sense of the distinction I was drawing between theory and poetry. The former seemed, almost by definition, to exclude the personal. But if I could take theoretical insights and somehow weave them into my reading, then I could apply a more flexible, responsive version of theoretical engagement. Rather than adopt-

ing a Grand Theory to explain the world, I wanted a Pick'n'Mix version
of my own making, gathering snippets from widely diverse fields of
inquiry, making unexpected links across disciplines. And within this, I
wanted to preserve a sense of my own involvement in the whole
process, which I saw as a creative one. I did not want to efface the reading self, or replace her with a critic. In short, I wanted a response, not
just a critique, but a response that opened up the poem and its effects
and made strange connections and gestures to new areas of inquiry,
rather than ironing out the contradictions of the text in order to impose
a masterful interpretation, or explain away its magic.[21]

Autobiographical Criticism and Poetry:
Problems and Limitations

To return, then, to the tidal edges. Look at a poem on the page. The
white spaces all around it signal loud and clear the potential roomi-
ness for interpretation. This is what I mean by the paradoxical combination of both compression and spaciousness: the poet compresses, and
in so doing, makes space for the reader to splash around. And now my
criteria for what poems do become clear: they hold contraries, they
express the ambivalence that prose cannot help overstating, making
too bold; poems can show that something both is and is not, at the same
time. And what of the critic's role? To map out some of the possible
routes that emerge, joining up whichever dots seem to most urgently
cry out to be joined. Of course this is a subjective exercise, in part; of
course what readers are doing is assessing the critics' creative skills,
and deciding how convincingly or imaginatively they have joined up
the dots. More insistently than any prose, poetry asks the reader to
make sense of it: to shape a meaningful prose narrative out of the white
expanse and the jagged edges. The trick is not to do so, not to fall for
it—not to formulate a meaning and reduce the poem to that. The poet
does not set out simply to perplex the reader, for the sake of it, working
out a code the critic then cracks. The job of the critic should be to piece
together several possible avenues of interpretation, to move onwards
from the first in order to try to see new configurations, rather than settling with one (the first, therefore likely to be the most subjective, the
one that comes—autobiographically—easiest) as the Truth. It is at this
point that the critic needs to look for some account of existent patterns
that come from outside herself—a different way of viewing the world,
that will broaden her own understanding at the same time as enrich
her criticism.[22] In other words, I want a more flexible, sensitive, responsive, critical approach, one that does not seek to reveal feminist mes-

sages, or explain away complexities, but that invites an expansion of the self; a model that proffers different reading positions, that challenges critic and reader to try on these unfamiliar perspectives as if their own. In this way, the poem stimulates empathy—even dialogue, of a sort, although in a written account such dialogue is necessarily silent.[23]

It seems to me that feminist reading models go only halfway in this respect, and that the reason is because of the paradoxically progressive and constraining effects of the personal, autobiographical voice. Western feminist literary critics are now all too intensely conscious of the limitations of their perspective: race, religion, sexuality, dis/ability, class, and ethnic diversity are all now recognized as aspects of identity-formation that fissure any earlier, easier notion of women's experience. One of the outcomes of this (tardy) sensitivity to the dangers of essentialism is the retreat into personal experience. In laying emphasis on the actual involvement of the critic, as an individual, in the process of reading, this partially meets the objections I raised earlier about objective criticism, but of course it also mediates against the kind of empathy I am advocating. It is at this point that the limitations of autobiographical criticism emerge most clearly. Annette Kolodny was one of the first feminist critics to stress the importance of the reading *process*, urging in 1975 that feminists "insist upon restoring to the language of critical analysis its sense of reading as process."[24] Suzanne Juhasz makes the same demand specifically in relation to poetry, in an article that was extremely important to me when I first read it during my research. She makes a more explicit plea for the validity of subjective input: "'What happened to me as I read?' 'How did it happen?' 'Why did it happen?' are essential critical questions."[25] It is probably no coincidence that, like Adrienne Rich, Juhasz is also a poet. Their accounts of reading are almost conversations with the poets in question, and expressions of gratitude for the guidance their work has given.

Juhasz concentrates on Anne Sexton's posthumous volume, *45 Mercy Street*. She deconstructs another woman critic's hostile review of the book, to show that the grounds for her criticism are subjective— ("emotional and personal"):

> Spacks doesn't like Sexton; doesn't like the experiences that Sexton brings out of the linen closet into the public consciousness; and most of all, doesn't like having to be identified with them, just because she, too, is a woman.[26]

Juhasz then proceeds to offer an account of her reaction to the poems. She is frank about the extent of her identification with the poet:

I can't set her up as a tragic heroine whose suffering does not
involve me. It is not only that I understand her pain—that it
touches my own—but that her pain makes me concerned about
her.[27]

She admits that there are some technical shortcomings in the poems, but
points out that the book was unrevised at the time of Sexton's death.
She reads the poems as poems of final despair, borne of the realization
that "poetry of self is not self-therapy and that she [Sexton] had tried to
use it for that purpose. Knowledge of the self, willingness to explore, to
reveal, is no salvation."[28]

Rich's essay is about Emily Dickinson. Her approach is more fully
autobiographical than Juhasz: she describes the car journey to
Dickinson's house, and is quite explicit about the need she feels to
somehow get inside Dickinson's head, to understand the mystery of
her poetry and her life. But as Schweickart points out, the essay makes
it clear that its author knows the danger of this potentially appropriative
desire, and also realizes that it is, in any case, ultimately impossible:
the poetry is "only a projection of the subjectivity of the reader."[29]

As Schweickart observes, both these essays depict reading and
criticism as acts of communication, rather than mastery; they seek not to
fix meaning, or explain the poems, but to explore them.[30] Both give
fuller attention to the actual process of reading, and their own involvement in that process. But there are problems too. The main one, in my
opinion, is that this model reinforces the association between poet and
persona: Sexton and Dickinson's lives are, it would seem, as compelling
and as needful of interpretation as the contents of the poems themselves. Women writers are well-accustomed to having their work read
biographically; Joanna Russ documents some chilling examples.[31] There
are problems with a critical strategy that seems to give further endorsement to this tendency; it makes it even harder for women to break free
of the literal I. It does nothing to counteract the essentializing implication of this line of thought: that women, caged in the subjective, can
only write about their own experience.[32] The second misgiving I have is
with the tendency to revere the poet and her work. Of course, in these
two examples, the critics were drawn to write precisely because of the
strength of their admiration for, and connection with the poets. But
what of poems and poets that do not mean so much to you? Do you
simply not write about them? If we proceed in this way, we will end up
with a body of gushingly appreciative criticism, which would tend only
to bolster our own opinions and ideas—an innate conservatism that
would do little to provoke debate and generate new emphases for fem-

inist thought. The third problem is the problem of autobiography. Juhasz focuses on a specific dilemma that she identifies (and identifies with) in Sexton's late poems. Her account makes no claims to be anything other than personal, but it inevitably circumscribes its own relevance in so doing. Since I am not facing the same issues in my own writing/reading life, the partial nature of her reading is very clear to me; I become impatient to find other elements of Sexton's poetry discussed—its formal range, perhaps, or a more radical attempt to disengage the poet from the poetry. Of course, as Schweickart notes, the nature of such critical practice is to be explicit about its status as just one interpretation: "the personal voice serves as a gesture warding off any inclination to appropriate the authority of the text as a warrant for the validity of the interpretation."[33] Nevertheless, this seems to me to be the fundamental disadvantage with autobiographical criticism: unless your reader shares the precise focus of your personal interest, she will quickly tire of it, and want evidence of more various perspectives. And if she does share your particular interest, this suggests a self-selecting consensual audience which hardly promises much in the way of lively dissent and debate.

A Practical Illustration of the Subjective Origins of Interpretation

What I have tried to do in this next section is to include the best of both worlds: a critical response that is conscious of the ways in which it is being influenced by personal and subjective ingredients, but is not constrained by or limited to them alone; a response that flits from one position of identification to another, testing out ideas, and following associations that the poem evokes. My aim is to hold off the moment of fixing meaning for rather longer than is usually the case. In order to give a clearer sense of what I mean, I have recorded my responses to a first reading. For this foolhardy attempt to practise what I've been preaching, I chose "The Beast" by Jeni Couzyn:

The Beast

In our house he stalks silent
on padded feet. He has left
cracks on the floorboards, gouged
chasms in my father's face, ripped
bloody rivers across his eyes.
My mother believes she has

tamed him. Nights, she strokes his coarse
fur, coaxes him onto her
bed, his huge weight
rocks on her chest. Purring like thunder
shakes the curtains. In pitiful mucousy
scratching her breathing
aggravates the night. There are
bloodspots on her pillow. Hers.
He's been king in our house
for thirty years now. I told them
–Don't keep pets, they will
devour you. Leave them
roam the wide bush. He heard.
He knocked me to the ground
with a massive paw
flexed his claws on my back
licked the blood with his bone-cold
reptile tongue. I cowered on the floor
screaming. His great jaws
smiled over me, yellow black-flecked
teeth had bits of
raw meat in them. His breath came in hot
foul smelling waves. Don't
show fear, said my mother, he
likes you. –He
lives here, said my father, he's
one of us. You'll have to
get to know him. I saw his arm was
scarred with claw marks
wrist to shoulder.
–He's old, said my father, be
gentle with him.
You'll learn.[34]

   Despite the temptations to tidy up my notes, I have not done so.
What follows is, then, the first draft: I found the poem (in text form,
rather than hearing it), in Linda France's all-female anthology, *Sixty
Women Poets*. Female experience, gender specificity is thus uppermost in
my mind—or at least I can hold fairly optimistic hopes that the poem
will at least not ignore the gendering of experience.
   What do I know about the poet? I have read an anthology she
edited, *The Bloodaxe Book of Contemporary Women Poets*.[35] The introduc-

tion reaffirmed links between women's ancient arts—lullabies, story-telling, etc.—and poetry. I imagine Couzyn as a sixties woman; I think I must have seen a collection of her poetry, with her photo on the cover—leggy, in flairs, long sixties hair. But the poem is in nineties typography; I'm not expecting it to be dated. All these tidbits are present somewhere in my mind as I start reading. They may, or may not, become relevant later.

The title—thoughts of *Beauty and the. . . .*

Immediately, personal pronouns—"our house," "he stalks." Who is speaking? I'm trying to get a hold on the text, to find a position from which I can make sense of what I am reading. I attend to/identify with the speaker, hoping for clarification. It is easy to presume the speaker is female—an unconscious link between poet and persona, which may be overturned later, but that the poem allows for the moment. My aim is to work myself into a position as close as possible to that of the speaker, so that I can understand the origins and intentions of everything she says. This is an act of imaginative empathy, imagining myself as her. (If I did not know the poet was female, would I have presumed the persona was male? If I was a male reader, would I be more likely to read the persona as male? If I was a male reader who knew he was reading a poem by a female poet, what then?) Even as I am striving for this empathy, I note certain features of the text.

The violence is striking—father and mother have suffered it, but what is described is their scars—"gouged/chasms," ripped/bloody rivers" (note geographical metaphors), an arm "scarred with claw marks." These suggest past wounds—something about bearing and surviving, about the memory of pain and fear being different from the experience of present terror. The speaker has also been attacked—scratched, as they all three have been—they are all physically marked by the beast. Its characteristics are very familiar—"his great jaws/smiled over me"; he has teeth with "bits of/raw meat in them," and "foul smelling" breath; he is a child's depiction of a beast, and there are hints of an ambiguous friendliness about him. He has padded feet, and he purrs, enjoys being stroked by her mother. Yet this is juxtaposed with descriptions of how she is affected by the beast—his great weight, bloodspots on her pillow—signs the child (?) might interpret as evidence of damage, yet does not quite do so. There's a curious lack of emotion from the speaker—terrifying events described in a toneless way; perhaps this suggests a deliberate dual awareness from the speaker—relating the drama from a later position of greater knowledge, hinting at its psychological, fantastical meaning. And then, the text reveals that the speaker is not a child—she's been around for thirty years (unless she is speaking of times before her birth), and she has warned her parents about keeping "pets." Yet the phraseology is child-like—short sentences, parallelisms, simple sentence constructions. There are four pieces of direct speech—from daughter, mother, and father (he says the most). All are commands/proscriptions/strong advice/warnings. Riddles, enigmas: statements that mean more than they seem to. That refrain, "said my father . . . said my mother." As in a fairytale, the tone is non-committal, and once you know the conventions of fairy-tale, you know to look for more than meets the eye, to anticipate unnameable danger. The beast—a staple fairytale figure, the mythic beast. Those gentle characteristics I've already noted, also present in *Beauty and the Beast*—woman as loving protector of an ugly, uncouth beast, its physical threat neutralized by her caresses—indeed, trans-formed by her love (this does not happen here—thwarted expectation; resisting closure). This beast, too, is king of the house (not of the jun-gle—the "wide bush" outside the home), yet the tale is unusual because father and mother are the actors. Father affirms the beast belongs with them: "he's/one of us. You'll have to/get to know him." (Is the daugh-ter included in that "us"? Or is she an outsider?) Fairytales set explicitly within the nuclear family lead inevitably to psychoanalytic interpreta-tions. Does the beast symbolize sexual desire? An untamable force, vio-lent, roaming; in this version unusually not owned by man or woman so not classically Freudian. Oedipal jealousy? The daughter ousted from the mother's and father's attentions, cast out to survive without their constant support. The beast usurps her place; she thinks she is fighting to protect her parents but really she is trying to regain their attention? There are elements of sadism; of the staging of a dramatic confrontation for the daughter, in which the parents let her down by siding with the beast. Throwing her to her fate within the patriarchal system—the ulti-mate betrayal from the mother—"he/likes you"—in the face of massive evidence to the contrary. Reminiscent of that bit in Winterson's *Oranges Are Not the Only Fruit*, when Jeanette thinks men are literally beasts: that women marry nice-looking young men but have no way of know-ing whether or not they have really chosen a pig or a brute.[36]

This encounter has the tone of a fantasy/dream. The child is caught up in the dynamic—but the idea of her being scared by wit-nessing sex between her parents is made less plausible by the oddly mature tone of her advice to them. Could the beast represent the conflict between her parents—in which she too becomes a casualty? Yet the wounds are so heavily symbolic,—blood, mucus, bloody rivers, scars. And the beast so insistently a physical manifestation—its bulk, claws, paws, breath. Why does the father get the last words? Or is that last line his? It could be hers. Are there allusions to specific figures—from myth, or other texts? I think (bizarrely) of Goldilocks and the three bears, and of the Honey Bunch bear. Of Deborah Randall's poem, "The Beast and Fiona"[37]—a lighthearted rewrite of courtship in which the beast is a pitiful, bedraggled wooer, mocked by his ladylove. Women poets demystifying the notion of Otherness? Man as bestial—in his ali-enness and in conventional meanings of masculinity as force, instinct, and physicality: domesticating, deflating the fearfulness. Marion Engel's novel, *Bear*[38]—relating the story of a sexual relationship between woman and bear—something about that unknowable remoteness, that differ-ence, being compellingly attractive? Possible readings—a feminist might read it as a poem about male sexual violence, men as beasts, but that would mean ignoring the mother's tenderness, unless that was taken as evidence of her enforced collusion. Drawing on psychoanalytic models it could be read as a poem about the absurdly false comfort parents offer children, reassuring them against all the evidence ("Don't/show fear, said my mother, he/likes you.") Returning to the relevance of the speaker's (indeterminate) gender, it could be read as a poem about the ways in which parents collude in sacrificing their young daughter—to violation, to patriarchy. (The threat in that last line.)

Clearly, these speculations are dependent on my intellectual auto-biography—perspectives I have been taught and have selected in pref-erence to others. (If I knew more about linguistics, I could have devel-oped an analysis of the syntax; if I had more knowledge of representations of beasts in literary traditions, I might have drawn on those.) In addition, such thoughts are informed by the way I react to the poem emotionally. Does it frighten me? Or remind me of similar feel-ings? Do I read the mother as victim or as powerful, controlling tamer? What do I feel towards the beast? What resonances does it hold for me? This is autobiographical stuff—useful, valid, but I keep a watch on it, make sure it does not overwhelm the rest.

Then comes the hardest part: trying to think in ways that do not come easily. Since nothing in the poem does gender the speaker, what happens if I make it a man? Then suddenly Oedipal implications emerge more clearly—young boy warning parents; his jealousy/bewilderment at the beast's intimacy with his mother in bed (compare Hamlet towards Gertrude's sexuality); his heroic confrontation with the beast; then the father's final words representing an assertion of his superior authority. In fact, it works better this way—as an account of male initiation? Or what about reading the poem from the position of the beast?

I do not want to interpret the poem as meaning something spe-cific: to crack the code, as I put it earlier. There is too much that I would have to omit in order to do so; somehow an explanation would detract from the layerings. If it were simple, it would not need expressing in this way, making use of dreamscape, fantasy, myth, and fairytale resonances. I know this sounds like a lame excuse: critics produce readings, they do not resort to such evasions. And yet it stands, and I have given a response, if not—yet—a critique. But as a lone response, it does not offer much. In a lively critical context, such tentative figurings could productively bump shoulders with others. In the seminar-room, it is possible to create such an environment. Students are still close to the text, and their experience of reading it; they can explore the interface between their own subjectivity and the text as a distinct, separate object, by comparing their reactions to others'. Interpretation does not have to be fixed in such a context; different emphases can coexist. But outside the teaching context, it becomes much harder to retain a sense of provisionality. My reading feels too thin, too much the product of one person. I miss the other accounts; the more confident, dissenting voices that would opt for some of these emphases over others, in order to insist on a meaning. I cannot contest meanings alone.

How can I transform this stream of thoughts into a tighter response, retaining the critical empathy I desired? I focus on the beast's symbolic meaning as sexuality—neither male nor female sexuality, but an unowned, untrammeled force: causing physical hurt and (perhaps? this is less explicit) pain, but, perversely, protected and endorsed by the very people it has marked so deeply. I reach this interpretation through the processes recorded above, making sure that none of the features I noted would contradict this reading. And alongside this process I am silently weighing up the idea: does it make sense to me? Is it true? And most importantly, am I in a position to know (does it deal with experiences I could have had)? A negative response to this final question does not invalidate my reading; it simply makes the perspective from which I am writing clearer. Do I agree with this presentation of sexuality? What implications does it hold for theories of gender and sexuality? Would it not seem to suggest that sexual instinct is somehow immune to material inequities—the combined effect of economic and sexual power, for example? And yet, does not the intimacy of the domestic setting suggest the poet was deliberately aiming for a tight, claustrophobic atmosphere, using the recognizable family drama in order to explore more psychological terrain? If I believe this to be the case, I should not be blaming her for the lack of attention to external power dynamics.

To extrapolate: what I tried to do was to think myself into the position of the speaker. In so doing I was not thinking of the speaker as Jeni Couzyn, nor did I lose sight of the fact that I was reading a poem; in other words, I did not entirely lose critical distance. I moved in and out of the speaker's viewpoint, trying out different perspectives. I delved around in my childhood memories searching for resonances, followed through any associations the poem evoked, tested out any theoretical models that seemed relevant, and tried to trust and pursue my intuitions. The points of sharp personal identification ("I felt like that") are not made explicit in the final written response. Nor have they been in this draft version, but that is not simply because I knew I would be publishing it; it is also because I do not usually need to write them down: they resonate across the whole reading experience, and their impact should still be felt in the final version as an extra layering.

This is not an autobiographical reading; I am not relating the poem to part of my life-story, nor explicitly revealing any details about myself. Readers may be able to deduce things about me from the reading I produce, but that is a different matter. Nevertheless, my personal involvement in the poem, as I read and as I tossed possible implications and associations around, is an essential ingredient in the process. When I was making up my mind about the validity of the poem's argument, I was testing it against my own values and beliefs. My subjectivity thus informs the reading process.

Paradoxes and Ideals, or Making a Virtue Of a Necessity

Apart from the incomplete state of these notes on "The Beast," the main difference between them and the accounts given by Juhasz and Rich is in the extent of the critic's visibility. Despite my earlier insistence on the subjective basis of all criticism, my own is not at all explicit in that stream of ideas/reactions. Perhaps if I saw myself as a direct inheritor of Couzyn's poetry, and felt a close affinity with her, my personality and position would have emerged more forcefully. Perhaps, too, if I were an experienced poet, I might wish to engage with her work in a slightly different—more personal—way. But here, instead of such an autobiographical response, I have recorded a provisional one: to show that no reading is the only or final reading, and to make very clear the limiting boundaries of my perspective. Would that I could divest myself of them, and merge merrily with the poem, frolicking in those waves as Freedman's metaphor suggests. This is the ideal I yearn for, and the process I always think I have been engaged in when reading, although it is not what the thoughts—the evidence on the page—record. There, the edges of my empathy are all too apparent.

Yet, for all its shortcomings, I believe this model can still be useful as an incentive to others, particularly those who feel uncomfortable committing their criticism to print. After all, does not this negotiation between text and reader lie at the heart of all textual criticism, and is it not precisely what students are expected to learn to do? Why do we pretend that we reach a stage where we can suddenly handle this relationship effortlessly? Why are we not more frank about the provisionality of our criticism, as well as our ownership of it? The yearning towards identification, and the simultaneous recognition of its ultimate impossibility: these are the two processes that seem to me to be absolutely central to a fuller critical practice. Without homogenizing female experience, or erasing difference, poetry can urge greater empathy—between women, and perhaps between men and women too. For it is the exercise of imaginative empathy that such poetry provokes, with the apparently contradictory awareness that empathy is only ever imaginary. In this way, such a critical practice guards against the arrogance of appropriation. The reader retains the subjective ownership of her perspective, as well as striving to transcend its blinkered limitations. The critic's personal involvement in this process enriches her writing by shifting the emphasis on to the poem's argument. It is, of course, a utopian enterprise, riven with contradictions. My excuse (naturally) is that I want the critic to work, like the poet, in the arena of such difficult and insoluble aspirations.

Notes

I wish to record my gratitude to Helen Bruder, for her patience and sympathetic interest during the—agonized—writing of this essay.

1. "I seek prose to relieve the gnomic anxiety of poetry, poetry to override the seeming clarity and control of prose. Prose has tidy borders on the page, poetry a tidal edge—no clear edge at all" (p. 17). "Border Crossing as Method and Motif in Contemporary American Writing, or How Freud Helped Me Case the Joint," pp. 13–22 in *The Intimate Critique*, edited by Diane Freedman, Olivia Frey, and Frances Murphy Zauhar (Duke University Press, 1993).

2. Suzanne Juhasz, "The Critic as Feminist: Reflections on Women's Poetry, Feminism, and the Art of Criticism" (p. 120), *Women's Studies* vol. 5 (1977), pp. 113–27.

3. Patrocinio P. Schweickart's essay, "Reading Ourselves: Towards a Feminist Theory of Reading" explores a similar project, and initially prompted me to consider the reading relationship in this way. It has been invaluable in the course of thinking about this piece. The essay was originally published in *Gender*

and Reading: Essays on Reader, Texts and Contexts, edited by Elizabeth Flynn and Patrocinio Schweickart (Baltimore & London: John Hopkins University Press, 1986), and is reprinted in *Feminisms,* edited by Robyn Warhol & Diane Herndl Price (Rutgers/Macmillan, 1991).

4. See for example, Jane Tompkins, "Me and My Shadow," reprinted in *Feminisms,* edited by Robyn Warhol and Diane Price Herndl (Rutgers/Macmillan, 1991); Nicole Ward Jouve, *White Woman Speaks with Forked Tongue: Criticism as Autobiography* (London: Routledge, 1991); Nancy Miller, *Getting Personal* (London: Routledge, 1991).

5. It is worth bearing in mind the sharp observation made by Deborah Cameron at the Glasgow feminist theory conference in 1991, in response to Nancy Miller's paper on personal criticism. Cameron pointed out that not everyone's personal accounts draw the crowds, or are considered as interesting as Miller's. The same holds true for the personal criticism offered by Rich, or Juhasz or—to take an Irish example, Eavan Boland in "The Woman Poet—Her Dilemma" (*Stand,* Winter 1986-87).

6. In her overview of recent developments in "personal criticism," Laura Marcus notes the popularity of a "self who seeks to mark her presence, but not necessarily to recount her history." I take this as referring to the same tricky distinction I am making between autobiography and subjectivity. She seems to reject such a distinction as ultimately untenable: distinctions between "the autobiographical, the confessional, the personal, the narrational, and so on, are not always clear-cut, nor is it always obvious where positional statement turns into autobiography." "Personal Criticism and the Autobiographical Turn," pp. 11–27 in *Political Gender: Texts and Contexts,* edited by Sally Ledger, Josephine McDonagh, and Jane Spencer (Hemel Hempstead: Harvester Wheatsheaf, 1994).

7. A good example (chosen from many) is Patricia Craig's recent review of Linda France's Bloodaxe anthology, *Sixty Women Poets* (Newcastle: Bloodaxe Books, 1993). She satirizes the collection as offering "a run-down of the whole female cycle," and complains that there are too many poems about "deep feelings," "women and babies," "all-pervasive fecundity" and female body parts. "Poems *by* women is one things, poems *for* women another" she observes acerbically—a revealing distinction that could, with the addition of a question-mark, stand as an alternative title for this piece. The review is published in *Poetry Review,* vol. 83, no.4 (Winter 1993/4), pp. 59–60.

8. Most of these attempts have been published by North American critics, and concentrate on their native poetry. United Kingdom critics seem to share my skepticism. Jan Montefiore boldly sets out to define a feminist poem in the opening chapter of her study, *Feminism and Poetry* (London: Pandora, 1987), but quickly moves on to less slippery slopes. Sally Minogue clearly feels that vigilant feminists have been out on patrol, terrorizing women poets, and forcing them into anodyne political correctness, but she gives few examples of these

missionaries. See "Prescriptions and Proscriptions: Feminist Criticism and Contemporary Poetry," pp. 179–236, in *Problems for Feminist Criticism* (London: Routledge, 1990).

9. In her study of nineteenth-century women poets and Romanticism, *Women Writers and Poetic Identity* (Princeton, New Jersey: Princeton University Press, 1980), Margaret Homans explained the dangers of too close an alliance between feminism and poetry, where poetry is seen as testimonial, experiential evidence about women's lives (p. 216). Nevertheless, in my account of the reading process I shall claim that this initial stage, in which the poem strikes the reader as offering authentic reportage, may be technically naive but it nevertheless has to take place in order for the reader to be fully engaged. It is during critical analysis that an appreciation of the fictive nature of language emerges.

10. In my opinion, Montefiore rather exaggerates this danger. Pointing out that radical feminist poetics risk "idealizing poetry as universal consciousness," she argues that "attention to the material, verbal aspects of poetry is liable to disappear in the vicinity of the ideal—or fantasy—of poetry as experience encountered at white heat" (p. 12, *Feminism and Poetry*). The example she picks is an extreme one and implies that attention to the reading process necessarily precludes intellectual rigor.

11. It is, of course, dangerous to offer sweeping generalizations about "contemporary women's poetry." I do not mean to suggest that all today's women poets write in this manner. I am thinking particularly of lyric and performance poetry, written in English and published or performed in the United Kingdom and Ireland over the last twenty years.

12. Male poets seem to make much greater use of regular meter and form: consider, for example, Tony Harrison's virtuoso control of the sonnet form, and his skillful classical imitations, or Simon Armitage's celebrated syllabics. There is a pronounced New Formalism amongst today's young male poets, a fascination with metrical control. It is tempting to speculate about the psychological implications of this clearly-marked difference between male and female poets.

13. Reader response theory, and the relevance of gender in these debates, are clearly beyond the scope of this article. Attention to the role played by the reader's sense of personal identity seems to have been largely overlooked until very recently. Among recent developments in this direction is the research conducted by Sara Mills. She distributed a questionnaire asking men and women about their responses to a "feminist poem" and found the men were far more reluctant to identify it as such, preferring to translate its contents into more easily universal themes. See "Reading as/like a Feminist," pp. 25–46 in *Gendering the Reader*, ed. Sara Mills (Hemel Hempstead: Harvester Wheatsheaf, 1994). Attempts to link psychological object-relations theory and the reading process strike me as particularly thought-provoking explanations for differing reading preferences and strategies. See "Texts to Grow On:

Reading Women's Romance Fiction" by Suzanne Juhasz, *Tulsa Studies in Women's Literature*, vol. 7(2), Fall 1988. While I was working on this article, a disabled friend, Sharon Mace, told me of the frustration she experienced during her English degree: her responses to texts were often described as being too subjective, because the able-bodied lecturers did not pick up on the particular aspects or implications that struck her most immediately. She reminded me—as I need reminding so often—of the caution with which I should be speaking about "female experience."

14. "It seems to me that—simply because of the ambitious poet's necessary struggle with language, form and reality—the most interesting thinking about the possibilities of radical feminist poetry has been done in the poems themselves, not in discursive or descriptive prose: even Adrienne Rich is far more subtle in her poems than in her essays" (p. 4, *Feminism and Poetry*). Poetry is not only a valuable resource for poetry critics: in the final chapter of her study of representations of the female body in nineteenth-century prose, Helena Michie turns to contemporary poetry to consider how today's women writers are tackling the legacy of Victorian taboos. She makes this switch in genre and period because, "poetry allows for a condensation of tropes that renders highly visible the rhetorical analysis of Victorianism which, in my view, serves as a basis for so much contemporary feminist writing" (p. 10, *The Flesh Made Word: Female Figures and Women's Bodies*, Oxford University Press, 1987).

15. This same gap exists between theory and prose fiction: it strikes me as another version of the poet/critic split I observed at the *Kicking Daffodils* conference. French intellectual tradition has never drawn such a distinction between ideas and invention, and the influence of this more unified approach is beginning to be seen. Susan Sellers makes the continuity of enterprise explicit by discussing the work of theorists and fiction-writers in the same study, *Language and Sexual Difference: Feminist Writing in France* (London: Macmillan, 1991). Nicole Ward Jouve has also helped contextualize the French approach in her writing on the so-called "French feminists." She points out that, in France, Cixous is viewed first-and-foremost as a writer and dramatist, not as a theorist. Further evidence of a change in approach is Geraldine Meaney's recent study, *(Un)like Subjects: Women, Theory, Fiction* (London: Routledge, 1993), which treats theoretical and fictional texts together.

16. "My objections aren't to the stringency of standards applied to women writers; rather I question the view of literature which sees response first-and-foremost in terms of hierarchical judgement. Presented with a poem, my concern is not to decide immediately whether it is good or bad, to speculate how to apportion the A's and D's over a spread including effort and achievement. Faced with questions of judgement, I do not rush out to fit the template of excellence over my poems and see how close the fit is. I ask who has drawn up these standards, and why? Will they include or exclude this poet—help to explain why they write as they do about this subject? Is there space for my pleasure as a reader?", p. 280 from "Mediums, Messages and Noisy Amateurs,"

in *Women: A Cultural Review*, vol. 1, no. 3 (Winter 1990), pp. 275–86. Regrettably, O'Rourke does not give any examples of this process.

17. "Love, mourning and metaphor: terms of identity," pp. 135–53, *New Feminist Discourses*, edited by Isobel Armstrong (London: Routledge, 1992).

18. Despite my anxieties, Gabriele Griffin helpfully applies French feminist post-structuralist ideas about the body and language to Nichols' poetry in an essay on teaching Black women's writing. Her essay, "'Writing the Body': Reading Joan Riley, Grace Nichols and Ntozake Shange," pp. 19–42, is in *Black Women's Writing*, edited by Gina Wisker (London: Macmillan, 1993).

19. I am aware of course, in retrospect, that what I conceive to be the poet's intention is actually largely my own invention. The same slippage is evident in Juhasz's approach, where she berates another critic for refusing to see "the norms that the writing has set for itself" (p. 118, "The Critic as Feminist," op. cit.). To what degree can a text be said to set its own norms and terms? This is a point of some creative confusion in feminist work on reader-response theory. It should be clear that my version of the reader is a partial attempt to reclaim the traditional liberal reader for a feminist practice. In this I am taking my cue from Nicole Ward Jouve, encouraged by her advice to the literary critic that, "however different your craft and your skills and your object, you are still in the same business as the artists themselves. The business of making sense of life which means as a first step making sense of yourself," p. 9, *White Woman Speaks with Forked Tongue: Criticism as Autobiography* (London: Routledge, 1991).

20. See, for example, *The Newly Born Woman* (with Catherine Clement), translated by Betsy Wing (Manchester: Manchester University Press, 1987); "Difficult Joys," in *The Body and the Text*, edited by Helen Wilcox et al. (Hemel Hempstead: Harvester Wheatsheaf, 1990).

21. Some of the qualities of this style are evident in Jacqueline Rose's *The Haunting of Sylvia Plath* (London: Virago, 1991). Her approach is full of unexpected twists and connections, an exhilarating read. On the issue of subjectivity, she does not offer much insight, closing her introduction with a teasing promise of revelations that never come: "I read Plath as a type of analyst of her critics and culture alike. If Plath is a ghost of the culture, one thing that will be clear in everything that follows is the extent to which she haunts me" (p. 10).

22. This combination of internal and external knowledge, both stimulated by the text (an external object) reminds me of Winnicott's description of the mother/child dynamic, in which the mother is (symbolically) both inside and separate to the child: "From the beginning, the baby has maximal intense experience in the potential space, between the me-extensions and the not-me. This potential space is the interplay between there being nothing but me and there being objects and phenomena outside omnipotent control." The process is about learning to balance subjective and objective knowledge. Winnicott notes that, in healthy development, "the child is able gradually to meet the world

and all its complexities, because of seeing there more and more of what is already present in his or her own self" (quoted by Juhasz, p. 244).

23. See Alice Templeton's equally idealistic model of the dialogic reading practice that Adrienne Rich's poetry demands, in "The Dream and the Dialogue: Rich's Feminist poetics and Gadamer's Hermeneutics," pp. 383–96, *Tulsa Studies in Women's Literature*, vol. 7 (2), Fall 1988. The reader, she claims, "must . . . choose to participate in the experience and to be acted upon by it despite the risk and uncertainty" (p. 290). In more practical terms, this emphasis on discursive practice has important potential for teaching purposes: sharing different reading experiences leads to enriched understanding of the text. But Templeton's approach implies, like my own, that feminist poems demand a greater degree of active involvement from the reader: that the critic bears a responsibility to the poet or poem.

24. "Flying and Fear Thereof," paper presented at the Modern Language Association National Convention, December 1975; cited Juhasz, p. 119, op. cit.

25. Juhasz, p, 119.

26. Juhasz, p. 120.

27. Juhasz, p. 121.

28. Juhasz, pp. 124–25.

29. Schweickart, *Feminisms*, p. 539.

30. Schweickart comments on the difference between this approach and that of conventional reader-response theorists. She notes the absence from Rich's writing of metaphors of control and submission: in this feminist reading practice, "the dialectic of control . . . gives way to the dialectic of communication" (p. 543).

31. Joanna Russ, *How To Suppress Women's Writing* (London: Women's Press, 1983).

32. Cf. Margaret Homans: "To place an exclusive valuation on the literal, especially to identify the self as literal, is simply to ratify women's age-old and disadvantageous position as the other and the object" (p. 218, op. cit.).

33. Schweickart, p.544.

34. *Sixty Women Poets* (Newcastle: Bloodaxe Books, 1993), p. 92.

35. *The Bloodaxe Book of Contemporary Women Poets: Eleven British Writers* (Newcastle: Bloodaxe Books, 1985).

36. "Slowly I closed the book. It was clear that I had stumbled on a terrible conspiracy. There are women in the world. There are men in the world. And there are beasts. What do you do if you marry a beast? Kissing them didn't

always help. And beasts are crafty. They disguise themselves like you and I. Like the wolf in 'Little Red Riding Hood.' Why had no one told me? Did that mean no one else knew? Did that mean that all over the globe, in all innocence, women were marrying beasts?," p. 72–73, *Oranges Are Not The Only Fruit* (London: Pandora, 1985).

37. Deborah Randall, *The Sin Eater* (Newcastle: Bloodaxe Books, 1989), p. 25.

38. Marion Engel, *Bear* (London: Pandora, 1988).

CONTRIBUTORS

The Seventeenth Century Collective:

Elspeth Graham is Principal Lecturer in Literature and Cultural History at Liverpool John Moores University. She has researched and published on seventeenth-century autobiography, especially women's, and seventeenth-century poetry, particularly Milton's. She also works on feminist and psychoanalytic theory.

Hilary Hinds teaches literature and women's studies at Fircroft College of Adult Education in Birmingham, United Kingdom. She has published on seventeenth-century women's autobiography, is currently completing a book on writings by women in the radical sects, and is also working on an anthology of women's writing from the period.

Elaine Hobby is Lecturer in Women's Studies at Loughborough University, and author of *Virtue of Necessity: English Women's Writing 1649–88*. Her research interests continue to be in this field, and she is currently working on a study of seventeenth-century female sexuality.

Helen Wilcox is Professor of post-medieval English Literature at the University of Groningen in the Netherlands. Her research interests are in the field of seventeenth-century literature, particularly devotional and autobiographical, and in the area of feminist criticism. She is editor of George Herbert's poems, and co-editor of *Teaching Women: Feminism and English Studies*, and *The Body and the Text*.

The members of the Collective have collaborated on a number of projects, notably *Her Own Life: Autobiographical Writings by Seventeenth Century Englishwomen* (1989).

. . . .

Johanna Alberti is a historian who works in adult education, mostly with the Open University. Her main interest is in the lives of interwar feminists, and she has published *Beyond Suffrage: Feminists in War and Peace, 1914–1928* (1989).

Linda Anderson is a Senior Lecturer in English Literature at the University of Newcastle Upon Tyne, where she also co-ordinates an

MA in Women's Studies. She is the author of *Bennett, Wells and Conrad: Narrative in Transition* (1988), editor of *Plotting Change: Contemporary Women's Fiction* (1990), and co-founder/editor of the journal *Writing Women*. Her book on *Women and Autobiography in the Twentieth Century* has been recently published.

Vicki Bertram is a Lecturer in English Studies at Oxford Brookes University, where she teaches courses in modern and contemporary literature. Her main areas of interest are in feminist theory and practice, "post-colonial" writing, and contemporary poetry in English. She is working on a study of gender in contemporary poetry.

Trev Broughton teaches Women's Studies at the University of York. Most of her work is on Victorian autobiography, but she has also published on feminist pedagogy and writer's block. Her current interest is in auto/photography as feminist praxis.

Ayse Durakbaşa completed her doctorate on Kemalist Feminism at the University of Essex in 1993. Since then she has been teaching at Mimar Sinan University, Istanbul. Her research for this book was made possible by the Fuller Fund, Department of Sociology, University of Essex. An earlier version of her paper appeared in German in the journal *L'homme* in 1991.

Gabriele Griffin is a Reader in Women's Studies at Nene College, Northampton. Her most recent publications include *Heavenly Love? Lesbian Images in 20th Century Women's Writing* (1993), and the edited volumes *Stirring It: Challenges for Feminism* (1994), and *Changing Our Lives: Doing Women's Studies* (1994).

Margaretta Jolly developed her interest in women's autobiography while studying at the Centre for Women's Studies at the University of York. She has since taught literacy and literature and been the happy assistant to the St. Pancras Living History Project: a group of elderly proud women who, through reminiscence, celebrate renewed dignity. She is currently completing her doctorate at the University of Sussex.

Ranjana Khanna is Assistant Professor of English and Women's Studies at the University of Utah, Salt Lake City. She received her D.Phil from the Centre for Women's Studies at the University of York, United Kingdom, and is currently working on a book entitled *Dark Continents: Feminism, Psychoanalysis and the Postcolonial Condition*.

Jane Rendall is Senior Lecturer in History at the University of York. Her publications include *The Origins of Modern Feminism: Women in*

Britain, France and the United States (1985), and she has co-edited *Sexuality and Subordination* (1989) and *Equal or Different: Women's Politics 1800–1914* (1987).

Marion Shaw is Professor of English at the University of Loughborough. She has written three books on Tennyson, recently completed with Sabine Vanacker a book on Agatha Christie's *Miss Marple* novels, and has written a number of articles on, mostly, nineteenth-century poetry and fiction. She is editor of *Man Does, Woman Is: The Faber Book of Work and Gender*. She is writing a biography of Winifred Holtby.

Sabine Vanacker is a Lecturer in Dutch Studies at the University of Hull. Her doctoral dissertation is on Women Modernist Autobiographers, and she has collaborated on Janet Todd, ed., *British Women Writers* (1989), and Virginia Blain et al., eds., *The Feminist Companion to Literature in English* (1990). With Marion Shaw, she has published *Reflecting on Miss Marple* (1991).

Nicole Ward Jouve is Professor of English and Related Literature at the University of York. She has published several works of fiction, and has written extensively on the work of Colette and Hélène Cixous, among others. Her collection of essays, *White Woman Speaks with Forked Tongue: Criticism as Autobiography*, was published by Routledge in 1991. Most recently, she has co-written with Sue Roe and Susan Sellers *The Semi-Transparent Envelope* (1994).

Judith Woolf is a Lecturer in English and Related Literature at the University of York. Her publications include *Henry James: The Major Novels* (1991), and *The Memory of the Offence: Primo Levi's If This Is a Man* (in press). She is currently completing a translation of Giacomo Debenedetti's *The Sixteenth of October 1943 and Other Wartime Essays*. She has also written several novels.

INDEX